Whereof One Cannot Speak

Whereof One Cannot Speak

Absolute Consciousness Beyond the Self

Peter Ralston

Lammastide

Whereof One Cannot Speak: Absolute Consciousness Beyond the Self is also available in electronic and audio formats.

Peter Ralston's Books are available through most bookstores. For further information, visit www.Lammastide.com or email: Ralston@ChengHsin.com.

ISBN 979-8-9876200-8-3 (paperback)
ISBN 979-8-9876200-9-0 (ebook)

Page design and layout by Chinook Design, Inc., www.chinooktype.com

Printed in the United States of America

Library of Congress Control Number: 2025924824
Library of Congress Cataloging-in-Publication Data for this title is available from the Library of Congress.

TABLE OF CONTENTS

Introduction

A MONUMENTAL UNDERTAKING

1 The name of this book, *Whereof One Cannot Speak,* is taken from Ludwig Wittgenstein's statement: *"Whereof one cannot speak, thereof one must be silent."* Sometimes people hear this as: about a subject of which one has no knowledge, one should keep his mouth shut. Yet this is far from what I hear as the real meaning of the quote. Instead, what's being said refers to that aspect of existence of which we can't even conceive, let alone speak—and yet of which we can become conscious. Here, we are already silent, since nothing can be said or even thought that matches this consciousness.

2 That being said, of course I will chatter on and on, attempting to communicate what I can, or at least point the reader in a direction for further contemplation where I can't. This book should *not* be your first encounter with my material—even though from time to time I will pull excerpts from my other books to help with the work we'll be doing here. If you want to tackle what's to come, you really should read the trilogy first: *The Book of Not Knowing, Pursuing Consciousness,* and *The Genius of Being.* And if you like, you can add to that *Ending Unnecessary Suffering* (which was originally part of this book). Without this background, what follows will likely not be understood in its proper context.

3 My purpose in writing this is to tackle overlooked facts and possibilities of the human condition, dive into the nature of life and death, and attempt to communicate a deep consciousness of the nature of existence. Again,

I am not intending to "dumb it down" for popular consumption or easy understanding—you'll have to put in the work to truly grasp what's being communicated—but I will do my best to make it accessible. It is extremely advanced and becomes quite complex.

4 My aim is to convey as best I can aspects of our reality that are missed by humanity given our shared assumptions and general level of consciousness. These limitations are commonplace because of our understandable, although distracting, focus on managing our lives rather than discovering the depths of the truth about existence—ours and everything else.

5 Certainly, I will have covered a few of these topics in other books, but I either want to reinforce a point or elaborate a bit more on them. I also want to contribute some deeply advanced new communications. Yet, this pursuit won't be very effective unless you can really experience the assertions for yourself.

6 Many of these assertions are nearly impossible to grasp because they run contrary to your accepted and assumed perceived reality, making them unacceptable, unbelievable, and inconceivable—whereof one cannot speak. Even though many upcoming subjects might seem detached from the reality in which you live—and remember, it's the reality in which you live that currently creates your world and experience, including any dissatisfaction you endure—grasping the whole story empowers you to make any attempt at conscious understanding real, rather than just a good idea.

7 When I was a young man of 19, I came across a Zen book. It intrigued me. I liked the stories and their cryptic nature. But it was clear to me that I didn't grasp any of it. Still, I ventured a ten-day contemplation period in the attic of the house where I lived at the time, trying to experience the 10 Bull pictures with Zen poetry outlined in the book. I stayed up in the attic alone all day, only coming down once a day for some food.

8 I was in college at the time and lived in a group house, and as a young man I knew very little about cooking. One thing I did know was that rice was

boiled and potatoes were boiled, so I put some rice and chopped potatoes into a pot of water and boiled them down to a sludge. I dumped that into my coconut-shell bowl, added some soy sauce, and took it up to the attic to eat. To this day I have that same Zen book, and somehow it has a soy sauce stain on it.

9 In any case, after about seven or eight days I had to admit that I really wasn't keeping up and I wasn't really experiencing whatever was being pointed at. That was a long time ago for me. Since then I have become far more conscious than I could have imagined back then. I bring this up because I suspect much of this book is going to be like that for you. It may not really make sense and certainly won't produce the consciousness necessary for you to share in what's being said. But perhaps it will plant some seeds and point you in directions you would never have considered without it.

10 The subjects in this book are divided into five basic parts: Parts I through III are the major parts, then Parts IV and V contribute a few more practical and grounded matters.

I. The Nature of Absolute Reality
II. Beyond Life and Death
III. Infinite Existence Is Absolute Consciousness
IV. The Stone and the Knife
V. New Perspectives

11 The scope is wide. What tethers these parts together is their contribution to your consciousness and to your experience. The most important thing is to contemplate the subjects, not just hear about them. It is not a book to just read, trying to absorb knowledge. Consider it like a long and detailed guided contemplation. Many assertions will be repeated again and again and again. Even if you think you've heard some point before, remember that unless you become directly conscious in what's true about that matter, you're not done with it. So, try again and go deeper.

12 Most of what's communicated in the first sections is primarily written for those who've had a direct consciousness of their absolute nature. "Yet, even with such foundation consciousness, the most fundamental points bear repeating many times because here we're going to go way beyond your nature and probe into the nature of all of existence. These assertions will bear repeating because it is easy to overlook them and not truly grasp the depth, profundity, and reality of what's being said—but instead have them go in one ear and out the other, so to speak. When you see me hitting something again and again, using various metaphors attempting to ground impossibly challenging material, it means you should take it seriously and push even harder to grasp what's being pointed at.

13 If you haven't yet realized this level of consciousness to some degree, then you won't understand much of what's said in these sections. You're welcome to read them anyway as food for thought, but allow them to be temporarily beyond reach. Perhaps just use them to fuel your intention to grasp what's true, independent from anything said—by me or by you or by anyone else. Even if you have had some degree of enlightenment, it will still take a lot of work and an increasingly deeper consciousness to grasp much of what's to come.

14 In my communications regarding getting beyond life and death, as well as grasping absolute consciousness, I reveal "information" that is nearly impossible to understand. But please don't take this as anything to believe or take on faith. You have to do the work yourself and find what you find, regardless of anything anyone has said (including yourself). I am simply putting it out as a reality that what I assert is true, but for you it must remain only a possibility—and perhaps something to consider or use to spur deeper investigation—until you get what's true directly.

15 Like I said, the material about death, existence, and consciousness is inconceivably difficult to comprehend because our collective experience of reality is founded on so many deep and overlooked assumptions that seem to be self-evident truths, and so the mind will tend to reject many of my assertions out of hand. It is the same with getting beyond yourself, seeking

an experience that is absent of, or at least independent of, your entire experience of self. This may not seem possible or wanted—just like death, or an end to you—but it is necessary for a deeper consciousness of existence. So it will take unprecedented openness and serious contemplation on your part to approach this subject.

16 It's totally OK if you reject something I assert outright and consider it nonsense. In some cases, I don't see any other way to relate to it given how the self-mind is designed. Some communications must sound like nonsense. Yet, I also don't see how they can be communicated in any other way. Perhaps that's my failing, and I implore you not to let my inability to express it in a way that reaches you to stop you from getting it. Still, being exposed to these assertions should give you fuel for new contemplations. I will do my best to make it as clear as possible; I simply request you meet me halfway—OK, *all* the way.

17 Although the absolute nature of existence is what's True, people are generally only interested in pursuing such consciousness as a fantasy, a belief system, or a form of entertainment. If you've read *The Book of Not Knowing* you can see why this might be the case. Our attention is on living life. It's not on pursuing what's true when what's true seems to do nothing for us in a practical sense. It only seems good for helping us get free of ignorance and for digging deeper into recognizing the nature of existence.

18 Attempting to tackle the absolute truth about the nature of existence may seem like just a philosophical endeavor or an exercise limited to mystical ideas or beliefs, yet it is actually the most real thing you can do. Despite the presumed limitations and the apparent abstract impractical nature of such consciousness, it can have the most powerful impact on your life—such as giving you access to becoming free of unnecessary suffering, becoming complete and happy in life, transcending death, and being freed of so many limitations, existential assumptions, misconceptions, illusions, and so on. It can even lead to an incredible depth of joy and humor. However, these occur only through the kind of deep consciousness you will confront here. To be sure, such results should be held simply as possible outcomes but not

the focus, because, as I often say, the truth has to be pursued for itself; otherwise you are pursuing the wrong thing and won't attain such results.

19 Shy of a direct consciousness of the absolute, there is much to become conscious of, much that can be done, and much that can be created in the life you live. Therefore, the last sections of this book provide some generally unknown possibilities that can empower you in your ability to create a more powerful and effective life. Hey, enlightenment isn't everything! ☺

20 Perhaps we could call the absolute the "context" for the "content" of life, and because we live solely within the content, the ability to step outside our experiences and see them for what they are provides a new way to relate to and live life. This includes ending suffering (see my new book, *Ending Unnecessary Suffering,* for a more in-depth look into this study), which I suspect will be everyone's favorite subject. Actually, I started that communication in this book, but it expanded so much that I split it off into its own book. I considered the material too useful for people to keep it buried in the pages of this book. People crazy enough to tackle this "unspeakable" material will be few, and ending suffering should be available to everyone.

21 I have found over the decades that telling something to someone, saying it once or twice, just doesn't work. It doesn't get through even the first of an endless number of mental walls in order to get to where it could make a difference. Therefore, in this book I am going to repeat myself in various ways until you are sick of it. But the hope is that in the end, you will finally get it, or at least get that you don't really get it.

22 If this is the first time encountering my work (not recommended), or even if it isn't, I recommend that after this introduction you start with *Chapter Eighteen* about how to contemplate and approach this work. It should help set the foundation for you to hear and contemplate what is about to come more effectively, so that you can get the most out of it. Even if you are an old hand, it wouldn't hurt at all to refresh the basic principles underlying this form of contemplation and investigation. Then come back and start from Chapter One.

23 At the risk of being even more repetitive, every book I have written has had the same purpose. That is to transform the experience of the reader in some way. It is not to convince them of some belief system, or to pass on some intellectual knowledge, or to entertain. It is to increase the consciousness of the reader about the subject matter and change their experience because of it—either learning more about what they already experience or becoming conscious of stuff that they never knew existed. That's my job. Given I've done my job, however, actually increasing your consciousness is up to you. That's your job. It is a deep and very challenging journey, so buckle up. It will take a lot of work. If you're not ready to do the work, you should pass on this book.

Part I

THE NATURE OF ABSOLUTE REALITY

This first part delves into some of the most fundamental aspects of our existence, the existential nature and condition of self and life. Although this absolute nature seems out of reach and rather abstract and not at all practical, if you are interested in the difficult task of transcending life and death that I present in Part II, such groundwork is necessary. It is not possible to approach a consciousness of the nature that is beyond death without understanding such deep and absolute matters.

Like I said in the Introduction, the first three parts are primarily written to those who have had some direct consciousness, at least a first glimpse. These parts walk you through some of the most overlooked assumptions regarding the human condition and experience, then push the envelope way past the breaking point. You need to make many breakthroughs throughout each chapter if you want to get any of this. I know this will be challenging, so let's start with some of the conundrums involved in sorting out your nature from your current self-experience, along with the difficulties encountered in trying to become conscious of these realities.

Chapter One

AWAKENING OVERLOOKED CONSCIOUSNESS

The Eyes Have It

1:1 One of our tasks in this work is to become conscious of who and what we really are, the true nature of our existence. This is often called enlightenment, as in the Zen tradition. Yet, such a quest implies that what we experience now as ourselves is not what we actually are at the very source or root of our experience. We might have to just accept that implication as a given in order to proceed—unless, of course, we already sense that we're not yet fully conscious of the real nature of our existence.

1:2 In either case, in such an undertaking, contemplation is in order. It is the usual vehicle to get us to our goal of becoming directly conscious of what we are—what we might call the true nature or essence of our existence. Many people think this is a daunting task beyond their abilities. But grasping your true nature isn't as hard as you may think. The only problem is you keep looking elsewhere.

1:3 Look at it this way: if you were an eye, you could only see what the eye sees. If you tried very hard to see yourself, how could you do it? You couldn't. Every action you'd take would be "looking elsewhere," and everywhere you looked would have to be elsewhere because it couldn't be you, since the eye can't see itself. The only way to get "you" would be to become conscious in the very place that you are. Can you see that this can't be done using any visual or mental faculty?

1:4 Trying to see yourself would be futile, and the only recourse you as an eyeball would have is to create a concept of such a possibility—given that as an eye you somehow had such capacity. But this is only a thought of what might be true, it is not an experiential consciousness of what *is* true. It is the same with you. Just stop looking elsewhere and simply become conscious of the very place you exist.

1:5 Don't insert: trying to perceive, experience, think, feel, sense, or any other activity. Those are all activities you *do*, they are not what you *are*. In your attempt to grasp you, however, don't try to avoid those activities; it is what your mind will do. Instead, strive to directly get to the source of the activities themselves: *you*.

1:6 You are right there. You may not be what you previously thought of or perceived as yourself, but you aren't elsewhere or mysterious. You are what is doing the "looking." You know you exist, and you experience yourself being, but you may not directly grasp the nature of your being. It isn't that hard to get, just get what's there. Get you directly.

1:7 Sorry if that sounds frivolous, or dismissive of your difficulties if you've been unsuccessfully attempting this consciousness—especially coming from someone who has lived his whole adult life with such consciousness. It is not meant that way. Instead, I am attempting to let you know it is not unattainable or inaccessible. If *I* can get it, *you* can get it. You are simply invited to see that all your failed attempts are "looking elsewhere," and instead be empowered to grasp the very heart of you. It is who and what you already are, nothing needs to change or be attained, the only extra ingredient needed is to become directly conscious of this fact.

You have *experience*, *you* are *you*.

You Are Not Two

1:8 Of course, there can be some tricky aspects to such a pursuit. There are overlooked assumptions that make it even harder than need be. For example, there is nothing you can manifest as or "be" other than something. If you are not "something," how could you be known or establish your "place" within existence? You couldn't—not without being something. Given you are a human you exist as a body and, in our modern culture, a mind. Whatever you find to be you—in other words, whatever you identify with as yourself—is what exists as you. There is nothing else.

1:9 You may be confused by such a statement since you've probably heard me say that your nature is nothing, that you are without element. Now it seems I'm saying you are only something. This is because you probably don't fully understand the real nothing to which I'm referring. This isn't surprising, as we will see in the upcoming sections. My communications in this matter can come out rather baffling and confusing at times.

1:10 As difficult as it is to entertain, when I say you are nothing, I really mean there is absolutely nothing there—no quality, no element, no dimension, no relative existence of any kind; you don't "exist." So, anything "there" would have to be something, wouldn't it? You appear to be there, to exist, so this is what is known as you and is how you are known at all. But in truth your essence or nature actually has no element—such nature doesn't exist in any form. This point is not only difficult to grasp, it leads to much mischief, so let's see if we can clarify the matter a bit.

1:11 When we entertain the notion that we may not experience who we really are, or take up some spiritual belief of a higher or ethereal existence, we will make a distinction between our physical or mortal existence and some other form of existence. The moment this happens—which may be an inevitable step when questioning or contemplating what you really are—immediately there is a distinction between one and the other. This provides the idea of "two entities."

1:12 Although this may be a preliminary distinction or stage in pursuing enlightenment, it is false. It can be said that to think you are a body-mind, or a character and person, is also false. But these two stances—that you are a body-mind or you are something else—are both erroneous.

1:13 So how is it possible to conceive this error, and to think what is correct in this case? It's not, that's the problem. Conception demands distinction, so we can't think or imagine this paradox because it's prior to any distinction. Everything experienced or known in any way is a "distinction" and so it is relative. That just means it is "that" and not something else.

1:14 This doesn't mean it is precise or clear—unclear, amorphous, and vague are distinctions also. All your perceptions, experiences, and knowledge occur solely as distinctions. They are also always relative, meaning they are in relation to what they are not. Up relates to down, fast to slow, smart to stupid, large to small, you to not-you, and so on. If they aren't "that" they don't exist as "that." An object exists in relation to other objects as well as to the space that contains it and surrounds it but isn't it. Do you get how I'm using the word *distinction*?

1:15 All of reality is known via distinctions. Therefore, when you consider that whatever you currently experience isn't your true nature, this immediately generates the notion that your nature is elsewhere, giving you the idea that your very being, or what you actually are, is different from what you experience as your self. By standing on such a notion, you can now wonder what your real nature is. Without such a distinction, why and how would you contemplate this matter? Where would you put your attention? You would simply accept your experience of self as your nature. But if you consider that it's not, you will, without thinking about it, conclude that your true nature is something else.

1:16 This notion might provide a way to proceed with our investigation by giving us a method to search out what we really are. But this must only serve us temporarily. We should be open to the possibility that it won't be where we'll ultimately end up, since by definition this is beyond our ability to imagine from our "pre-conscious" perspective.

1:17 But the function of creating this distinction is to have a catalyst—something applied to make a change that itself doesn't remain after the change. As I wrote in another book, introducing something temporarily that allows a process to move forward is the point of the story of the wandering Abdul:

> Abdul is traveling with his camel in the desert. He comes across a heated inheritance dispute among three brothers. Their father recently died and has left them seventeen camels, decreeing that half should go to his eldest son, a third to the middle son, and one-ninth to the youngest. But seventeen camels don't divide up easily in that way. To solve this dilemma, Abdul donates his camel to the dead man's estate. Then, with eighteen camels, they can divide them with half (nine) going to the oldest son, one-third (six) to the middle son, and one-ninth (two) to the youngest, thus totaling seventeen. Abdul then takes his camel back and goes on his way.

1:18 Our purpose for considering that you are not what you experience or know as yourself is to use this concept as a temporary goal—an inserted camel, so to speak—without fixating on it as a final goal, but rather as a useful stepping stone. Although it may create the possibility for this kind of deep contemplation, it also forms the false idea that your nature is something separate from yourself. Yet we're talking about the true nature of yourself, not something else. There are not two you's. There is only you—and truth to tell, there isn't even that, except as a distinction.

1:19 What is the absolute nature of your very existence? It turns out that through direct consciousness you discover that what's really true is that your "nature" has no element to it whatsoever. A word of caution, however. Whatever idea you may have had of what I just said, that's not it. The actual consciousness is absolutely not any thought that could possibly arise. I speak about this nature just to continue with the communication about the common dynamic of imagining you are two. Since your nature has no aspect at all it can't be pinned down as a something, because in so doing it would then have an aspect to it—which makes it a particular thing and not another.

1:20 Certainly, this then makes it sound like your true nature is something other than yourself because yourself is chock-full of aspects. So how can you understand the statement that it isn't? Although you could say that your nature is itself and not what it's not, the paradox is that it is also not separate from anything. This is challenging to understand, so perhaps a metaphor will help.

Carving Up the Uncarved

1:21 It might still seem as if I'm suggesting that we live in two worlds, but they are actually the same world. One is the absolute nature of this reality—of which we are generally ignorant. The other is the relative nature of this same reality—this is the world that we know.

1:22 Just as a way to "think" about the matter, we could say, metaphorically, that one aspect is like an infinite uncarved block, and the other is what's carved out of the block. Without carving the block into pieces, the uncarved block cannot be perceived in any way, since there is nothing to perceive and no one to perceive it. The carving—or making of distinctions—creates a relative world, and so perception becomes possible, as well as necessary for life. In this imagery, we can see that although these two domains—representing the absolute and the relative—seem to be different, the nature or substance for both is identical. We're simply ignorant of this nature; we only experience the carving.

1:23 If we move closer to the truth—still using the metaphor imagery to ground us—we can begin to entertain the fact that "consciousness," or existence in its absolute form, is the uncarved block. This means every relative distinction, such as self, objects, bodies, awareness, and everything else that exists or could possibly exist, is of this same nature. They are forms of existence or consciousness. They are simply limited forms of absolute existence because they are finite and distinct. They have boundaries and, by definition, are not whatever they are not—that makes them relative.

1:24 But consider the possibility that absolute consciousness, which is the same as absolute existence, is still the very nature of everything that is relative—it just shows up as limitation. Because we only perceive or experience the relative—since it is the only thing that *can* be perceived—we are restricted to knowing only these limitations. Stopping there, however, we fail to grasp the infinite or absolute nature that is the foundation for it all.

1:25 Where the metaphor falls short is the fact that our imagined infinite uncarved block is really relative. Because we can't actually imagine infinity, all we can do is at best produce a conceptual image of some infinite objective substance. If this "substance" is infinite, however, and all that is, it doesn't stop anywhere or have any boundaries at all, so there is no way to perceive or experience it. Being infinite, it can have no location or space or substance, because it actually can't exist as anything relative in any way—that is what the carving is all about.

1:26 Yet, when it is carved up, then there is one thing and another, and they are finite because they do stop somewhere. In this way, one element can perceive another. As one of those elements we can perceive the carved-up stuff. But we are only perceiving the carving itself, in other words, the "outside" of the substance at the point of distinction, but not the substance itself. As with our uncarved block, we don't perceive the real "substance" of existence, just the distinctions that are made out of this substance, the limitations that arise when carved up in order to create something. Can you follow this?

1:27 On the other hand, without the carving, there is no need to perceive anything because it is all one—or, actually none. There is nothing to perceive and no function for it to serve—not to mention, once again, that in this case perception is not possible. Beyond the analogy, try to imagine that all of this complex existence of space, objects, and life, in some unimaginable way, arises from and shares the same nature as an absolute consciousness that itself has no aspect or element. At the same time, don't confuse anything that can be thought or imagined as the absolute.

1:28 To use another analogy, start by acknowledging that space must be infinite. Even though we can't conceive of this infinite nature, we see it encompasses, and will always encompass, everything objective. Although we can only see the objects in front of us, we also grasp that space is as much a part of the objects as it is of empty space. Space fills everywhere, whether in the form of an object or in the form of the absence of objects—in other words, the distance between objects. Yet, what is the real nature of space?

1:29 Concentrate on this for a moment and experience that the nature of space includes all that you perceive in the objective world. Yet, the absolute nature of space is overlooked and not what you think or take for granted. Even as you think about infinite space you really just imagine great distances with the concept that it goes on forever. But this is not grasping the real nature of infinity. If you acknowledge space must be infinite, and therefore absolute, that should change your sense of its nature a great deal. Although you can't picture or imagine infinite space, you can grasp that it must go on forever, since if it stopped somewhere, what is on the other side of that? So, you can see it can't ever stop; you just can't conceive of it not stopping.

1:30 There is really no way to get around it, even if it is inconceivable by the mind: you must conclude that space includes all of objective existence and yet isn't itself relative, it is infinite. Don't confuse the distance between objects as space; that is relative. Space is the "context" that allows for objects and distance to exist. Therefore, this nature, like the nature of the uncarved block, is absolute and without character or relativity. It really is absolutely nothing, and that is how it can be infinite. Grasp that because infinity can't have boundaries or distinctions, it has no location or element, it doesn't stop anywhere and yet contains all that does stop.

What would you call this nature? *Nothing* is as close of a word as I can come up with. Although you can't imagine infinity, and so can't imagine the real nature of space, it presses you in a direction that requires deeper contemplation.

1:31 Just so, I'm asserting that existence or consciousness is infinite and is the nature of it all, and so we can't imagine the real nature of what I'm calling consciousness either. This consciousness is not restricted to awareness or mind. It is infinite in possibility, because it is the blank slate, so to speak, upon which existence can occur. But just as I call the nature of infinity nothing, I'm calling the nature of existence a consciousness that shares this same absolute nothing nature. Don't get hung up on the names, they are just the best I can do using the English language to point to something inconceivable and not found within any language.

1:32 Our difficulty in grasping this lies in the fact that all our thinking, imagining, and perceiving exists solely within the relative. Here, we will always hold the absolute and relative as different realities. What we're missing is the fact that we're not talking about a different reality but the very nature of all reality. Our problem is simply not being fully conscious of this source-nature of existence.

1:33 Since existence manifests only as the relative, this is what we perceive. But think about it. Although we tend to think of the absolute as rather ethereal, not practical or grounded in objective reality, we can see that the absolute remains and is unshakable no matter what happens or what exists or changes in the relative. Just as with our infinity analogy, we see infinity is completely unchanged no matter what occurs or doesn't occur within objective existence.

1:34 Our entire perceived reality could turn to dust and it wouldn't in any way change the absolute, which is unchangeable. Everything that exists relatively is only one of infinite possibilities—there is no end to the possibilities of carving up the block, so to speak. If something can be one way, it can be another. That means relativity is also infinite, and infinity is an absolute.

The absolute is the only constant in the universe and is impossible to alter in any way, because there is nothing at all to change.

1:35 Every element of existence must arise from no-element. Can you see that? The fact of relativity—the existence of elements and aspects—doesn't in any way change the absolute nothing or no-element in which it takes place. Since this possibility must have no distinct element, we could call it nothing. Yet this nothing is not the absence of something, nor is it in contrast to something or to everything. There is actually nothing we're talking about. It doesn't "exist." It is the nature of existence.

1:36 All of existence is relative. One, two, none, more, everything, something else—all are distinctions in the relative domain. As a matter of fact, every possibility in the entire universe and beyond, and every possibility to come, will always exist within the relative. The most universal and grand event or possibility is still relative. That's what makes it universal and grand, because it's not specific and mundane. Any time we imagine or experience another possibility or reality, we've already created relativity no matter what it is we imagine or experience. The absolute is simply the nature of all of it, we just may not be conscious of that fact.

1:37 We can't say that the nature of existence is something new or different or something at all, even though it is the nature of everything that is. This really leaves us with no distinct possibility. Since this possibility must have no distinct element, we could call it *nothing*. This is difficult to grasp, and that is why we use the metaphor of the uncarved block.

Trying to Grasp the Nature of Existence

1:38 The absolute nature of existence is not what's *known* as existence because what's known or perceived as existence is restricted to the distinctions we make through perception and interpretation, and every distinction always takes some limited form—otherwise it isn't known. The true nature of existence, on the other hand, *is* existence, and not any one distinction or all distinctions taken as a whole. That may be difficult to understand, but that's because understanding depends on distinctions.

1:39 As much as we "live" that our perceptions and experience *are* reality—and we're not likely to be moved from that position—it really can't be. For many reasons, it is pretty much inevitable that what we experience is far too limited to represent the ultimate nature of existence, which must be beyond or independent of perceptive-experience. What's worse, knowing this won't change our perceived reality because that is also beyond our limited capacity.

1:40 You need to grasp that this nature is not different for any aspect of existence. It is the same nature for you, others, life, objects, space, mind, emotions, concepts, and everything that exists in any way. Do you see that existence—whatever that is—*is* existence, so any aspect therein must share the same nature, which is existence itself? But how can that be? All those things are so very different in character and substance. Yet, as we saw in the metaphor of the uncarved block, the absolute and the relative are not inconsistent or in different "places," so to speak. It just seems that way.

1:41 The absolute is the true nature of relative existence. It is the nature of the very stuff that we experience. As another analogy, we could think of it as follows: in a dream the whole world, and everything in it, is only a function of and completely contained within the mind that dreams it. This "mind" could be said to be the real nature of the dream, and everything that is perceived within the dream is of this conceptual nature.

1:42 In a dream, all that is "known"—a table, a person, light, the cat, running, feeling sad, etc.—is solely made up of the distinctions created inside the dream. So, what seem like distinct objects and activities all share the same nature that is this "mind" and really don't exist on their own as they seem. We can also see that this nature (mind) and perceived reality (dream) are not separate or in different "places." Not a bad analogy, and it gives us another stepping stone toward grasping this point.

1:43 It is difficult to make the leap that what we perceive as objects, thoughts, feelings, and so on may be of a nature that is quite different from the assumed nature we experience. What is even harder to entertain is the possibility that all these distinct experiences share the same nature. That's where the analogy becomes useful. We see in the dream analogy the possibility that what seems to be of one nature is actually another.

1:44 In our case, the nature of all we experience is an absolute that I might refer to as absolute consciousness or absolute nothing—just so we have some way to refer to it. But, keep remembering that the reality of this isn't the same as whatever comes to mind when using those words. The assertion is that the nature of all that we experience has no element even though it is the nature of all elements.

1:45 To be clear, we don't have to remove or deny anything we experience in order to grasp this nature because it's already the case. Again, as an analogy, we may not be able to see past an object that impedes our view, but that doesn't mean that space is impeded at all, or that space is not an aspect of the object itself, or that space is not infinite. We just can't see these facts from our limited perspective, but we can grasp them.

1:46 Of course, your consciousness of this is what matters. Believing any of it doesn't do a thing to increase your consciousness or help you directly grasp the reality such ideas try to represent. Paradox makes such points challenging to understand. Even becoming conscious of your true nature doesn't at all provide a consciousness of any other aspect of existence—unless of course you experience yourself as others, life, objects, and so on. But you don't. So even your first few enlightenments will probably not resolve your mind's struggle with this paradox.

1:47 It might be possible to become conscious of the nature of everything all at once—but it is extremely unlikely. This is because we live in a world of distinctions, and each element that is experienced as reality is experienced differently and as uniquely that. When we grasp the nature of one domain or subject matter, we rarely directly grasp that this very nature applies to everything. That's why we usually require enlightenment after enlightenment before we begin to connect the dots. And remember, believing in such a thing, even after an enlightenment, is useless. You have to do the work and get it all directly, otherwise it doesn't count, because then it is only a thought or extrapolation or belief and not direct consciousness.

1:48 None of this is very practical regarding life concerns, so you may not be interested in pursuing such consciousness. Normally, most of your energy is devoted to either managing life or trying to make your lot in life better in some way. Although such activities are very important to you, they exist in a very different domain of focus than trying to grasp the truth.

1:49 On the other hand, you might have some interest in finding out what's true. But if you accept whatever you experience and however you conceive of the world as true, or all that is true, there is no motivation or openness to question or investigate it. Without such an opening, your focus remains solely on personal concerns. Although this myopic focus may sound reasonable, the challenge is that when you live completely "inside" life concerns—doing your best to improve your lot—you are limited to too many assumptions and reactions that make even your life goals more difficult than need be.

1:50 When you experience the nature of self and life, you have access to new possibilities in relationship to life's complications. This alone doesn't resolve all your concerns—though depending on your depth of consciousness some experiences may fall away as dysfunctional and unnecessary—but it does create a new and more open perspective. Life is a relative domain. Being conscious of absolutes doesn't change the demands of relativity, it simply changes your relationship to these demands. In any case, the absolute is challenging to understand. There are some basic reasons why this is so.

Ignorance

1:51 Our biological nature makes us learning machines from birth because we begin life in complete ignorance. By design this creates some overlooked existential consequences. Without really understanding the dynamics behind these consequences, we still feel them in the background, and this results in blaming ourselves for deficiencies ill-defined.

1:52 Beginning life in complete ignorance and with virtually no skills or capacity to take care of ourselves, we are required to fill in our ignorance and to "learn" the skills necessary to manage life. Beyond what "comes with the package" at birth through genetics, in order to learn basic physical, conceptual, and social abilities we use trial and error and imitation. When it comes to crafting a self—which we really have no inherent idea how to do—we probably also use trial, error, and imitation, trying out various learned human features until some identity begins to form.

1:53 Over time, and with much (often forgotten) effort, a great deal of learning and development indeed unfolds. But what's missed in all this is that every piece of knowledge, social skill, understanding, and mental ability that we acquire is invented. Many are adopted inventions from our collective human culture, and much is self-invented.

1:54 For example, clearly language is a shared invention that we learn, depend on, and live within, as are morals, values, traditions, and so on, and none of these existed before they were invented by us collectively. Beliefs, opinions, assumptions, perspectives, etc., tend to be self-invented—but are clearly culturally and socially influenced—and we can see that no belief existed prior to it being thought and adopted.

1:55 Once again, one of the central inventions that arises in all of this is one's "self." Consider that what you identify with and experience as "you" is something that you crafted and designed. But just like all the other learning you did, your attention wasn't on the fact that you were creating yourself but on the self you were trying to become.

1:56 So, without noticing, you remained ignorant of your role in fashioning yourself, since from the beginning your awareness never turned in that direction. The resultant "person" you now identify with simply became your self-experience, with all your perceptions and attention looking out from this experience as you attempt to manage life from moment to moment. This is another overlooked dynamic.

1:57 Even the fundamental consciousness—what we might call "who you really are"—that exists throughout your self-conception is lost within the amalgam of adopted skills, mental activities, and identifiable characteristics you adopted and came to think of as yourself. The primal awareness of your unfettered and unattached source-existence remains hidden from view within your experience until you directly experience who you really are—grasping directly your existence without identity, history, or process.

1:58 At this point you might begin to contemplate your essential nature, or *what* you really are. But that isn't commonly done because, as has been said, your awareness and efforts are naturally devoted to managing life, and not to grasping the source of your self-experience. Although you might think that knowing who and what you are is the end-all to consciousness, it isn't. It is only the beginning.

1:59 Many of us are still a ways from such foundational breakthroughs, but whether we have made them or not, our experience remains stuck in what we could call the self-mind. Although we started life in complete ignorance, we've learned a great deal and so naturally assume that all the learning we've done has solved our condition of ignorance. Yet, when we look more closely, we can see that it hasn't. This second point may seem to be a false statement on its face because we also assume that our learning is all that *can* be done, and since we seem to know so much, how can it be called ignorance?

1:60 Yet, when asked what is life, or death, or how did we come to exist, or what is the absolute nature of existence, and so on, we find no direct genuine conscious experience that answers any of these questions. We only find speculation and belief, and these do not rise to the level of direct personal consciousness. So, it turns out that we are just as ignorant as we were at birth about the foundational realities of self and life, and that everything "known" has been learned and is not an inherent or direct consciousness of these essential matters.

1:61 Because of this ignorance, and the fact that virtually our whole experience of self and world is invented and adopted, we have a nagging background sense that there is something wrong with our very person. We try to cover up this sense by inserting beliefs and convictions, by gathering more knowledge, by piling up opinions and assumptions, or perhaps by working to become competent and successful. But none of these actions alter our foundation sense that something in ourselves is incomplete, and perhaps broken; they simply bury it.

1:62 This condition of existential ignorance doesn't just tend to lead us to a sense of ill-defined personal lack, it also means that in order to fill in the gaps of what's unknown in these areas we require some other activity to substitute for direct knowledge. This is most often done through adopting beliefs, opinions, convictions, assumptions, and the like, forming what seems to be a solid version of reality. But if you look closely, you'll see that all those activities are concepts.

1:63 Beyond these "faux" forms of knowledge, as a community or culture we are further pressed to create inventions that serve to coordinate our interactive efforts and organize our perspectives, thus creating a great deal of our perceived world. Yet, these inventions are not seen as inventions, and we should note that no invention is a direct consciousness. Such consciousness is about grasping what's existential and inherent, not what's invented. In this pursuit, it's essential that we know the difference.

Chapter Two

CHALLENGING ASSUMPTIONS ABOUT REALITY

2:1 To help educate you in some of the foundational understanding needed to delve into the more difficult material about life and death and the nature of absolute existence, consider the next couple of chapters as a sort of Consciousness 101.

Inventions

2:2 Although pretty much no one knows it, no matter what beliefs, ideas, perspectives, or assumptions you have about anything, they are inventions—which means they are not existentially real. Anything that is conceptually generated to serve a purpose cannot be an inherent aspect of existence, and obviously, these conceptions are not objective. Clearly, they were not aspects of existence before their invention.

2:3 This is not to say that you have much of a choice about whether or not to adopt many of these inventions—self, society, culture, language, mind, interpretations, and more—because that's where most of the world in which you live is created. If you want to participate in this world you need to adopt, or at least know about and be able to make the distinctions that are the inventions that make it possible. But that doesn't make them real. As a kid if you wanted to play in the game of make-believe you had to adhere to what was made up in order to play the game, but it was still make-believe. It is the same with all this, it's just not known as such.

2:4 Most people have a hard time getting that many experiences such as language and self, mind and society, are inventions and not existential or objective realities. So, to tackle this we need to grasp that these "inventions" are actually conceptually generated.

2:5 But they seem so real, we use them every day, and most of our lives are lived through them. It really seems as if language is a natural, almost biological function of our reality. Self certainly seems self-evident, and present as a real and solid experience of our person. How can these "lived" experiences be inventions?

2:6 To get how this is so, start by grasping that at some point, just like cars, phones, and refrigerators, language didn't exist and then it did. Clearly, it only exists because we created it, and it lives within the fact that each individual has learned it and uses it. In this way, it becomes a constant part of our everyday lives and a familiar and commonplace activity. It also produces so much of the experience needed in order to relate to others and live a social life, and probably to make a living. Language even appears to become the centerpiece for our thinking or mind through our internal dialogue.

2:7 The importance of language isn't in question, the fact that it is an invention is the point. We know that phones, refrigerators, cars, and so on are clearly objective inventions, and they are probably also central to our lives even though they are inventions. Conceptual inventions are no less central, and no less invented.

2:8 It may be harder to grasp, however, that your "self" is an invention. But let me clarify. Here, we are not talking about your existential nature—whatever that may be—nor the existence of your body. In addition to these, you have an experience of being an inner self, the "one inside," the conscious entity you identify as not your body but perhaps residing within it. This is largely based on and founded on the idea that you are at the source of your perceptions, and this experience is reinforced by the existence of your internal dialogue—which we have already seen is itself an invention.

2:9 From these kinds of conclusions and assumptions a conceptually generated "experience" of you being a self-residing-within-your-body, and usually inside the head, becomes a taken-for-granted and central aspect that constitutes the core of your self-experience. But I claim this too is an invention. (More on inventing the inner-self later.)

2:10 This point also applies to society as a whole. Social reality is invented. Society is based on agreements and values, culture and a collective identity, and in our modern societies many added contributions exist—such as a shared language, how we think of mind, the invention of an unconscious mind, human rights, even what it is to be a self, and so on. When we look into it, we see that it occupies the largest slice of our personal experience and world. Again, all of this is conceptually generated to serve a purpose and so is invented.

2:11 Grasping that these shared and powerful experiences are inventions is one thing—and we may have no desire to stop using some of them, even though many inventions are dysfunctional and unnecessary, and cause or contribute to our challenges and pain. If we don't experience them as generated, we can't change or stop doing them. Even our perceptive-experience of the real world is crafted around many such conceptual inventions.

2:12 Can you see this dynamic operating in your experience? To be clear, these conceptualizations are most often not experienced as minor or superficial activities. In your personal world, conceptual inventions create the experience of your self, your beliefs, your world view, your self-view, and so on. These are conceptual activities created by you. They are inventions—and therefore can be changed or eliminated—but they are not known as such. Consider this point, don't just gloss over it.

2:13 Certainly, there are many fundamental and agreed-upon inventions we share that make our interactions workable—language, politeness, general rules of engagement, shared values, and so on. Although they comprise most of the shared world in which we live, and so are difficult to change, some are ineffective or damaging; and it's useful to consider what those might be. Likewise, there are many self-inventions that are dysfunctional—prejudices, judgments, projections, opinions, blind beliefs, assumptions, jumping to conclusions, points of view, and so on. These should be scrutinized and ruthlessly challenged.

2:14 It can be hard for us to sort out which is which in our own case, since whether useful or dysfunctional, both are accepted as our self-experience and view of reality. Yet, with critical inspection and detached observation, we can begin to discern which personal mental activities are detrimental to our overall well-being and growth. Many of these kinds of self-inventions are found in our beliefs and assumptions, perspectives and cosmologies.

2:15 To be clear, "cosmology" is a word I use to loosely refer to our personal views about how the world and reality work. This is generally made up of adopted belief systems and unrecognized assumptions about the nature of reality. Beliefs and assumptions that aren't aligned with what's true or factual are rarely useful or effective, and are often dysfunctional. Yet, if we don't recognize them as inventions—and therefore as conceptually produced and something we are doing—we can't drop them.

2:16 In some cases, dysfunctional beliefs might be rather obvious, such as a belief that you are worthless, or that all others are evil liars. Rationally, you can see that these kinds of beliefs will limit and degrade your experience of life. But even though you might be able to recognize that some belief is disempowering, you may not be able to easily drop it because you still believe it. See the rub? Only when you can get that it is something you are doing, and that you don't have to do it, can you stop doing it.

2:17 There will be beliefs that seem justified and serving self-preservation that are neither. These can be beliefs you're attached to simply because you want to be—even if unconsciously—not because they empower you. But this reality is overlooked. You may also well have cosmologies or perspectives that darken your world or push you into a dysfunctional corner. But without these invented "realities" a much more open relationship to life, which includes many more possibilities, could be available.

2:18 To pursue this introspective work, one question you can ask is: does this "invention" (belief, view, assumption, perspective, opinion, et al.) really empower and free me, or does it limit and degrade my experience? Remember, everything you experience should be up for inspection. Within this conceptually invented domain what you choose to take on creates the degree to which your personal world is free, successful, or satisfying. Most people have no idea that they can change long-held beliefs and assumptions. For them, it seems that such things are fixed and simply a reflection of what's real. But they aren't. You can stop generating any invention.

2:19 To further delve into this world of inventions, let's look at several inventions that aren't known as such. Instead, they are simply held as aspects of existential reality. When we press deep down into such overlooked realities, we create another crowbar to pry open more doors to the truth.

You Exist Because of Not-You

2:20 Making a rather abstract point more personal, your entire experience of existence is relative. This means you completely depend on what you are not. You only exist because of not-you. Clearly, when you draw a circle the inside and outside of the circle are created at the same time. Just so, when the distinction of self is created, not-self must be and is created simultaneously—they are the same event.

2:21 Your very experience of being a self is exactly the same event as experiencing not-self. Contemplate this until you grasp the reality of it. You can't experience existing as a self without experiencing the existence of not-you, and you can't experience being a sentient self without the existence of other sentient selves. Yet, this latter assertion about the self might be a bit harder to grasp.

2:22 It shouldn't be hard to grasp that without a not-you there can be no you. Even if you are the only thing that exists in the universe, there must be something not-you. If you exist in empty space, the empty space will be not-you. Because everything is relative, there must be a distinction of you and not-you in order for you to be experienced at all. But why can't you exist simply alone in space without another "you" having to exist?

2:23 A sentient self needs a world of "selves" in order to exist. Without the context of sentient "selves"—what could be called a social context—there is no way a single self can exist. This is something like without the context of numbers, no single number can exist. Can you see that you can't have a 1 without the existence of 2, and so on? Just as a number can't exist on its own but needs the domain of "numbers" to exist, so it is with a self.

2:24 As a specific self-reflective sentient experience, you exist only in relation to other sentient selves. The existence of an object or even a creature is not the same thing as a self. Self is a distinction within experience that is not just a distinction between objects. You make the distinctions of table and chair but neither is considered a self. Your "self" exists as an individual conscious entity identified as a particular person.

2:25 You can't be an individual unless there are other-selves from which you are distinct. The distinction of self and "other" immediately creates a social world, and this is where your existence as a self is created and resides. Whenever the distinction of sentient beings is created, a social context immediately comes into existence—which simply means a new world arises that is composed of sentient beings that can communicate.

2:26 If you were the only "entity" that existed, you would have to be all that is—at least entity-wise—wouldn't you? What contrast could there be? How could you identify yourself? In relation to what? How could you be self-reflective? There would be no language, process of thought, emotional reaction, culture, values, society, or anything else that could possibly form a you or isolate you as an individual, because all those things depend on a social context in order to exist—and a social context depends on a you and an other.

2:27 You couldn't be an individual because you wouldn't be separate from any other entity. There would be no other to relate to or interact with, no known "reality" beyond simple existence. Of course, like the uncarved block, if you were all that is, then nothing would exist—there would be no distinctions and so no relativity.

2:28 The thing to get is that your entire experience of reality and self only exists within the relative—your experience is completely relational. This is true about every aspect of your world. When it comes to your self-experience, this experience occurs in relationship to other selves. Without this relationship your experience of yourself and your internal activities could not arise as it does.

2:29 For example, notice the role language plays in your self-experience. Most of what you call the activity of mind is probably made up of internal dialogue, which is commonly held as "thinking." When you look into it deeply, however, you find that language exists only because of others. Without others there would be no language. Yet notice how much of your entire daily experience occurs in language, in your own head as thinking, or as actual communications with others. This entire world exists only in relationship with, and only because of, other sentient selves.

2:30 A self needing selves to exist might be difficult to understand, but it is something you can contemplate. If you can't get this existentially, you should at least be able to see that the identity that you experience as your self was constructed in relation to others—parents, culture, learning, and observing and interacting with others. This relationship with other selves created what you determined a self to be, and also comprises what you identify as *your* self.

2:31 You should be able to grasp that every thought, sense, feeling, object, perception, sensation, and everything else that exists in any way is a distinction and is relative. All known existence is relative. Therefore, this clearly includes your experience of yourself. You only exist because of the distinction and fact of not-you, and as a sentient self you exist in relation to other sentient selves. Consider your self-experience in that light.

2:32 Beyond this fact about self-existence, let's continue by challenging an assumption we live within that is so taken for granted as to seem to be an observable truth about our natures. This is that the most essential aspect of ourselves exists in what we experience as an "inner-self." Yet, this inner-self is not what we think it is. It is an invention.

The Inner-Self Is an Invention

2:33 Where do you locate yourself in your experience? It seems that almost all humans experience their "private" self, their inner self-awareness, as residing inside their body and usually inside their head. Can you find this sense of an inner-self right now in your experience? This location is usually taken for granted as the "seat" or "place" where you exist.

2:34 When you talk to yourself or have a thought, where does that take place? Is that the place where "you" reside? Do you experience yourself as occupying a private inner world, living within an internal state to which only you are privy? Isn't this where you locate "you" as a conscious entity? Isn't this place and this "one" the most important and necessary living element for you?

2:35 I've talked elsewhere about living inside and why it seems real, but the real nature of this seemingly existential condition is rarely grasped. As the title of this section states, the whole notion, perception, and experience of being an internal self-object is an invention. How can that be? It seems to be self-evident and obvious. But we fail to notice the reason it's obvious is because we assume it to be existentially true and necessary, and this assumption creates the very experience that makes it self-evident.

2:36 But ask yourself, can you find this "one behind the scenes" that you never really see? If you have done lots of contemplation you can attest that, try as you might, you can't find this one directly. Why is that? You may keep assuming you can find it but are just unable. Yet, you still can't find it. This is because it isn't there.

2:37 Don't take my word for it. Give it a try, and a try, and a try, until you are convinced for yourself. You can experience what's there, and you can become conscious of who and what you really are, but you can't find what's not there. That's because this inner-self-object is an invention, and it's not shared by all creatures.

2:38 It shouldn't be too hard to imagine that a tree or single-cell organism has no such internal world or notion of an inner-self—even though we tend to project the inner-self notion onto all living things because we assume it is the essence of all creatures, just as we assume it's an essential aspect of ourselves. Yet without standing on such assumptions, we can also imagine that a tree has no self or mind, and no inner world.

2:39 It isn't difficult to imagine the tree has no internal dialogue because we experience it as having no language. Just so, an animal that has no conceptually constructed language also has no need nor impulse for an inner-self or the notion of an internal state to arise. We should be able to see it living simply as a body perceiving its environment, which defines its world.

2:40 So, it also shouldn't be too difficult to conjure up the idea that at one point humans themselves had no such isolated sense of an inner self. If we extend this to the idea of having no "mind"—or internal state—this may be harder to imagine because we assume mind is fundamental to the human condition. Yet consider that long ago humans, or human predecessors, had no language, so like the tree or animal they could not be talking to themselves, and that activity is a major contributor to creating the notion of being inside and having a mind. Couple that with a total lack of wonder about what might be at the source of perception, and we see no inclination to create a notion that anything other than the body itself is perceiving.

2:41 Imagine an ancient culture where people lived as their bodies, without any separation or division between mind and body, much like most creatures. Then, imagine someone from a culture like ours coming into their midst and suggesting that the self is really an inner ethereal self-object (to be served), or a soul (to be worshipped), or higher self (to be aspired to). What do you think would be the reaction by these ancient people?

2:42 More than likely they would see these attempts as not only unnecessary but as unhealthy. Why divide oneself from the organic nature that produces existence in the first place? They may well see this as a sick addition to healthy living and reject it outright. For us, such a perspective represents a very different reality since we live as if the inner-self idea is the holy grail, and is existentially real. But let's rethink the matter.

2:43 The body is the only objective reality that indicates an entity. Inventing a new distinction such as a soul or conscious entity doesn't change that, it just muddies the waters. If this self-activity is indeed a fabrication it would be useful to know how it came to exist. Obviously, it has to be constructed through concept, since with the invention of an inner-self the physical body has already been rejected or bypassed. Yet, this inner-self is still held as some kind of immaterial object, even if unfound, and we miss the irony of that. If you don't accept the assumption that you are some entity within, and not simply your body, you challenge something very fundamental for you, don't you?

2:44 Once again, we see that prior to inventing the distinction of an inner-self-behind-the-scenes, there is only a body and the activities of the body. We can imagine that at some past point for us, like the animals, knowledge of anything inside the body was absent, and likely of little concern. If the body were opened up we'd find only organs and other physical features. So where is this internal state or inner person to be found?

2:45 It's not there, nor is it experienced unless it's invented. But how can such a clear and obvious experience, that pretty much everyone shares, be an invention and in this way not inherently or existentially real? The fact that everyone shares in this experience might make it seem like it must be inherent in and a function of the mere existence of being human, like an organ that is a given. Yet, pretty much everyone shares the experience of language, and clearly language is an invention. Therefore, we see that just because experiences are shared doesn't make them inherent.

2:46 So, how does this inner-self get created in such a non-random way? In the ways I've already described elsewhere, but to briefly recap: a thought forms that one's location is at the source of the perceptive faculties and resides as an immaterial "object" within the body somewhere. This idea of an "immaterial object from which consciousness arises and resides" remains assumed rather than inspected, and thus becomes held as the real-you behind the scenes.

2:47 Yet when you begin to thoroughly inspect and attempt to directly experience who you are, you discover that you can't find this self-object, try as you might. The reason you can't find it is that it existentially doesn't exist. It is an invented assumption that forms into what seems like an experience, and this assumption has spread widely throughout humanity—as have many, many other assumptions.

2:48 You perceive a body but only assume there is an unseen internal entity at the source of or "behind" bodily perceptions—this internal self is probably seen as either an aspect of the body or as distinct from but living within the body. When deeply inspected, both body and mind can produce fascinating results—you can discover many interesting and overlooked dynamics here. But no matter where you look in the objective world or what you find, this search still doesn't reveal an inner-self.

2:49 If you stop assuming the shared conclusions drawn from imagining that you are located behind the perceptive organs and associated with the reproduction of your own voice within, and simply stand on objective reality as the foundation, you can see the real nature of this inner-self. Stop assuming and generating the activity that makes it so, and no inner-self exists.

2:50 If not inside, where is the self? If not simply a body, what are you? That can remain an unanswered question for now, and still you are able to recognize the false nature of the inner-self—that it is an activity you are doing rather than a fact of your essential existence. Think about it: if you didn't have any thought or concept that you are within, if you didn't assume a location behind perceptive organs, what would you experience?

2:51 Even within the relative world, we don't need an inner-self in order to exist or to live successfully. Living within this assumption as if it's an essential aspect of oneself isn't useful. Perhaps inventing and using a distinction such as "mind" might create certain benefits. With this invention, we create a new domain of distinctions and relate to matters in new ways that produce new results. Whether these additions are beneficial or not depends on what they are and what they do. But it is never beneficial to accept even such an invention as "mind" as an existential reality rather than what it is, which is the creation of a new context in which to hold a domain of experience.

2:52 On the other hand, being ignorant that an inner-self-object is an invention and an assumption doesn't appear to have any benefits but does have many consequences. Primarily, it defines the life and world that is lived as yourself, thus making your self-sense smaller and more isolated. It leads to much mischief and a detachment from being responsible for your private inner "behavior," tending to reduce your sense of responsibility and overall integrity. Living with such a distinction isn't necessary, but if you do, I recommend that you at least fully experience it as an invention and not as an inherent aspect of your existence—and if you're going to live inside this inner space, at least "clean up your room."

The Nature of Mind

2:53 Since mind seems so central to our self-experience let's take a deeper look into its nature. It might sound like an absurd statement to say that the mind doesn't really exist. But, difficult as it might be to grasp, like the inner-self, mind is also an invention. It is an activity not an existential reality. If we can see that our private inner world is created, it shouldn't be out of the question to consider that mind might also be a conceptual creation. But it takes some serious contemplation to break free of these deeply accepted foundational assumptions.

2:54 From *The Book of Not Knowing:*[1]

> Although culturally we accept mind as part of our experience and existence, it's good to note that no one has ever seen one. Consider the possibility that before the distinction of "mind" was invented by ancient cultures, there was no "mind." People didn't perceive it, think about it, talk about it, or experience it. We like to think that "mind" still existed and people were just ignorant of it. But is that true? Since we don't know what mind really is, it might be that it doesn't exist except as a created distinction.
>
> Try to imagine a world in which you had no "experience" of mind—no thought of mind, no word "mind," no reference to mind, no idea of a "place" where thoughts and emotions "reside," no concept at all that there is such a thing. What would life and experience be like without the distinction *mind*? Mind is an invention in our perceptive-experience that serves to indicate and create the notion of an "internal state."
>
> If we can recognize mind as a created context for experience, we see that this allows for a new domain of distinctions that couldn't occur before this invention. The content of this context is the distinctions that constitute all conceptual activities—ideas, beliefs, concepts, fantasies, imagination, memory, emotions, intuition, and so on. Even our reference to "the mind" (as if something is there) is content, not the context of which I speak. And neither the context nor the content is an object.
>
> Relative to this matter of mind, the only object present is the brain. We may attribute the workings of mind to the brain, but in our experience mind isn't an object, it's an activity. We tend to as-

[1] Peter Ralston, *The Book of Not Knowing* (North Atlantic Books, Berkeley, CA 2010)

sume, without much thought, that there is somehow a "mind-object" filled with "conceptual-objects." Yet in our experience, we only find mind as activities, not objects. When we grasp the nature of mind, we see that nothing is objectively there. If we were to open up your skull and look into your brain to search for the number four, do you think we would find a "4" in there? No, we would find a lot of tissue and blood.

2:55 It might be difficult to grasp what might have existed prior to inventing the idea and distinction we call mind because we live within an assumption that everything we experience was an aspect of being human from the beginning, and people before us may have just been ignorant of these things. But this isn't true at all. Many human experiences and whole perceived realities didn't exist until they were created at some point.

2:56 It is interesting to note that language was invented long before mind was. People talked and wrote before generating the idea of the existence of an inner conceptual domain. If we think human experience has always been the same throughout history, we aren't being very imaginative. Consider that human experience has probably changed radically over the millennia, building upon as well as eliminating whole domains of invented experience.

2:57 Perhaps it would help get a handle on this phenomenon to look at a relatively new set of distinctions becoming a part of our accepted human reality. Consider all the concepts that began primarily with Freud that we unthinkingly bandy about in Western culture today. Whether or not one embraces his ideas, after barely a century, it's nearly impossible to think "pre-Freud." To paraphrase the poet W. H. Auden (from as early as 1939): *To us Freud is no longer a person, but a whole climate of opinion under which we conduct our different lives.* Did "unconscious mind" exist for people before the term was popularized by Freud? Obviously not in people's experience.

2:58 The so-called "unconscious mind" was created pretty much in the same way as mind. That means neither existed prior to their creation. I remember a story told by a graduate student of psychology. He had a professor that fit the image of a typical Freudian with accent and all. One day when the student went to the teacher's office, the professor said, "Do you believe in zee unconscious mind?" The student was taken aback, knowing that the entire domain of psychology is based on this idea. So, he said, "Of course." The professor, looking over his glasses, said, "I don't."

2:59 Imagine before the notion was created that there exists a part of the mind inaccessible to one's daily experience, likely no one thought there was anything in their experience that wasn't known and obvious. It might seem like this aspect of mind was there but not known or accessed, but is that true? Perhaps it's just a new way to look at experience. This might be the same for the so-called conscious mind. In various forms, the distinction of mind or something similar has been made by almost all cultures, but even these aren't all the same distinction. This tells us that it is an invention particular to the civilization that creates it.

2:60 Have you ever seen a mind? No, no one has. It is not something observable and exists only when the distinction of "mind" is made. In other words, you might say that the body exists as something observable and inherent to being human, but why say there is mind? In western cultures the ancient Greeks noticed that there seemed to be something in experience that is not the body and not objective. From this they invented the notion of mind, and off it went into history.

2:61 Imagine what it would be like if you lived in a world where there was no "mind." You may see people all around, and even talk to them and interact with them, but where would you see or observe a mind at work? Currently, you imagine there is a mind operating behind people's actions, but without the distinction of a mind-behind-the-scenes, their actions would simply be their actions.

2:62 You may ask, "But doesn't mind exist even if we don't make such a distinction?" OK, *where?* You are postulating that mind is some *thing* that exists somewhere and awaits your discovery. But that assumption only arises from an experience in which mind already exists as an aspect of being human.

2:63 Mind isn't an object, it is the context for an activity. This activity is called conceptualizing, and it is very creative. Whether this creative nature is good or bad, effective or dysfunctional, is open-ended and depends on what is created. Inventing the context of mind may be useful in some ways, but it is far more powerful to grasp that it is a human invention rather than accept it as a fixed objective reality.

2:64 Core principles of the human condition, such as this, are very difficult to understand because we have such a hard time grasping anything outside our own fabricated "reality"—which, by the way, has been built upon millennia of humankind's conceptual inventions. Consider that, prior to the context of mind, something like perception would be considered a bodily function, such as the eye "seeing" or the ear "hearing." There is no need for mind there. Perhaps, if a thought arose, it wouldn't be a "thought occurring in the mind"; it would be the body knowing or reacting, or whatever related distinctions might be made within the human experience at the time.

2:65 The point is, the invention of mind creates a new way of looking at experience, and so how we see the world. It provides new tools and distinctions and domains that allow us to view awareness and experience in a different context, giving us the ability to invent stuff on many levels. The new abilities that arise from this invention have a powerful influence on our entire experience. Therefore, we should know them for what they are and not take them for granted as true and real in themselves.

2:66 But consider, what is an experience of reality prior to all the inventions we've developed over the millennia? Quite a contemplation. I doubt that saying more will add much clarity, so I'll leave it there.

An Historical Look at the Evolution of the Self

2:67 We have been exploring quite a few overlooked assumptions, many of which probably seem very abstract. So, let's back up to move forward. We tend to view all of this intellectually and conceptually, imagining that some immaterial world of mind and self exists independent and unmoored from the physical world. Let's challenge that notion by considering the evolution of the notion itself.

2:68 Imagine that through the human evolution of the brain, a new level of conceptual ability arose. Because of this ability, and using this ability, humanity created an ethereal domain that might be called the mind, and then separated the experience of the mind from that of the body. Since the notion and experience of the self is founded on and related to this ability, we also assume the self is independent from the body.

2:69 Consider the possibility that all these assumptions are false. It is the body that is the source of the self, it is not separate or independent at all. The brain creates activities that become known as concepts. The thing about concepts themselves is that they aren't objective, even though they are often thought of that way. This gives us the impression that there is another domain occurring besides the body, but there isn't.

2:70 Sobering thought, isn't it? That's only because we have become accustomed to thinking about this reality in a certain way, and it is based on a lot of assumptions and conclusions. Open up to the possibility that the brain is doing self via the synaptic activities that create concepts, therefore there is really no self independent from this activity.

2:71 This is challenging to get, so let's go way back and consider all this from a biological and evolutionary point of view. It's not important that the specifics or details of this argument are accurate but simply that the flow is viable. This unfolding story is just to prepare us for a new possibility usually overlooked.

2:72 Let's start with the beginning of life on this planet. We hear life started in some kind of primordial ooze that enabled simple single-cell organisms to arise. Imagine being a single cell. Here, we can easily see there is little complexity, and no mind or conceptual capacity. But now consider multi-cell organisms evolving. How could that come about?

2:73 Imagine that a collection of cells bunch together by chance, or by forces and circumstances pressing them into a bunch, or because this gathering served some survival function. However it comes to pass, these could well be just single cells bunched together. We can imagine that perhaps the cells inside the bunch might be required to do a different job than those on the outside. The outside cells are exposed to the environment and light, and so may develop a thicker cell wall and capacities to deal with the environment directly. The inner cells, lacking light and with less exposure to the environment, would change their makeup in order to relate to that condition.

2:74 We can see that in this scenario the differentiated cells would each take on different jobs, and a dependency on each other would arise. As this body of cells grows in complexity, some system of passing nutrients and whatnot throughout the group would need to occur for each group of cells to survive, and so systems would be created—for example, a way to pass oxygen and nutrients to all the cells would be needed, as well as the disposal of built-up toxins.

2:75 Now imagine some grouping evolving into a plant. Here, we see specialized cells doing different jobs becoming part of a whole organism, and the miracle arises of using chlorophyll to help capture the sun's energy to fuel the plant. This whole domain is still composed of strictly objective matter, using what's there—light, minerals, water—to create and sustain life.

2:76 After plants become abundant, a new organism arises—a creature or animal that feeds on plants, using the plant's captured energy to fuel itself. Along with the ability to eat plants—usually requiring a mouth and digestive system to absorb nutrients—these creatures have to develop some sort of perceptive capacity and mobility in order to do that job.

2:77 Since generally plants don't move around, the animals feeding on them would need to be able to change locations. You can see a huge leap in complexity is needed, developing many specialized cells acting to supply all the necessary components—from perception to find the food, movement to get to it, and ways to absorb it. These varied components must act in coordination to be able to do all that is necessary. This likely requires some sort of brain and nervous system.

2:78 After the plant-eaters develop, predatory animals arise that now feed on the plant-eating animals, taking their nutrients and energy for use by the predator. This further requires not only perceptive abilities but hunting abilities as well, and hence some form of problem-solving capacity. We can see that we fall into this category, even though we can eat both plants and animals.

2:79 In the increasingly complex creatures, specialized cells form perceptive organs, as well as many systems performing coordinated and interdependent jobs—circulatory, lymphatic, nervous, endocrine, muscular, and so on; and organs accompanying these systems do particular jobs—skin, liver, kidneys, lungs, heart, spleen, intestines, brain, and so on. This becomes quite complex, but the main feature that pushes humans apart from other animals is its brain. One thing to keep in mind, however, is all this complexity is still simply made up of single cells, and in our case, starts with a single cell multiplying into many. The complexity doesn't change that, so don't lose track of this fact as we go.

2:80 From all this development, the human brain becomes incredibly sophisticated. For our consideration, the main point to all this is what this new brain creates. Aspects of the human brain form as if a new "organ" that produces a new function, which in short could be called abstract problem-solving. Other creatures started down this road, solving problems related to physical survival. But this new ability becomes quite complex and abstract, and eventually this problem-solving ability creates a "self" abstracted from the body. Yet, how might that come about?

2:81 This conceptual domain created by the human brain is constantly solving problems—just take a look at the mental activity that never ceases in your mind and ask what "problem" is it addressing? Be it minor or major, you should see that the brain is indeed doing that activity. As the human brain evolves, it develops an ability to solve problems that don't exist, and abstract problems that only occur in imagination. This alone creates a whole new domain.

2:82 One of the things that occurs in this new abstract and imaginary world is the idea that this conceptual world exists independent of the physical world. After all, it seems that way, since the "concepts" that arise as activities, even though produced by the brain, don't seem connected to the physical and in themselves are not objects or solid in any way. How might this separation between mind and body come about?

2:83 After we are born, we have only ill-defined perceptive activities going on, without knowing what any of it is. But as we start to sort them out, at some point we distinguish between the set of experiences and perceptions over which we seem to have control, and those we don't control. In this way, because some perceptions seem related to a location and some impulses appear to control the body's movements, eventually we identify ourselves as being a body.

2:84 Once we relate to being a body, this sets up the notion of being separate from other objects that are not our body. As our conceptual capacities increase and we become more and more abstract and speculative, the notion arises that the self is not just the body but a non-material aspect seemingly separate from the body—although it's overlooked that it is brain activity (body) producing such notions in the first place.

2:85 Having created the assumption that the self is separate from the body rather than being the body itself, we attribute perceptions as being received by the self, not the body, and so it appears that this inner self is located behind perceptions. We may acknowledge that perceptive faculties are a function of the body, but this is why we place ourselves within it. This is followed by the idea that the self is the source of conceptual activity, and so either this self shares the same nature and substance as concept, or it has some nature prior to concept, resulting in the idea of an immaterial inner-self of an unknown nature.

2:86 In this way, building on the conclusion and assumption that this self is the source or receiver of all that is experienced and perceived, and immaterial in nature, our selves become completely abstracted from the physical, and the unfound inner-self-object is born. The fact that the body is the location for all perceptive organs is overlooked, and a sense of some non-objective inner-self-object becomes the accepted and shared "experience" of most humans.

2:87 Since we are constantly problem-solving, and one problem that arises is not knowing who and what we really are, we intellectually set out to answer these questions. But since, in the end, whatever we conceptually come up with turns out to be unsatisfactory, we may also begin to question where and who is at the source of all this perceiving and deciding, which continues to be unknown. As we search to find this unfound and intangible self, we can't find it—yet, we still insist it must be there since it seems self-evident, and more importantly, it seems to be "us."

2:88 Because we continue to desire and imagine great things for this assumed but imagined self, we start to make up fantasies. We imagine that we are a higher self or a soul, and so on. This may give us a transcendent view of ourselves and our reality, but it doesn't advance finding this one or its nature. We've mistaken a false notion of self for some divine entity. It might feel good, but it is nonsense. This "problem-solving" ability has run amok and postulated and concluded all sorts of things that aren't true.

2:89 From all this, our "self" experience seems to exist as some entity detached from the physical. This is supported by the fact that we think and imagine and yet can't find where these conceptual "experiences" come from. Since we have detached ourselves from the body and assume we reside unfound within it, it's not hard to imagine we must be something other than what is conceived and what is perceived within "the mind"—although we often confuse those activities with ourselves as well—and to consider our "real selves" as the unseen source of these activities.

2:90 Could this be the source of the myth of the garden of Eden? By leaving the physical or animal kingdom and inventing some new mental domain that separates us from our objective and biological reality, we become imprisoned within an isolated and false reality—the "self." In any case, we've gotten ourselves into a real pickle based on an assumption that we all share. This whole false conceptual reality is reinforced by humanity, our community, and by religions and spiritual pursuits of all kinds. No one challenges this assumption, it is simply the starting place for all the rest.

2:91 Regardless of the evolutionary development that may have taken place, and the unfolding of social conventions, the present assertion is: the development of a brain that can work to solve problems, even in fabricated abstract and imaginary worlds, produces activities that eventually lead to the idea of the self. This self is only an idea and a conceptual invention. To go deeper, we are required to continue to investigate the domain where this idea germinates.

Why Is There Endless Brain Activity?

2:92 As you begin to consider that the main function of your "cerebral" brain could be encapsulated as "problem-solving," you may have been able to validate this notion for yourself as you have watched your brain working. The problem-solving activity of the brain isn't just an ability, it is a feature, and this feature seems to relentlessly do its job. Watch what your mental activities are constantly doing. What is that? We might call this activity *solving problems.*

2:93 Many, many of these are easy to solve and so may not seem to be a problem at all. Feeling your nose itch? How do you solve that problem? You scratch it, and probably barely notice both problem and solution. But what if your hands are fully occupied carrying stuff, now the problem becomes more apparent, doesn't it? What solutions pass through your mind? Put down the stuff to free your hands to scratch, lean over and rub your nose on the wall, ask someone to scratch it for you? Whatever. It's not that every problem is difficult, and many are rather unconsciously acted upon, but consider that they are still part of this activity.

2:94 Interpreting what something is that you are perceiving, thinking about what you should say to someone, calculating how you're going to manage your time today, deciding what to make for dinner, imagining a better life, or working out how to deal with a scary scenario: these kinds of problems are constant and normal, and most often easily solved—it is just the function of your brain doing that job. But they are all simply aspects of this problem-solving capacity.

2:95 Even the fantasies, stories, and little imaginary movies you run, if not seeming to directly relate to a problem, are at least keeping you from being bored (a problem), distracting you from your current reality in some way for some reason, and keeping you connected to a social world and the activities of life, though these activities are just acted out conceptually. They may also directly relate to some problem-solving—trying out various possibilities, or working out an issue be it physical or social, and so on. Even the apparently trivial imaginary activities that seem to run aimlessly through your head may be needed for maintaining a self, but we'll get into that in a bit.

2:96 Look at each mental activity that arises. What problem is it solving? It could be easily solved having a ready-made solution available, or it could be difficult and in need of finding or figuring out some way to handle the challenge. The arena of problem-solving stretches from the physical to the social, from relationships to abstract considerations, and everything in between.

2:97 Though I'm calling it the problem-solving aspect of the brain, that doesn't mean the solutions we come up with are effective or that they don't create many more problems than they solve. As a matter of fact, when we pay attention we see that a great deal of our mental activity is rather feckless and useless, but it goes on nevertheless. Have you ever noticed that the brain just doesn't seem to stop, ever? At least while you are awake. It goes on and on, and stuff often seems to come unbidden. But intended or not, this activity is ceaseless, even when it doesn't seem to make much sense. Why?

2:98 Study your endless thinking and imagining. It can show up pretty clearly at night when you are in bed but aren't sleeping, or at other times when you don't have much to do but to think or imagine. As you watch this activity you might see it's challenging to stay on one subject for long. Instead, the mind will move from subject to subject, sometimes following a theme and sometimes jumping to something seemingly unrelated.

2:99 What are all these apparently random endless stories and images that jump from subject to subject all about? It is hard to fathom why thought after thought continues to spring up without a great deal of logic to it. What's going on here?

2:100 Consider that the brain contains a huge amount of stuff—thoughts, memories, images, music, stories, imagination, and so on. It is all there in each moment but is usually only accessed as specific images or stories one at a time. The idea here is that whatever is thought in this rather unconscious way is already in the brain. But when something is accessed, connections are often made with other stuff, since its job is to relate many disparate aspects into some "problem-solving" activity in order to imagine various possibilities or outcomes. So it can jump from subject to subject in seemingly random ways, sort of like brainstorming, without regard for immediate practicality. It needs room to move in all sorts of directions to create an activity and environment that can "solve problems."

2:101 As an analogy, imagine the brain is like a container full of trillions of marbles, each marble a thought or image or memory, and they are all there just waiting in the brain. When you reach into this container to pull out specific marbles (reaching for something deliberately, or randomly grabbing whatever is touched upon), you come up with a scenario those marbles represent. Sometimes as you grab related marbles you can also scoop up one or two marbles that are nearby but not related to the group, and this gives you a non-sequitur or weird idea.

2:102 There appears to be some volitional impulse to produce or search for specific thoughts that relate to an intended subject or pursuit. But conversely, sometimes it seems thoughts and images arise randomly and unbidden. In either case, on purpose or not, your brain is ticking away constantly, generating this conceptual activity.

2:103 Perhaps the reason our thinking and imagining, internal dialogue and problem-solving, are constant and ceaseless activities, isn't so much about what's produced by these activities, but rather because they are needed for something else to exist. What could that be? If the self is a function of concept production, then it is necessary to maintain this activity in order to maintain a sense of self—or perhaps they are the same thing: the existence of the activity may be what creates the distinction of self. In this case, the activity doesn't have to produce anything useful, it just has to take place.

2:104 The activity doesn't have to make sense or go anywhere specifically or practically. It can—and will for self-survival purposes—but it doesn't have to in order to produce a self (the experiential locus for what needs to survive). It simply has to continue as an activity because the idea of a separate self is based upon the existence of the activity itself. Further, the brain producing concepts that are abstracted and unmoored from physical reality or immediate perceptions gives the impression that there is something other than the physical at work. From this conclusion the "problem-solving" nature of the brain imagines there is a non-physical self that is in charge of or at the source of this activity. So the result of such conceptualizing isn't as important as the fact the conceptualizing is taking place, keeping up the impression there is a self behind it.

2:105 We've seen that prior to such a conclusion we are likely to simply stand on the distinction of self as a body. From here, if a distinction is made that the self is not the whole body but rather is a function of the body, then the self is seen as an aspect of the body directing and managing gross physical life. This could be considered a function of the brain alone and so still tethered to the physical. Yet if this activity is also considered to be the source of concepts, and this source is unfound, a mystery arises. From here, it is just one small step to the idea of a non-physical inner-self-object. Either way, physical or not, the self becomes an assumed reality.

2:106 Just as the internal dialogue—based on language—keeps a "self and other" present by engaging in an activity that is based on this distinction, so does running conceptual perceptive images (movies, stories, music, etc.) keep the presence of the self locked into the assumption of being located at the source of perception—even though the occurring perception may be conceptual—thus reinforcing and maintaining the assumption that the self is an unfound object of some kind behind the scenes. Again, overlooked is the fact that no location or immaterial self-object has ever been found.

2:107 The brain keeps trying to solve the problem of what and where a self is and so makes observations and conclusions based on the information it has, the foundation of which is largely based on a perceived objective world and millennia of accumulated human assumptions. Yet, none of our beliefs or conjectures seem to ring the final bell of truth. Because our problem-solving abilities have stalled out in this area, and success eludes us in finding this self, conceptual and immaterial possibilities are entertained. Thus we have detached ourselves from being restricted to the objective and instead imagine we must be some non-objective entity. Once this happens we go down roads of assumptions and conclusions from which we build a perceived reality that isn't true. But since this conceptual reality provides the accepted explanation of our own existence, we maintain it and experience it as if it's true and occurring. In fact, it is only occurring because of the generation of imagined concepts producing an assumed world that we accept as real.

2:108 At this point it should become clear that without such activities constantly occurring, the self-mind could not exist. Since we identify with the mind, we can't let that happen. Even attempting to drop it all and just experience a reality without self or mind—and so being without any conceptual activity taking place—we will still make such an effort entertaining by giving it contemplation status, and even that attempt quickly slips away to merge again with some form of mental activity. 'Tis a conundrum.

2:109 Again, imagine the existence of a culture where the self is only a body, and the idea of creating a distinction of some inner self or soul is considered unhealthy and destructive. What would be experienced by that society?

Whatever it would be, would be quite different from the world we assume, don't you think? Yet, it is a viable possibility. What do you think is really the case?

Is There Consciousness Independent of the Brain?

2:110 **Guided Meditation: Creating Thought**

Have a thought right now, just make one up.

Great. Thank you.

What created the impulse to have that thought?

If you didn't really do the exercise but simply read it, go back and spend some time to actually do it and consider it before going on.

2:111 Can the brain do that by itself? If the brain goes through mechanical synaptic processes, does it direct itself or is there some other "component" at work directing the processes, as we tend to assume? We can see that simply hearing and understanding the instruction then following it can easily be a mechanical process, perhaps like a computer with AI. Still, for us, there seems to be something prior to having a thought, but we can't see what that is, and this creates a mystery. If it is the brain itself that is creating an impulse to have a thought, what is that physical activity and how does it come about?

2:112 At this point, we are advised to remember Occam's Razor: *when faced with multiple explanations for a phenomenon, the simplest one is usually the most accurate.* So what would the simplest explanation be in this case, requiring the fewest assumptions or complexities? Clearly, the body and brain creating the thought of self is the simplest explanation, no need to invent a whole new ethereal domain to explain it. This doesn't mean it's true, but that is it most likely.

2:113 Still, we have not answered the question of how particular thoughts, especially abstract thoughts, arise. There is at least a possibility that some form of consciousness exists independent of the brain, or is inherent in the brain itself, that provides the impulse to think or question. It is unknown if this is true, but the possibility exists. Some form of "consciousness" seems to be the source of the impulse to generate specific conceptual activity, but this form may be the brain itself or some other physical or objective manifestation and not what we assume. Whatever is true, it is most probably not whatever we might imagine.

2:114 Entertaining the notion of an independent consciousness of some sort, we are tempted to then create an inner self, or soul, or some such, but this takes us backwards to the superstitions we are attempting to transcend. On the other hand, even though our thought or image of what's true in this case will most likely be wrong, it is useful to entertain such a possibility in order to continue to openly investigate, but not draw conclusions one way or the other too quickly. It may be that the possibility of such consciousness is nearly impossible to get a handle on.

2:115 It is also probable that the idea of some "consciousness" independent of our brain activity is simply a function of the brain itself. Yet, it is still hard to find what is true, be it physical or non-physical. Unless we can clearly grasp something that is independent of the body, it is only a myth, and we don't want to go down that road again.

2:116 Our human culture has already created the idea that we are separate from the physical world and the body, but there is no real evidence this is true, and our assumptions and conclusions are not realistic enough to base our existence upon them. So in our investigation, we need to ground our existence in the body as our starting point—because without it we have no evidence of existing at all. We need to further acknowledge that just as objective reality is not subject to our interpretations or mental shenanigans, as a body we also exist independent of such conceptual activities.

Body

2:117 If we are simply a body, our next question might be: what is the body? We experience the body as an animal and as real. This is our starting point, but clearly we still don't know what that is. On the other hand, don't forget the body is still just a sack of cells. It may be complex, with many groups of specialized cells able to do various jobs beyond merely being a cell unto itself, but it is still nothing but a large collection of mindless cells. That should tell us something, but not everything.

2:118 The body is the only proof and manifestation of a you existing at all. Yet, we don't know what a body is, or what any objects are, any more than we know what awareness or a self is. Although we are very grounded and certain about the existence of both body and objects, we are not so sure about the self.

2:119 It may be aggravating, but we understand that we can't base our investigation upon what we desire to be true, or on what is useful to us, or what we perceive, and certainly not what we think. Again, starting with the body as our only existence, we've seen it's likely that our problem-solving abilities are responsible for creating abstract possibilities that suggest we may be some ethereal being residing within the body. But since this immaterial self object is not founded on anything but conjecture and conclusions, we can rule that out, because if it's true we should be able to find it, to experience it, or become conscious of it. But we can't.

2:120 Although we seem to exist, jumping to the conclusion that we are some immaterial object separate from physical or objective existence just doesn't cut it. It isn't useful. We are far better served by putting the genie back in the bottle, eliminating all the conjectured conceptual hoopla, and simply letting the self be a body.

2:121 You may have missed a leap we made in all this, from the rational and almost scientific argument being laid out so far to something more mysterious. You are left with an inability to find what you are. If you're a body, then what is that? If you're not a body, then what are you? You need to clearly find what you really are to solve this problem. If you're not directly conscious of your nature and the nature of existence, you will be unable to solve it and perhaps not know where to turn—unless you just take my word that you don't exist and your nature cannot be found within what's conceivable, but that doesn't increase your consciousness at all. I see no way around it: difficult as it may be, you have to become conscious of what's true, and not just choose a side or a belief.

2:122 I'm going into all this because in our cultural evolution as humans we have gone down a road of assumptions that aren't true. That road is to imagine we are an ethereal being, a one within, a soul, a witness, and so on, and assume this indicates our nature. Even those that have had their first few enlightenment experiences are usually still stuck in this myth. Because a shared assumed existential foundation dominates mind and experience, the whole idea of a self still exists even with some degree of enlightenment. Such a partial direct consciousness is still about "you." Among other things, I'm trying to free us from this myth.

No Perspective Is True

2:123 One impediment to dissolving myths or any other invented reality is the fact that all humans view the world a certain way. Each of us has a perspective on what life is and how it all goes down. We view life based on self-concerns and self-interests formulated around the belief systems we've adopted.

2:124 No matter what you think is going on in the world and in your life, it will be based on your perspective—*how* you view it, and *why* you view it that way. It will be formed around a framework built from your beliefs, assumptions, values, culture, past, and so on. Most people have a hard time clearly discerning their own perspective because to them it seems they are just observing the world. But this is far from true. Looking more carefully you should see that you have a particular viewpoint and a specific perspective of the way it all is. The thing is no perspective, no view, is true.

2:125 I know this is likely not going to be a popular assertion. Yet, it's not possible that any view can be true. This might be very difficult to get, because we only grasp stuff through the filter of our perspectives. But we can see that any perspective is based on the conceptual stuff mentioned above and more, and that stuff is all invented and adopted by humanity, our culture, our family, and ourselves. This limits the view to made-up stuff, not to what's inherently true.

2:126 I'll bet you can get this more easily by looking at others and how they get it wrong, or at least seeing their views as views and as unnecessary. But consider it must be true for you as well. And all perspectives are conceptual in nature. It is "knowledge" formed in the mind and interpreted by an already biased individual. In this way, no perspective can actually be true. But it goes much further than that. It is existentially not possible for any perspective or world view to be true.

2:127 Of course, we could be more or less devoted to pursuing what's true. We might work hard to be honest and to perceive what's true as best we can. And this will be a much more powerful and different experience than any other. But even then, our view can never match the existential nature of reality, if for no other reason than a view is always one-sided.

2:128 For example, we view an object from only one perspective, one side, and can only see what's visible to us from that perspective, that physical point of view. We don't see the other side of it or under it, and so on. If we could view the object from every angle and every side infinitely, we would have more information and a much different perspective about it. But even then, we still don't see it from the inside, nor do we see its real nature, or see it for-itself. It is the same for all our perspectives on reality. Intellectually we can understand this limitation, even though we can't seem to transcend it. Yet, our challenge is even trickier than that.

2:129 Our subjective perceptions might be up for grabs as to their ultimate validity, but we have to admit that the objective world must be without alteration and so we're perceiving what's true, aren't we? Well, maybe not. Certainly, there is a seemingly solid foundation offered by the physical world and we respect its nature as not subject to the whims of mind and perspective.

2:130 Yet, we see that we add a great deal to what we perceive no matter how much or how little information or data we have about it. Just as we are unable to see objective reality from every viewpoint, inside and out, we have to admit that an ant or a bird or any other creature will not perceive the same object as we do. This tells us our perceived reality is always self-created, and not simply a reflection of what-is but a function of the viewer.

2:131 Beyond these limitations, it's not possible for anything formed and limited to represent the real nature of existence. No perspective can occur without being formed and so limited. For you to personally experience this may seem out of reach or perhaps it just seems irrelevant. I appreciate that sentiment. Yet, you still may be able to recognize that whatever perspective you have, it is not absolute or completely free from bias.

2:132 You can also grasp that your particular perspective could change, and probably has changed from time to time, and so can't be inherently or existentially true. Yet, if you miss why your changing views demonstrate that they can't be existentially true, you may not grasp this point. For reality to be inherently or existentially true it can never change or be subject to various views, because it is what IS. That means it is not created temporarily or to serve some end, therefore it is not an activity that comes and goes. The truth of existence must be absolutely what-is, beyond any changes. Get it?

2:133 Although some perspectives are more empowering or effective in real life, none are themselves true. Once we know this, when we are stuck with some emotion or mood or outlook that causes distress, and we don't seem to be able to get our feet under us to manage this experience well, it is useful to know that even our strongest and most demanding view is not in itself true. In this way, we are better equipped to drop it, regardless of any overwhelming pressure to stay with it.

2:134 Beyond any practical applications of this assertion, the upcoming mass of material needs you to challenge your perspectives as you proceed. Remember, hard as it may be to confront, no view, no perspective can be true—not even yours. Hold it as only an attempt to grasp some matter, see it as a temporary placeholder, while partnering with the possibility of grasping whatever is true directly.

Chapter Three

MOVING TOWARD THE ABSOLUTE

Pressing Beyond Inventions

3:1 So far, we've touched on several overlooked experiences we live within as if they are inherent or existential aspects of our reality when they are actually inventions. In Part II we'll see much more that is overlooked, especially in the form of deeply shared existential assumptions that create our experienced reality. But understanding the depth of these upcoming unconventional assertions rests on being able to experientially recognize the invented building blocks that constitute much of our perceived world.

3:2 Although you can stop generating any invention, some might be useful to keep, while others are not. Either way it is powerful to truly get and genuinely experience that they are all inventions, whether used or not. No matter how many experiences are really unnecessary inventions best tossed, or how great and powerful some inventions are, none are objectively existent, and so they can't ultimately be real. Their reality exists as an activity you are doing, not something that just *is*.

3:3 Whether ultimately real or not, when we investigate our mental or physical domains thoroughly we discover an incredible and brilliant complexity to them. Yet most people spend their lives without such exploration and merely take much for granted about the world in which they live. For example, the human brain is far more ingenious than most of the thinking that comes out of it.

3:4 The complexity and interconnected intelligence that seems to comprise a bee colony, or the complex inner workings of a computer, pale in comparison to the human brain. This brain is what produces all that we experience, including concepts and ideas and all that we call mind. Yet we only access understanding the brilliant design of the brain indirectly through science and research. The end product of this effort is a knowledge that takes the form of ideas, concepts, and images of what's true about the very organ that is producing those concepts. But we don't access it personally by directly experiencing our very own brain.

3:5 Imagine what might be different in our world if we did. To do so, however, we'd be required to match the intelligence, complexity, and effectiveness of our own brain within our conscious-experience. We assume we can't do this because we don't do it. Yet we have to admit that we are quite close to and intimately connected with our own brain, self, and body. What's to say we can't become conscious of the real nature or intricate dynamics that exist in the very place we experience *being*.

3:6 Such a notion isn't considered possible by our culture, but possibilities exist outside the assumptions of any culture. Consider that whatever you are, you can become directly conscious of it because it *is* you; and whatever life and existence are can also become directly conscious to you because you are alive and you do exist. These would be direct encounters, and not merely inventions—and if we discover that any of it is invented, a direct encounter will reveal that as its nature.

3:7 A direct encounter is quite different from most of what occurs in the domain of your mind and experience. It is not having an idea, belief, assumption, conclusion, conviction, image, conjecture, feeling, perception, sense, knowledge, intuition, or any other form of experience that comes about through indirect means. It may be hard to understand, but indirect means the "information" coming into your "consciousness" is not the thing-itself but an activity—a representation or an effect—that is independent from the subject even though it seems to be related to the subject.

3:8 All perception, thought, and experience is indirect. This is just saying the perceptive-experience you have of something is not the same as the thing-itself. For example, when you see something you assume—and live as if—the perception is the same thing as what's viewed. But sight is a function of light bouncing off an object and you interpreting the light. This means the "data" gathered by the light stimulating nerves in the eye are funneled through interpretation and association to make sense of it. Any one of those activities makes it indirect. Without the light, you have no experience of the thing whatsoever, and even with the light you don't have any information that isn't carried by light. Yet, no matter how many indirect perceptions, concepts, or other activities are added to the mix, it will still be indirect—because it is.

3:9 When it is direct, it isn't dependent upon anything but the subject itself, because it *is* the subject itself. See the difference? This is not a common distinction. Everything perceived or experienced is indirect. The only exception might be having an insight where the subject hits one's consciousness without a middleman. This, however, is still a function of mind, and not the true nature of the subject, but it indicates the direction of a direct encounter.

3:10 We can divide this direct-encounter distinction into two possibilities. One is a direct consciousness of the absolute or true nature of some aspect of existence—this is also called "enlightenment," what I usually refer to as direct-consciousness. The other is gleaning what something is, or is about, in a relative sense. We could call this a direct encounter in the relative domain.

3:11 Here we can even directly experience an invention. That means we grasp the invention *as* an invention, even while we are using it. This provides a very different perspective of and freedom from just living inside of it. In any case, personally experiencing the truth of a subject and getting what it is for-itself could also be called a direct encounter.

3:12 Simply said, grasping the truth of something directly for yourself, not based on hearsay, belief, conjecture, or anything else, could be called a direct encounter within our relative reality. On the other hand, becoming conscious of the true nature of any aspect of existence—self, other, existence, life, etc.—is a direct-consciousness of the absolute truth. Neither of these are inventions, or subjective musings. In both cases the direction is toward what's true.

3:13 Ultimately, the depth of consciousness we are pursuing here is based on a direct experience of the absolute nature of existence, so our pursuit must include grasping the absolute. Although that may sound abstract and inaccessible, or rather grand and special, it's simply the nature of existence prior to what we perceive and experience as reality. So, let's look more deeply into what is meant by the absolute.

The Absolute

3:14 One thing that isn't an invention is the absolute. But it sure sounds like an invention, doesn't it? Perhaps we think it is simply a philosophical notion or metaphysical idea. It seems far away and awfully grand. How could this not be an invention? The ideas, fantasies, and concepts we have about the absolute *are* inventions. But the absolute itself is not. So first we need to pull the word down from the clouds.

3:15 The absolute, here, simply means it is not relative, it is what's true at the root bottom, the very nature of existence. Try not to hear "absolute" as something grand or exalted, and certainly not as inaccessible. As an analogy, imagine that the temperature referred to as absolute zero is simply when all atoms stop moving completely. We can see that when temperature heats up, atoms move faster, and when it cools down, they move more slowly. This creates a relative scale of hotter and colder. But when we get to absolute zero the atoms stop moving altogether. That takes us off the scale. You can imagine that encountering such a shift in condition would be a radically different experience because there would simply be no activity going on at all, just the stillness of existence.

3:16 Although this is just an analogy, and absolute consciousness is not the same thing as absolute zero, if we hear absolute in this way it might help make it less mysterious. We simply have to step off all relative scales. The essential nature of existence already exists independent of relativity, therefore, we simply need to become conscious of what's already true.

3:17 When we attempt to tackle absolute consciousness, however, we will naturally try to understand or experience it. Although a necessary endeavor, these efforts cannot succeed on their own. *Understanding* and even *experiencing* is not the end of the story, and for such absolute consciousness, obviously, we need to get to the end of the story. But this might not mean what we think it means.

3:18 There may be some confusion about this in the sense that one could imagine being conscious of the absolute means to know absolutely everything. This is not the case. The idea of knowing everything is actually a relative matter and won't happen.

3:19 Why won't it happen? Because *knowing* and *everything* are both relative distinctions, they are limited forms of experience. Knowing can go on forever, meaning that new distinctions and creations, learning and discovering, can occur infinitely. Therefore, such knowing can't ever be reached since infinity doesn't end. Infinity is an absolute.

3:20 When we speak of absolute consciousness, we are talking of being conscious of the absolute nature of something, not being absolutely conscious. Here we are simply conscious of the true nature of existence, and this is where it steps out of the relative. Yet, again, this direct-consciousness is not dependent on mental understanding or perceptive-experience because those faculties are relative, and the absolute is not. The good news is that we can actually become conscious of the condition and nature of our own existence directly without intellect or perceptive-experience acting as intermediaries.

3:21 This consciousness is done directly by "you"—your real nature—not by your mind or your invented self—neither of which are capable of such consciousness. The kind of understanding and conception that allows learning and gathering knowledge to take place is a function of mind, making all knowledge an addition to your self-experience rather than inherent in it. Therefore, such knowledge is indirect no matter what it is. It is never a direct-consciousness of what's true.

3:22 Whatever is true about the nature of existence—an existence able to generate the complex mechanisms that allow for inventions and knowledge to occur in the first place—was true before any knowledge or conceptual invention or understanding was ever created. Direct-consciousness, on the other hand, enters the absolute because it is the very "thing-itself"—not an understanding of it, or a perception of it, or even an experience of it.

Let's go to the dictionary to look at what's said about the absolute:

- something that exists without being dependent on anything else.
- ultimate reality.

3:23 Existing without dependency on anything else means it is not relative. Relative demands a this and that. For example, up depends on down, good depends on bad, objects depend on space, self depends on not-self, and so on. One cannot exist without the other. Any distinction cannot exist without the existence of whatever is not that distinction.

3:24 When I speak of the absolute, I'm referring to what is absolutely true about the nature of existence. It's good to remember that when it comes to you this absolute nature *is* you—what you really are—rather than what you experience or perceive. This nature is beyond and not limited to your "self," because it is absolute, yet it is still your nature. Grasping you directly means you are conscious of the very source or essential nature that you are. It's like grasping the "substance" of the uncarved block, whether carved or not. This "is" exists prior to trying to experience or perceive something—it is direct.

3:25 At this point, you may well be thinking something like: "maybe no absolute really exists, it is just a fantasy, and reality is simply what I perceive and know of as reality, and this absolute stuff is just nonsense." I truly appreciate the power of such a view. It's true that what people hold as the absolute is just fantasy and nonsense. Beyond that, however, we must acknowledge that something has to be true, and absolutely true, even if it isn't how we think of it. Yet, as discussed here and in the trilogy,[2] there are all kinds of impediments to our seeing what's really true. So I invite you to stay open. Without denying them, be willing to move past such reactions.

Absolute versus Relative

3:26 An absolute defies understanding because it's prior to any method of understanding or conception. It also defies being reduced to any kind of perceptive-sense for the same reason. Our ability to think about the matter is cut short because the absolute can't be reduced to anything relative, and distinctions—which are always relative—are essential for creating any domain of thinking or perception. This is not to say we should try to stop perceiving or thinking, just that we should allow for a new consciousness to arise that isn't limited to those activities. The absolute isn't found in any distinction, even though we are right now making a distinction called the "absolute" in order to consider the matter.

3:27 Before we go on, it may be useful for me to further clarify that I use the word "distinction" in an unusual way. The dictionary definition suggests that distinction is the difference or contrast between similar things or people. Although this somewhat applies to my use of the word, it is far too limited. What I'm referring to with the word "distinction" is nothing less than everything.

3:28 A distinction simply means that whatever we are talking about—an experience, an object, a thought, an action, a fantasy, or anything else—it is that

---

[2] Peter Ralston, *The Book of Not Knowing* (Berkeley, North Atlantic Books, 2010); Peter Ralston, *Pursuing Consciousness* (Berkeley, North Atlantic Books, 2015); Peter Ralston, *The Genius of Being* (Berkeley, North Atlantic Books, 2017)

and not something else. For example, when an object exists it is solely that object, it is not any other object, or the space around it, it is not light or fear or a conundrum. That is how it gets to exist. If it is not distinct from not-it, it can't exist.

3:29 Do you get how I am using the word? Everything experienced in any way is a distinction, its mere existence is that distinction. It's important that you understand what I'm saying when I use this word. [For more on distinction see: *The Distinction of "Distinction,"* Chapter Twenty-Four in *The Book of Not Knowing,* and *What Is Distinction?* Chapter Three in *The Genius of Being.*] Now, back to our consideration.

3:30 Everything—bar none—is not only a distinction, it is always relative. If you know it, understand it, feel it, sense it, or it exists in any way, it is relative. Relative simply means "in relationship." It is me and you, this and that, here and there, something and nothing. All of these are relative. Once reality is formed, it is relative. It has to be, because whatever the form is—no matter what it is—it is not something else, and that makes it relative and distinct.

3:31 What you understand and can conceive is always relative and so never absolute. You cannot understand or conceive absolutes. For example, try to imagine infinite space. Notice that you can't. The best you can do is imagine lots and lots of long distance with the idea that it goes on forever, but you can't conceive of this forever because it doesn't stop anywhere. Whatever you conceive or imagine, notice it is not the reality of infinite space. You can understand the idea but can't experience the reality. This is because infinity is an absolute, and its true nature is not relative, and not what you think. Do you see how it's not possible to accurately conceive of absolutes?

3:32 You can, however, become conscious of what's absolutely true, because such consciousness does not depend on conception or perception. Yet, when you grasp that an absolute is not in any way relative, you will still make a distinction to represent the absolute, and the distinction itself *is* relative, because you have created a domain of the absolute and a domain of the relative, and so have created a this and that once again. See the rub?

3:33 The absolute doesn't take sides. Ultimately, there really is nothing here. But this too can be misunderstood. If you say the absolute is nothing and not something, then once again you've made it relative. It is nowhere else, it is not other than the relative. There is not some ethereal world or mystical place where the "absolute" lives—that would just be more relativity. We aren't really talking about anything here. There isn't one speck of a subject either here or absent from here. It is the true nature of here, and this is inconceivable.

3:34 That doesn't mean you can't grasp it. You simply can't understand it or conceive of it. Understanding and conception are limited or relative forms of consciousness. You can become directly conscious of an absolute, but you won't be able to "picture" it or relate to it outside of making some relative distinction.

3:35 **Let's do a thought experiment:**

Imagine that nothing exists except infinite space. There is not one element other than space and your awareness of it, even you don't exist as an object, just awareness.

First, consider that you don't experience space, you experience distance instead. How do you normally perceive space at all?

Perceiving an object, you notice the distance between you, as an object, and it. Since you perceive objects all around, you are aware of distance all around and call that space.

You imagine that you can perceive space without objects since you can think about the notion of empty space without visible objects. Yet, if you stop taking this assumption for granted, you can notice that your imagination has a three-dimensional component that is objective—as if this space is filled with some ethereal substance—which likely extends out only to the limits of your perceptive capacity.

This can be hard to grasp because we generally imagine objects as solid and distinct substances. Yet consider that air is objective, even if we don't see a distinct substance to it because it is invisible to the eye.

But now, in your space without objects or substance of any kind, what can you perceive?

Notice that you can have no perception or conception whatever of anything, since there is nothing there—meaning there are no objects at all—and so you can't even perceive the space. Think about it.

Try to get that a *concept* of space is the only thing that could possibly suggest any idea of space—and that could only occur as a memory of having perceived objects previously. If you hadn't, you could not even have a concept of space.

In fact, you would actually have no perception of space whatsoever. Soak in this no-space space and try to grasp its nature.

Notice, here, you experience no element, quality, or aspect—so much so you can't imagine it or think it. This can be challenging to get because it's rather impossible to conceive that, without reference to any object existing, there would be no perception of or even an idea of space. There would be nothing that could be perceived.

So, your awareness and perceptive-experience would have absolutely no discernable element to it, you wouldn't experience anything and would have no reference or location; and without any conceptual activity—which would have to be based on a past formation that no longer exists—there would be nothing at all going on.

3:36 This thought experiment offers a sort of "consciousness" of existence that is very different from what we normally experience. It isn't a direct encounter, but perhaps it does create a way to approach grasping the limited nature of perception and comprehension, opening a door to overlooked possibilities.

The Unthinkable

3:37 Even after your first few encounters with an absolute, you are clear that you've become conscious of the true nature of something. Yet, you'll still make a distinction that this nature is not something else—such as your true nature isn't your personality or mind. In a real sense this is true, but in so doing you've made a distinction that isn't actually the absolute consciousness you encountered, although it's the best you can do at the time.

3:38 At the moment of your "enlightenment"—of whatever subject you directly encounter (and the very fact that we are talking about "subjects" creates distinctions and relativity, but hold that to the side for now)—you find no conflict or separation from the thing-itself. But then your mind immediately joins in, and when that activity occurs, distinctions will arise in relation to your new consciousness. They won't be correct, but you're likely not to notice that because your consciousness is true and your mind is simply trying to contribute something thinkable. But consider, how can you limit or squeeze an absolute into any distinction, into any thought, or sense, or feeling? You can't!

3:39 It is useful to know that any distinction you make can't and won't be the absolute itself. It will be a relative event. But as we saw with the uncarved block, as the distinction itself occupies your attention and perception, you will likely miss the fact that even this distinction is of the same "substance" or nature that is the absolute. Whatever your mind comes up with, however, it cannot be absolute even though it is trying to relate to or understand this breakthrough. Although this mind activity may be a limited form of consciousness, in such a direct encounter you will likely not grasp that fact because doing so requires a much deeper level of consciousness.

3:40 Yet armed with this understanding you may be able to stretch your "mental" cognition to include a representative presence of this direct-consciousness of the "untouchable" absolute, and not take such a distinction—understanding, experience, or imagery—as anything but a placeholder for something beyond distinction. It's a little like how in language we use sounds or shapes to bring to the fore a distinction that has nothing to do with the sound or shape used. But without using a word to communicate something, that distinction isn't brought forward into our awareness. Although the absolute is not itself a distinction, the best the mind can do is use a distinction that refers to this consciousness, while simultaneously recognizing that the distinction itself is not the consciousness to which it is pointing.

3:41 The absolute Truth and your cognitive awareness of this Truth are not the same thing. The absolute is what's True, the real nature of "existence." You can become conscious of the true nature of any aspect of existence such as you, another, life, an object, or existence itself. But this still isn't likely to be the complete absolute Truth—where there is nothing left to become conscious of—even though it is absolutely true. The limitation lies in the limited depth of your consciousness, not with any error in your encounter.

3:42 After many enlightenments, you start to piece the whole together. Instead of simply grasping the nature of this and the nature of that, you can begin to create a consciousness in your experience that more closely represents this absolute nature, rather than just forming another mental invention. At some point, you learn to live with the limitation of mind and stop trying to get the mind—and therefore perceptive-experience—to do a job it can't do. Instead, you remain directly conscious of what can't be thought.

3:43 As Wittgenstein so eloquently said: "Whereof one cannot speak, thereof one must remain silent." This is not to say that one can't be conscious of whatever is being talked about, so the statement is not an excuse or a place behind which to hide. Obviously, the quote implies that something is "known" that can't be spoken. And the reason it can't be spoken isn't at all because "it just can't be put into words," but because it's not possible to even conceive.

3:44 Remember, conception and understanding aren't everything. They are just limited forms of consciousness. Unfortunately, that's all most people have access to and all they think is possible. But they're wrong about that. They simply have to transcend the limitations of mind to grasp a consciousness that precedes mental inventions. In order to do that, however, you must be willing to be wrong about everything you think and experience as reality, including the way the world works. Most people have a very hard time entertaining such a possibility.

3:45 Imagine a "consciousness" that is so intrinsically capable it is able to create the context of "mind" and the distinctions of experience, including conception and understanding. It is reasonable to assume that some potential exists prior to everything perceived or experienced that inherently has the ability to create such domains. What is *that* reality? What is the nature of existence before anything is created, before meaning, before life, before the big bang, before the universe, before time?

3:46 Absolute consciousness is not elsewhere. It is physical existence. It is mind and perceptive-experience. Even though its nature is without element, this nature also applies to all that is elemental. It exists right in the same place that everything exists, but not *as* any *thing*. It is the true nature of everything, and there are no aspects to this nature, not even space or nothingness. It is not separate from existence, it is the nature of existence. It is Now, and there is nothing here at all. All existence is contained within non-existence. Or to say it another way: "thereof one cannot speak." But one can become conscious.

Experience versus Consciousness

3:47 One of the reasons so many misunderstandings can take place about these subjects is due to a very challenging dynamic extremely difficult to discern even by those who have had enlightenments. I have already touched on this several times, but it bears repeating. To sort out this dynamic, let me further make a distinction between "experience" and the "consciousness" that arises from enlightenment.

3:48 Perhaps I should first clarify what I'm referring to as experience. For this discussion, experience is everything that you are aware of—what you perceive, feel, think, assume, believe, sense in any way. Anything that comes into your awareness I'm calling perceptive-experience. A subset of experience is what you have going on within your internal state, including your interpretations of everything. I'm calling this conceptual-activity "mind," which influences everything you experience. Mind and experience constitute the world in which you live, and it is everything that is occurring or known by you in any way, including yourself.

3:49 When an "enlightenment" occurs, this new consciousness is not the work of the mind, even though the mind is the main tool used to pursue such consciousness. The consciousness that arises or awakens is not an "experience" and does not occur within your mind. It is directly gleaned by your real nature, prior to any activity. Again, this is what is meant by "direct."

3:50 When this occurs, however, the mind or experience is deeply affected. Some related experience will immediately arise as an activity. This is almost always fused *with* the enlightenment and frequently mistaken *for* the enlightenment itself. Yet, what the mind does isn't the same as the sudden increase in consciousness, it is just the impact that consciousness has had on your mind. This can be difficult to understand or even grasp because understanding occurs within the mind and is either conceptual or experiential. But neither of these are direct-consciousness.

3:51 As long as the mind and self are active—creating the context for experience—both comprehension and experience will take place consistent with this self-mind. Mind and experience will always remain the foundation of your awareness because they are key aspects of and necessary elements for survival and life. That is why it is so difficult to grasp an unbridled consciousness free from any marriage with the relativity of experience.

3:52 As I've communicated elsewhere, I recognized early on that most people who've had enlightenment breakthroughs mistook their new-found consciousness with the forms that arose in their minds immediately afterwards. I called this the Lava Syndrome, using the metaphor of an erupting volcano, suggesting that breakthroughs will harden into a new form of rock as soon as the lava cools. This happens with any breakthrough, because experience always degrades into concept. What's usually missed in this metaphor is that with direct-consciousness the "breakthrough" is not formed in any way, and any conceptual-forms that arise cannot match this consciousness. Like I've said, this isn't a dishonest impulse but a mistaken one.

3:53 The mind will do its best to form something related to the consciousness—not knowing it will fail. The mind is so open and pure at that moment, and is so affected by this consciousness in such an unprecedentedly freeing way, that it will feel as liberated and authentic as possible. From this place, whatever is created or formed—so that there is some distinct experience you can relate to—will be held as an enlightenment "experience."

3:54 The overlooked operative word here is "relate." The mind creating some way to relate to this consciousness immediately degrades the absolute consciousness into a relative experience. Perceptive-experience divides reality up into distinctions, which is necessary for life. But within these distinctions direct-consciousness is not to be found. What is found is a "state" or "experience" that is related to your breakthrough but is not the consciousness itself.

3:55 I don't want to give the impression that direct-consciousness is in any way inaccessible or needs to be vast or immense to be real—as we've seen, vast and immense are *relative* distinctions. There are many "minor" as well as "deep" enlightenments, and they are all true and can be direct conscious breakthroughs. A more minor or partial enlightenment is no less true, it is just limited and not very profound in its depth. This is hard to understand, I know.

3:56 To explain this, I often use the following analogy: if water represents a consciousness of the truth, a thimble full of water is indeed water, it is truly water. But it is not the same depth afforded by grasping an ocean of water, or infinite water. They are all true in that they are all water, but what one grasps with a thimble is different than what one grasps with an ocean. This might not clear up how or why this should be so, but it helps ground the mind in something thinkable. It is still detrimental to place the mind in search of something colossal—this is only an ideal and a mistake. I am simply trying to point out something hard to grasp, and this tends to lead us to believe it is inaccessible. It can certainly seem mysterious at times.

3:57 For example, one of the rather mysterious aspects for me shows up sometimes when I'm facilitating others. I can have something in mind to get across about the nature of some form of consciousness, or a new distinction not generally made by people, or an insight or what-have-you, and communicate it fully, having nothing more to say on the subject. I might look into my experience for more but find nothing. It seems I'm finished and have run out of anything to add. But then if someone asks a question, or sometimes even just says something like "What?," a flood of material can come pouring out.

3:58 It is difficult to say where such new communications come from, because previously looking into my mind and experience I found nothing to contribute, it was completely empty. When another mind enters with a question or response, however, suddenly what wasn't previously there springs to life. It seems to arise instantly in relation to that mind. It's as if consciousness, when confronted by this alternative perspective of reality—which is placed over and against what seems obvious to me as a direct-consciousness or an authentic experience—tends to reveal what needs to be addressed in order to clarify the matter to that perspective.

3:59 This puzzling dynamic aside, the main point here is that what occurs within the mind or awareness or perceptive-experience is not a consciousness of the absolute, and apparently this is difficult or almost impossible for people to grasp. Any direct-consciousness will affect your mind and influence your experience, and these will relate to the breakthrough, but they won't be able to match it or represent it in any way that is accurate.

3:60 That's because all experience and perception exist within the relative domain, and the absolute is not relative and so impossible to "think" or "perceive." This will always be true of the absolute. Since almost no one—including those claiming enlightenment—really knows this, much mischief can occur and misunderstandings abound when it comes to such matters.

Leaping Beyond

3:61 Trying to convey what is not possible to convey, of course, isn't possible—whereof one cannot speak. But I will toss out a few more nuggets in a futile attempt to convey what's unthinkable. The first point is possible to get even though it has to be done existentially, which isn't common. The last point is only accessible with direct-consciousness but does offer an extremely unconventional view that reeks of paradox impossible to square away, yet might be an interesting confrontation nevertheless.

3:62 It is very difficult to point to a new experience when there is no shared reference. Therefore, in order to do the next exercise, drop all assumptions except that you exist. Normally people's sense of existence is founded on their history and identity, and their character as a person, but drop all that for this exercise. Here, focus just on the bare-bones sense of your mere existence, not as something in particular, or as what you experience, just that you exist, unknown and unseen, the mere existence of you without form. Can you do that?

3:63 **Guided Meditation: You as a Distinction**

Put attention on your awareness of this moment. Don't single out anything, just be aware of all that you perceive now. Don't think about it or assume anything. Be open. Get that you have a distinction in your experience that is you, and you have a distinction in your experience that is everything not-you.

Just have those two distinctions in your experience. Don't single out anything perceived, just dwell on the fundamental distinction and experience of the existence of you and the existence of not-you—don't worry about specifics.

Concentrate on this you and not-you. Grasp experientially that not-you is always right there with you. No matter what you experience it is either you or not-you, and in every moment if there is a you there is not-you, if there is not-you there is you. They are inseparable.

Get this like an experience until you find yourself solely within the distinction of you and not-you—like you exist as a "thought" that you exist. Not-you also exists as a "thought" that is experienced. When you can experience no separation between you and not-you, except as a thought that there is a you and a not-you, soak in this experience and open up. Don't assume. Be inside of this experience as it occurs.

When you've done the best you can with that, ask: what is the real nature of existence without any me or not-me? What is the nature of existence itself?

3:64 Consider the following statements:

You are not your mind, you are not different from your mind, you are not other than your mind.

You are not your body, you are not different from your body, you are not other than your body.

You are not the world, you are not different from the world, you are not other than the world.

You do not exist, you are not different from existence, you are not other than existence.

3:65 The kind of understanding that allows for such statements to be heard as anything but gibberish can only arise after gleaning a direct-consciousness of you, body, mind, and world. Within a relative experience there is no way to understand this except as strange statements that are clearly impossible. But it does offer the notion that the Truth is of a nature that embraces paradox.

3:66 Please excuse my attempts to convey something impossible to convey. You are invited to seek out the truth for yourself, disregarding anything I've said. But perhaps something said has helped point you in a direction you wouldn't have considered heretofore. If a direct-consciousness of what's true isn't of interest to you, and you don't see the benefit of attaining such consciousness, then simply pass on all this.

3:67 As I said, I offer it primarily to those who have devoted time and energy to such a pursuit and mostly to those who at least have had their first "kensho" (first glimpse) and beyond. This is also true of Parts II and III. Then we'll end with more practical material. I started with these difficult subjects because it might help you really dig into the matter of life and death, and the truth about ultimate consciousness. It will also help you benefit from more practical stuff to come, because without a freed-up and detached context from which to view the reality you experience, you will remain stuck inside this reality and so not be able to master it properly. All that aside, let's wrap up this enlightenment stuff by having a look at some of the pitfalls that attach themselves to such an endeavor.

Chapter Four

CONFUSIONS AND MYTHS REGARDING ENLIGHTENMENT

The Enlightened Ones: What They Are and Aren't

4:1 There are quite a few people claiming something called enlightenment. Yet there are many myths, lies, and misunderstandings surrounding this matter. For me to speak precisely about what enlightenment is, or who is really enlightened, is absurd. It isn't possible with any real accuracy. What is possible, however, is to try to clear up some of what isn't enlightenment or the result of enlightenment. Also, it might be useful to point to some of the signs of the presence or absence of this consciousness, and to point out that there is a difference between the person and their enlightenment.

4:2 Again, as I've said, enlightenment is becoming directly conscious of the true nature of existence, or any facet of existence. Direct-consciousness means there is no method or perceptive faculty used, there is no separation between your consciousness and the Truth—that's what makes it *direct.* This is not a function of the mind or any faculty of the mind, such as cognition, feeling, intellect, intuition, conclusion, etc. Yet, to the mind, it is seen as the best "experience" to have—even though the consciousness itself is not an experience.

4:3 As I've pointed out, the mind will be affected by this consciousness, and so in that moment a new experience will arise that is often confused with the enlightenment. I know it sounds like grasping the nature of existence would be a perceptive-experience that you become aware of, but it's not. That's why such direct-consciousness is impossible to understand unless it occurs for you personally, and this fact opens the floodgates for misunderstanding and misleading mischief from others claiming such consciousness.

4:4 When trying to sort these things out, it is useful to separate the person from the enlightenment they claim. One myth about enlightenment is that a person will be immediately transformed by it, and always in the same way. This might sound reasonable because the Truth has to be the Truth and can't be different for different people. The problem is that what's also true is the mind and self-makeup that existed before the enlightenment are left more or less intact after it, and these minds and selves are all different. Some substantial changes will occur, but complete freedom from mind and self while maintaining a personal life is unlikely in the extreme.

4:5 Although the consciousness itself is free from the self-mind, this self and mind will still remain active. This self-mind is a human attribute created as a way to persist and to manage life, and as social creatures this especially applies to managing a personal social life. Our lives occur through the activities generated by both self and mind.

4:6 The self-mind involves making distinctions, ordering reality, and identifying with a locus and an individual. Although it's possible for this to change radically, and can be very different from person to person, it will tend to follow the basic patterns that have been created throughout one's life, and will also follow cultural foundations because this is the world in which our lives take place.

4:7 Still, the freedom supplied by direct-consciousness creates the possibility to transcend all this by seeing it for what it is, and yet most people who've had one or even a few enlightenment breakthroughs do not transcend life or self—though, given the enlightenment is true, they will recognize that all forms of these activities are themselves not existentially true. Such consciousness, however, doesn't mean the person is freed from a self-identity, and so they will tend to act out life generally as they would have previously, based on their built-up personality.

4:8 Just bring to mind people who claim enlightenment, or who you think are enlightened, and notice that each is very different from the others and each has a unique personality; and this personality—other than some changes in perspective and perhaps temperament—is undoubtedly generally like it was before they had any awakening. After enlightenment the trajectory of their lives can take very different paths—from great contributions to humanity, to solitude, or just waiting for life to end—depending on the person and their mental state and intentions. No matter what path they choose, however, they must still act out life until they die.

I didn't come here of my own accord,
and I can't leave that way.
Rumi

4:9 Let's look at some examples of people who may or may not have had some degree of enlightenment. William Shakespeare demonstrates through his ingenious plays a possible consciousness freed of cultural assumptions and an understanding of how the human mind works, as well as many insights regarding life. He may have simply been a genius in his field, but it is possible that he also directly grasped the nature of mind and life, and so had a capacity to relate to them in ways most people don't.

There is nothing either good or bad,
but thinking makes it so.
William Shakespeare

4:10 I've mentioned elsewhere that there are indications Leonardo da Vinci likely had some enlightenment, simply because of his capacity to create outside the norm in so many areas, and his ability to think in uncommon ways freed of the fetters of norms and assumptions.

Among the great things which are to be found
among us, the Being of Nothingness is the greatest.
Leonardo da Vinci

4:11 A direct-consciousness can make great contributions more accessible to the creative and committed mind of particular people, such as the above possibilities. Yet the real point here is that a drunken bum on the street may also have had an enlightenment experience. This flies in the face of the fantasies and myths surrounding such breakthroughs—that's why I mention it. There is nothing inherent in having a direct-consciousness or two that prevents the overwhelming drives and attachments a person might have from drawing them into what we might see as a wasted and degraded form of life. I doubt it is the norm, but I suspect it has happened.

4:12 The thing to get is that enlightenment doesn't guarantee the way life will unfold for someone. It does tend to move it in certain directions just because of the nature of such consciousness. The trend is toward honesty, freedom, and compassion, with tendencies toward transcending binding human assumptions and conditions. But this is not guaranteed and really depends on the degree and depth of the consciousness, as well as the character and agenda of the individual.

4:13 Trying to understand the effects of enlightenment using those that claim enlightenment may not be the best measuring stick, since their claim may or may not be genuine. Even if they have had a direct-consciousness of some kind, the depth of this is up for grabs, and what they do with it can be empowering, misleading, or just self-serving. What a person does and how they do it depends on the person—their mind, assumptions, past, culture, intent, and their purpose for doing it. It is actually likely that most people who "preach" about enlightenment will have a hidden agenda in operation that has nothing to do with whatever consciousness they may have.

4:14 For example, I was asked to watch a woman with a large following who claims to be enlightened. I watched, and although she had a good presence and emanated certainty, in my view what she was doing was totally self-serving. She was not really facilitating or empowering her followers. Instead, she was "laying down the law" that she has worked out and pushing a cosmology that she invented as if it were true. Her work with people didn't really support them to grow or become conscious for themselves, but instead she pressed them to get that they were wrong. She seemed to always have to be right and be seen as better than others, even though this was all couched in a "spiritual" presentation. So, she didn't really have students but "followers" who simply believed in her proclamations.

4:15 This kind of disposition is not rare, it is actually frequently the case. I have personal knowledge of "teachers" mixing invented cosmologies, or adopted belief systems, with what should be genuine and pure contemplation or investigation. This confuses people because it becomes unclear what is an honest pursuit of the truth and what are simply claims being made or beliefs held. Imagine how much damage might be done, in many ways and on various levels, by those in positions of leadership who push personal beliefs and agendas rather than keeping fidelity to the truth.

4:16 Other examples might include people who've become famous because of entertainment-show exposure or by accessing other social means to get noticed. Regardless of the depth of their consciousness, the fame and authority that accompany their communications undoubtedly provide them with a much higher status and platform in the eyes of others than is real or deserved. Again, such tendencies are not unusual, they are the norm. Any enlightenment experience is inevitably not complete, and one's head can easily be turned by the adoration of fans and followers. What is more enticing than the admiration of others? Not much, and people with some degree of enlightenment aren't immune to this draw. These elements should be taken into account.

4:17 When listening to such people it is important to be clear about what their communication is actually doing, and not get lost or distracted by interesting-sounding rhetoric. In the end, is the communication empowering or not? Does it just entertain and resonate with your beliefs, or does it push you toward self-discovery and the truth? Most people open to such communications have a hard time discerning the real from the false, or recognizing the difference between liking it and grasping whether it is truly empowering or not. Yet, paying attention and asking these kinds of questions go a long way toward recognizing what's there.

4:18 Of course, there are just straight-out charlatans. But the point is even such partial consciousness doesn't demand that people be truly honest about their communications, nor does it mean that what any individual comes up with, or invents, is true. People mix personal and cultural assumptions and inventions into their assertions all the time. It's very hard to stay clear of such influences, and people who have not had such breakthroughs will have a hard time knowing what is true and what is just tagging along for the ride because of the beliefs and mind of the person speaking. Remember, there is a big difference between the person and whatever consciousness they may have—those are not the same and shouldn't be conflated.

The Ramana Conundrum

4:19 One of the challenges and confusions we find in most spiritual practices, perhaps all, is mixing cultural assumptions and personal beliefs with the Truth. Some practices are solely belief systems and not relevant to a discussion of becoming conscious of the Truth. Yet even those that are founded on pursuing some sort of direct-consciousness or enlightenment inevitably contain overlooked cultural influences polluting the communication—if not at first, certainly over time when the practice is passed down to those attempting to realize what's offered rather than having realized it as did whoever founded the practice.

4:20 When Ramana Maharshi took on teaching, even if reluctantly, he had had a deep direct-consciousness of the nature of self. His work was insightful and tended to cut through bull and fantasy. But eventually even he fell back onto cultural relations to food and diet and other beliefs that relate only to his culture. His well-meaning explanations can also be easily misunderstood as stages necessary for enlightenment. Neither food nor culture is "true" or necessary, but for even one of the best of us, such beliefs infiltrated his teaching.

4:21 When we think of Zen we often think of neatness and well-swept walkways or raked stone gardens. We might picture a zafu and robes, perhaps some beads as part of Zen paraphernalia. Do any of these have anything to do with Zen or the truth? Of course not. They are primarily Japanese cultural aesthetic values and traditions, and these got mixed in with their way of structuring Zen as a practice. No robes or any dress that was current only in years past has anything to do with the pursuit of the truth, nor do any of the other trappings that are associated with a practice.

4:22 Dancing with bells, shaving your head, adopting a peculiar diet usually originating from another culture, changing your name to one from a different language thinking it makes you more spiritual, wearing special clothes, developing a specific posture, and so on—none of these things has anything to do with the truth or becoming more conscious. There are many trappings that get mixed into spiritual practices that have nothing to do with an honest pursuit of the truth. In some cases, they may have a nice effect on the mind, or help one focus, but this isn't the truth or an intent to get to the truth, it's managing your experience. In many cases, they are just ridiculous and unnecessary affectations that have nothing to do with the truth or its pursuit.

4:23 When we add cultural assumptions to our pursuit, it blurs and distorts our view and intent. Imagine adding the common American idiom "lift yourself up by your bootstraps" to a practice. The sentiment has come to mean "be responsible for your own success," but if such an adage were to pollute a spiritual practice then people would buy boots and try to lift themselves into enlightenment. Think it will work? Of course not! You can't actually lift yourself from your bootstraps. But people may try for a long time, and will fail, thinking this is what they need to do and they are just unable. Can you see the parallel here? Mixing cultural or personal values, traditions, beliefs, or trappings with a spiritual practice or the pursuit of the truth is always a mistake.

4:24 This applies as much to any newly invented practices as it does to the traditions. Intellectual arguments, psychological additions, freshly minted models and theories, declarations and conclusions, and believing in hierarchies are all just as faulty and misleading. They are independent pursuits that may or may not have any value, but they are not a pursuit of what's true. They are a pursuit of what's thought or claimed to be true, and that is a vastly different pursuit. In some cases, perhaps most, they just encourage spinning mental wheels with more beliefs and ideas. Pursuing imagined outcomes—which in the end are just claims, conclusions, and theories—is a mistake, because it doesn't embrace the open-ended possibilities necessary to pursue whatever is true no matter how it fits with any belief system.

4:25 Diet, fantasy, beliefs, assumptions, imagination, culture, traditions, rituals, costumes, cosmologies, drugs, ad nauseam do not and cannot lead to enlightenment or to discovering the Truth. They may or may not get in the way, but they are not a commitment to discover what's true. Instead, they are something to believe in or do, with the mistaken idea that they are going to produce an awakening within you. They will not. They are at best unnecessary "jewelry" and trappings that just distract from the real work of consciousness. At worst, they are traps dooming a practitioner to a fruitless ritual of pursuit, thinking it will produce results it cannot, and therefore wasting your time and giving false hope.

4:26 Getting past the pitfalls of any practice and focusing on the real intent—which is to directly and personally grasp the truth for yourself—leaves you with a task but not an answer to your search. So, you will remain ignorant of the truth until you aren't, no matter how learned or sophisticated you become within any practice. Enlightenment or absolute consciousness can only be done directly. Indirect methods won't cut it—although some may assist you in keeping your attention on the effort until you make a breakthrough.

4:27 This is not to say the opinions or conclusions of an individual are more valid than believing in blind traditions, or that the self is the best arbiter of the effort to discover what's true. You may well benefit from the honest assistance or facilitation of some practice or person because they can help you step outside your insular world, point out things overlooked, or expose you to possibilities you would not come up with on your own. Yet, in the end, it is always your responsibility to become conscious of whatever is true, no matter what anyone, including yourself, says.

4:28 Some innocuous trappings or rituals that have been attached to a practice may not get in the way of pursuing the truth and might even help the practitioner's mind to focus or ground their efforts. The point is, none of these attachments are true, and it's best to understand them for what they are, and see them at best as tools to be used and tossed, and as ultimately unnecessary. It is also useful to see that many of them are detrimental and obstacles to your pursuit, or perhaps just sirens leading your attention in a wrong direction.

4:29 Still, you have to make the attempt no matter where it leads you. Just be alert to any accessories, assumptions, or beliefs that might pollute a genuine investigation. In the next part, trying to tackle the reality of death and the real nature of existence and life is a very tall order—one of the tallest orders we can take on, and one that has had no genuine understanding throughout the history of humanity. So we must allow ourselves to be a bit audacious, being open to the possibility that we can make headway where the great thinkers of the past could not. Our commitment must be to the truth, however; beliefs won't do. We must be willing to delve into the inconceivable and even the illogical, which are seemingly insurmountable barriers and may be why no one (or at least very few) has cracked this enigma heretofore.

Part II
BEYOND LIFE AND DEATH

You are probably filled to the brim with insanely challenging stuff already. But you ain't seen nothing yet! So, buckle up. The next two parts are far more difficult. There is no quick fix or easy solution to the most challenging subjects humans have encountered since we first developed the ability to ask questions. Reading what's to come is a huge undertaking, understanding what's said is even more difficult, and experiencing the truth of it all is a task that demands your whole heart and soul. Of course, it's your choice whether or not you take on this task, but since you've been reading this book and have come this far, you are obviously interested and courageous enough to go forward.

I will attempt to lay out a step-by-step explanation, working our way toward an incredibly deep consciousness unlike any human experience we've shared heretofore. To foreshadow the overarching conclusion to all this, spoiler alert, *you* are the problem. The challenges to being deeply conscious exist because of the self. This is one of the sticking points of the whole human experience, to think we are individuals and actually exist as separate selves. But this is not really true.

Notice how we gravitate toward such statements as "I think therefore I am," or "I am that I am," and see these as positive and profound assertions. Yet we miss the obvious arrogance that is at the base of this whole matter. It is all based on the existence of "I," which doesn't exist. Becoming conscious beyond the self provides a totally new experience of the limited reality in which we are stuck. But as I said, this is a challenging subject to address for many reasons.

Chapter Five
WHERE WE STAND

5:1 Let's face it, the chances of actually transcending life and death are slim. Clearly, we have no desire to let go of life. Instead, we are completely committed to it. Because of this, we tend to ignore and avoid even the thought of death. But we really don't know what life is and have no understanding or acceptance of death beyond fantasies and ideas. That said, let's proceed.

5:2 Throughout this study you will encounter many unconventional and unknown facts about your experience that will blow your mind, and you will be exposed to realities that almost no human even knows are possible. You should have many insights along the way. The journey itself will be transformative, but unless you attain the deepest level of consciousness the final goal will remain elusive.

5:3 Even having had a few enlightenment experiences won't do it. You'll have to have a much deeper level of consciousness to accomplish such a goal. Shy of that, however, along with your many breakthroughs, you'll still end up with a road map for pursuing this level of consciousness—given you wish to commit to such a thing. So the study and journey, even though extremely challenging, is worth the effort.

5:4 Commensurate with your work on transcending life and death, you will also discover how to be complete while living life. This alone will make a huge difference in your self and life experience. So, even if you fall short of the ultimate goal, you'll benefit greatly by delving into the assertions to come. Throughout this study, from time to time, I will draw from past material when helpful or needed, to prepare you for more difficult material to come because many of the upcoming assertions will not only be new but unprecedented, and we'll need a shared foundation in order to proceed effectively.

A Most Difficult Subject

5:5 Life and death are obviously about existence and non-existence. But for us it is really about *our* existence and the end to *our* existence. This connects the subject of living and dying to what we experience as ourselves. If we are not conscious of a nature that is not alive and cannot die, then we will just cease to exist at death. Are you conscious of anything about you that is independent of life and death? Most people aren't.

5:6 Transcending life and death is a very difficult and a very uncommon thing to do because it has no social rewards, is not related to what serves a self, and isn't a part of our culture or our experience in any way. The task in front of us is immensely difficult and not at all popular or common. People do not want to confront or even think about death as a real inevitability for them. We push it into a "future that will never arrive."

5:7 Yet, it will. We don't want to confront this because it means the end of ourselves, completely—despite all the myths and bullshit to the contrary. There is a relationship between our denial and avoidance of death, and our sense of isolation and aloneness. This may seem like a stretch, but it isn't. Still, we need to know more about self, other, and death in order to connect the dots in this case.

5:8 Of course, in attempting to tackle this ultimate and most fundamental subject matter—your existence and non-existence—there needs to be a good deal of contemplation on your part, and this contemplation must take place throughout the communications to come. Take each assertion made and contemplate it until you can find it in your experience or have an insight about its nature. You need to become immersed in the experience in which you live, as well as grasp your experience in ways that are true but inconsistent with your normal way of perceiving things.

Death as a Doorway to Consciousness

5:9 We might wonder what is the use of focusing on death? It seems a dreary subject. The only reason it seems dreary, however, is because we are wed to life and persisting within it. This seems like a no-brainer—what else would we be wed to? Yet, how can we really understand life unless we understand death? After all, they are the flip sides of the same coin.

5:10 Perhaps we'd prefer to focus on improving our lives, and maybe the only reason we engage in pursuing an increase in consciousness about anything is thinking it will improve our experience in some way. For tackling the depth of this work, however, we have to get past such a limited focus.

5:11 Remember, Ramana Maharshi and Gautama Buddha were both motivated by death and not the search for "enlightenment," and certainly not the pursuit of improving their lives. As a teenager, Ramana was affected by his father's death and became obsessed with his own. Lying on the floor, he went through acting out the process of dying, asking what is left when this goes or that goes? In the end, he had a deep enlightenment of his true nature. When he got cancer in his old age and simple treatments failed, he refused more serious attempts to save his life, reportedly saying, "Why are you so attached to this body? Let it go" and "Where can I go? I am here." Such a disposition may need more explanation and understanding in order for us to grasp what is being said deeply enough to also free ourselves from death, so we will do just that.

5:12 Siddhartha Gautama (usually known as Buddha) was a prince who led a sheltered life as a young man. Upon leaving his palace and confronting old age and death for the first time, he ended up making his mission in life to deeply understand and become free of both life and death. This led him to the deepest possible consciousness humanity has acknowledged. We also see in the story of Jesus that he allowed himself to die rather than save himself, showing a transcendence of self-survival.

5:13 It seems some of the heavy hitters in consciousness work began with a focus on death. Death does cut through all the spiritual fantasies and bullshit people can get caught up in. Perhaps it can offer a doorway into the real nature of existence.

What to Expect

5:14 Remember, to make breakthroughs and pursue deepening consciousness you must read this whole book as a contemplation throughout, no matter what subject we happen to be addressing at any given time. Take it all seriously. The chances are slight you will achieve the depth of consciousness needed to grasp the deepest parts of this work. Yet the more you experience the simpler or more understandable assertions, the better equipped you will be to tackle the absolute nature of existence, and therefore life and death.

5:15 Consider hearing this like a very different kind of contemplation, and in Part II, keep your background focus on the possibility of transcending life and death. Take this material on as if there is no input from me, and you are doing this all alone, coming up with subjects to consider and contemplating them yourself. There will be deep and difficult subjects to tackle, but it is imperative that as you listen you contemplate whether or not any assertion is true, and work hard to experience it directly for yourself.

5:16 When you hear something we've already addressed, don't hear it the same way you did the first times—and I will repeat myself. Don't just intellectually hear what's being said, look at a repeated subject as an opportunity to continue your contemplation of it and work even harder to truly grasp it or grasp it more deeply. When something is repeated it is because it needs repeating, and it should be approached within the context of all the new material that has been presented up to that point.

5:17 Anyone who has read *The Book of Not Knowing* more than once can attest that each time they read it they grasp more stuff than they did the time before. That's because as your consciousness grows you become increasingly capable of recognizing communications that would not even register previously. In my old school I had the staff participate in the main consciousness workshops every time we did them. Over the decades not once did a staff member say they had gotten it all and it was just repetitive. Instead, more often they shared their new depths of consciousness and their excitement about grasping material that had eluded them up to that point.

5:18 When you hear some assertion again, ask yourself: do I deeply experience what's said, do I have insight into its nature? If not, then more work needs to be done. Actually experiencing the matter or having an insight will change your experience of the subject. It won't be the same as the world of just hearing about it—it will be a different reality. If it's not, you haven't really gotten it in a way that will transform your experience. Remember, it's not enough to hear or even understand an assertion. You must isolate what the subject is in your experience, and then look into it, taking the time to investigate the matter experientially until you make progress.

5:19 Transcending life and death is close to the ultimate consciousness any human can attain. You will tackle new assertions that virtually no human has even heard about, let alone experienced. Know that this is nearly an impossible task for a human. Everything you know and are will likely resist this possibility; your mind will reject, ignore, blank out, merely believe—or more likely disbelieve—much of what will be asserted, especially as we get deeply into it. It might sound like a good idea, but transcending life and death is not a walk in the park. It may be the hardest thing a person can do.

5:20 In the beginning the material may be difficult but you can grasp it. The next three chapters start with pretty gettable material so as to lay down a foundation, getting us on the same page before we proceed further into the deep end. I will go over stuff you may have heard before, but I need to create an experiential foundation that you can recognize in order to ground our work. As we proceed, however, the material runs into impossibly challenging subjects that only leaps in consciousness can resolve.

5:21 Again, throughout I will repeat and repeat and repeat what may appear to be the same assertions. Your job is to make sure you deeply experience the matter, not bemoan the fact you heard it before. This makes it an ongoing contemplation. There may be times when it feels overly repetitive and a hard slog. Consider this aspect rather like a mantra, to be visited over and over. On the other hand, if you completely and directly experience the assertion, then just revel in hearing about it again and enjoy the freedom and insight you have in the matter. If this is not the case, listen more carefully and work harder to experientially grasp what's being communicated.

5:22 To be clear, throughout Part II we will be working on two goals. Grasping how it is we create our experience of reality and becoming complete with life is one of our goals. The other is grasping the absolute nature of existence and transcending life and death. These are not the same goal. I don't want you to be confused as I keep switching back and forth between the two. Remain clear on this, and remember to keep each as its own goal. Stay with the progress being made in your understanding and consciousness for each as they unfold throughout this basket-weaving of subjects.

5:23 Remember, you must set out to prove these assertions for yourself directly. Whether successful or not, make sure not to turn any of it into some kind of belief system, especially the stuff about death and the absolute. If you find yourself doing that, then just toss it all out, and start from scratch on your own. If you turn any of this into a belief system I'll kill you, and then you can find out about death for real. ☺ Are you clear on this point?

5:24 Although so much may seem out of reach, there will be a lot that you can grasp, and no matter whether you obtain the ultimate possibility or goal, you will be exposed to and experience assertions that few humans have tackled heretofore. Again, your mind will be blown, and you will have a different view of life and reality by the end of this work. There is much you will get, even if you fall shy of the ultimate goal, so it is worth the effort. Let's begin.

Chapter Six

EVEN THE EASY STUFF IS HARD

Self-Obsession

6:1 As you start down the road of investigating life and death, acknowledge that the starting point is you. Notice you are obsessed with yourself. Watch. Your attention is always on you or coming from you and everything perceived or experienced is related to you. Right now this is the case, isn't it? Can you experience your obsessive focus on your self, right now? This is such a fundamental principle for all experience it is overlooked. Don't overlook it.

6:2 Throughout your past, can you find a time when you were not in the picture and central to whatever was experienced? Even in those rare moments when you might have had all your attention on another or an event, you are still the one perceiving it, right? You are still there in the background as the one experiencing the event. Don't you seem to exist all the time, and aren't you the most important aspect of all existence? In your world, aren't you the center of the universe?

6:3 Do you get that you are self-obsessed, self-oriented, self-centered, and truth to tell, very often selfish? Can you find anything in your experience where you are not the central character? You are the one managing life. You are the one doing everything you do—you are the one eating, walking, talking, thinking, feeling, emoting, and everything else, subtle or gross. You constantly care for your welfare, avoid pain, and seek comfort.

6:4 You are upset when your feelings are hurt. Why? Because you experience yourself as a social entity and think this social-self is important. Therefore, everything said to you is all about you and your ego, your identity. Don't you hold that the person you are is special and important, and wants to be loved and not criticized, etc.? Do you think this is real, or is it just a mental fabrication created by you trying to manage your self-image and self-esteem and protect your ego? Look into it.

6:5 Even if you can't see that such reactions are there to serve you, at least you can see that you are central to everything you experience, right? They are *your* feelings and *your* reactions, and it is always about you, no matter what you attribute as the cause.

6:6 Can you experience that you exist largely as a social being, and therefore your self-experience is mostly a function of the human community? Consider that this is a false reality, an invention and an activity. This social activity is not existentially real. Yet, all your experience is based on this very self. If your attention is ever on anything other than you, you still hold that you are the one giving the attention. Can you find anything that isn't about you? I'm not talking just about what you experience, I am also asserting this is about your very existence. You think you exist and are real and necessary. This is completely taken for granted and accepted as the true condition of being. Entertain the notion that it is not real or necessary—that *you* are not real or necessary.

You are the problem, not the solution.

6:7 Can you see that the fundamental principle of being self-obsessed will totally bias and dominate all experience? Do you get this like an experience that is real for you? Can you find anything that is true outside this context, this self-obsession? Even if you can't, notice you still hold that something must exist outside and independent from your self and self-experience, correct?

6:8 Discovering whatever that may be requires the ability to look outside your self and outside all social content and context. Can you do that? Is there any possibility of experience not of your own making? That would mean whatever is experienced, "you" would *not* be the one experiencing it. Sounds strange, doesn't it? Realizing this possibility would demand becoming conscious of experience independent of your own self and mind.

6:9 Now, consider that experience and even awareness do not have to be dependent on you. You are invited to entertain the idea that life, consciousness, and reality exist outside and beyond your self and your self-experience. You assume the existence of yourself is behind everything you perceive and think and do, yet this might not be the whole story.

6:10 You acknowledge there is a reality outside of you, because you experience a vast domain called not-you. But notice that even everything in that domain is related to you, and you think that you are the one perceiving it. If there is another possibility of experiencing reality outside of your experience, you don't know, because you are stuck in a world of self.

6:11 Perhaps probing into some of the basic foundations of this self-experience would be useful to help us find a way to get free of it. Recognizing what we are stuck within is the first step to getting unstuck. Acknowledging the forces and dynamics that push us into a non-random world of needs and desires, fears and resistance, self-concept and self-preservation, empowers us to eliminate such self-created dynamics, or at least relate to them differently and with more detachment. Since when we consider life and death we are considering *our* life and *our* death, we see, once again, that the self is the main feature. We need to get beyond this self in order to attain a much deeper consciousness.

Being Alone and Meaningless

6:12 If we are going to transcend life and death, it would be useful to know what life is and what death is. But guessing, concluding, or believing just won't cut it. Since most of us won't have access to a direct knowledge of these existential subjects, we need to find another route to success.

6:13 Toward that end, we can grasp the reality of life by looking deeply into what constitutes our experience of it, and by getting free of our deep assumptions about life and the meaning of life. Likewise, we should confront the overlooked and resisted reality of death. With these two foundations, we can proceed to create a new understanding and experience of, and so relationship with, life and death.

6:14 We may not need a direct-consciousness of the true nature of life to begin tackling this issue as it relates to our goal of transcending it. On the other hand, it would be useful to understand that life really doesn't exist, that it has no meaning, and for humans it is basically a generated, albeit powerful, conceptual experience. This experience is almost completely generated by the mind and exists conceptually as a fabricated reality, something like an illusion superimposed upon our perceptive faculties. But we don't need to grasp this to proceed—it is only useful because it provides freedom from our many primal assumptions about life. So consider life in that light.

6:15 Entertain the possibility that life itself has no meaning, since meaning is a human conceptual invention, and life existed prior to the existence of humans or human conception. Take a moment and let that sink in. It is an obvious fact once seen, but it is easily glossed over without grasping the experience that life really has no meaning.

6:16 Also, consider the possibility that what you experience as life, and especially your life, is not what it seems—that what you experience is superimposed upon your perceptions by giving meaning to everything in relation to you, and then imagining a drama unfolding that is only created by your self-mind. (For a more in-depth look into this reality, see *The Book of Not Knowing,* and others. I won't spell it out here.) Without these activities added to life, what would remain?

6:17 As impossible as it may seem, we need to grasp that our experience of life is an activity of mind. We think it is biological, but besides not knowing what biology really is, we need to examine more closely where a personal life exists. It exists for us primarily in our self-awareness and social concerns—which encompass far more than we usually think.

6:18 Saying life is meaningless might go down better if we see the activities of life as something akin to space rocks bumping into one another. Unless we give it some, we see no meaning or significance to this activity. We usually know nothing about such cosmic activities, and they hold no thought or concern for us. Consider life is something like that, a meaningless activity that we apply meaning to because of our focus on and commitment to survive as a self. For us our real concerns about life are social. Beyond assessing the mere threat or benefit of something for physical survival, isn't this where most meaning is applied?

6:19 It may be challenging to grasp, but the world of a social reality arises the moment a sentient self and sentient other have been created. After that, everything that results from this distinction is social. From this social context an immense of experiences and realities arise. Think about it. If we took all social meaning out of life—and in so doing eliminated all value, significance, comparison, importance, reactivity, the idea of destiny, the need to attain, feeling like something is missing or wrong within ourselves, concerns for what others think of us, and on and on—what would be left? Seeing life without all that stuff, we'd see life very differently, wouldn't we?

6:20 If our goal is to transcend life and death, we need to recognize that all this hoopla we're attached to and take so seriously as our personal life and drama is just that—a meaningless activity. We see ourselves and lives in a story we imagine describes both self and life, yet the end of this story is not something to make a fuss about. It has no meaning and isn't important except to ourselves. Grasping this allows us to more readily be able to let it go. If we are going to accept the reality of death, we need to be able to do that.

6:21 When you die you die all alone, all by yourself. Why is that? What overlooked experience and assumption does this reveal? It points to the fact that your entire self-experience is already alone. You were born alone, but with an inherent drive toward others and life, and you will die alone, without that or any other drive.

I'm the one that's got to die when
it's time for me to die.
Jimi Hendrix

6:22 Throughout life we're alone, living in an isolated private inner world. This fact is known by us, but the experience of being separate and alone is felt as a malady that should be overcome. We struggle with taking care of our individual and separate self while trying to remedy this sense of being alone and isolated. Do you think this dynamic might influence your experience of life and yourself?

6:23 We've jumped into this topic pretty quickly, already confronting life as a meaningless activity and ourselves as being isolated and alone from birth. That's a lot to take in in such a short period of time. So perhaps we can back up a bit and take this one step at a time.

6:24 Given we are alone, where is it that it seems we could possibly not be alone? Trying to solve the problem of being alone is found solely in the social domain. Having warmed up to our task, let's begin to look into our social experience more deeply.

I Is Us

6:25 Looking into our self-experience—that which will die—we may find it useful to see how it came to exist. Unknown to us, what we experience as a self is actually a function of shared human inventions and assumptions. Although we might start life as a rather blank slate, quickly we work out an identity to take our place within this human world. As we do, we overlook the fact that there are consequences for adopting the many assumptions that go along with becoming a part of this world. But that's a lengthy story, so let's start with our most core condition and look at how it's built.

6:26 On some deep level everyone experiences themselves as separate and isolated. But this is a condition that has to be created before it can be lived. What we don't see is that inherent in the social world we adopt are assumptions that lead to this outcome. We fail to grasp that what we experience as a self is a construct and an invention of our social reality. Even though we think we exist as an individual that simply sprung up from the universe, as if from spontaneous generation, this isn't true at all.

6:27 Being busy living life, we overlook the fact that our self-identity is really a social function and that a society and culture exist only within the people who make it up. When we look at it impartially, it's plain that culture is purely conceptual—there is no culture outside the minds of the people who comprise one. Instead, we live as though individuals and cultures are separate events, as though somehow our social reality exists apart from us. This is a bit like thinking a forest exists independently from the trees.

6:28 Our culture is made up of our collective perspectives and values, our assumptions and beliefs, our methods of thinking and behaving, and so on. Since we're born into a culture and a society, we can no more avoid being shaped by it than we can avoid being the product of a gene pool. Our culture, our community, our society is you and I—and everyone else. A social world exists within all of us as a shared accepted reality. It is one of the most basic factors in the framework from which we perceive the world around us. (Note that in this work, references to society, culture, and humanity are all basically referring to the same activity and dynamic.)

6:29 Many shared assumptions are foundational to our perceptions. We can't help but take them for granted, which makes it difficult to recognize how much they dominate our entire experience of self and environment. No matter what we encounter, much of our interpretation of the event or object or person is predetermined by the assumptions that unconsciously shape our perceptions. Core shared assumptions bind us all and are as common and natural to us as the air we breathe. These assumptions are shared beliefs adopted not from personal choice but simply as a result of being part of humanity.

6:30 Even various subcultures, regardless of their differences, are founded on the same basic assumptions. It may sound as though these assumptions are somehow force-fed into our thoughts and perceptions, but our indoctrination comes about quite naturally in the process of growing up.

A few examples of generally overlooked human assumptions:

- Perceptions reflect reality
- I am in here and you are out there
- I am an individual
- I must survive
- You are not me
- We all live inside bodies as inner self-objects
- I am located behind my perceptions
- Life is necessary
- Objects are not-me and are rather insignificant compared to me
- Life should mean something
- I'm special and unique
- and so on

Most or all of these assumptions probably just sound self-evident, don't they? You likely never thought of them as assumptions but merely as observations or givens of your existence.

6:31 Such foundational assumptions are reinforced at every turn and simply fall into place like basic "truths" that dictate the nature of our experience by shaping our interpretation of whatever's perceived. They simply appear as perceptions and observations rather than assumptions, don't they? By calling them assumptions I'm obviously implying they are not true but are instead generated by an activity of mind that is shared but unrecognized.

6:32 On top of foundational human assumptions we also have many beliefs that come from our culture and family. Since these assumptions and beliefs are shared by everyone around us, we don't recognize their considerable influence. It is like being a fish in water unable to recognize the water. Hard to fathom, isn't it? But begin to entertain the possibility that this is the case.

6:33 Since the birth of humanity, people have created many phantom worlds in which to live. In fact, our most powerful inventions are not technological at all; they are conceptual. Every culture needs structure and values in order to function as a cooperative effort, and commonly held beliefs and assumptions provide a shared reality in which to be and interact. But for this work we must think beyond such limitations.

6:34 In response to the questions of existence, such as "Who are we, and why are we here? What is life, and how did we come to exist? And what happens when we die?" a staggering number of belief systems, values, religions, cosmologies, and worldviews have been invented, lived, and taken very, very, seriously. For the most part these "inventions" occurred organically or collectively over a period of time, but despite their unpremeditated beginnings, they are inventions nevertheless, and none of them are true in and of themselves.

6:35 By design, the modern human mind craves knowledge, especially in places where we can find none. When faced with an absence of information, we'll make something up—we will believe and assume. This tendency appears to be universal—in every culture, some set of beliefs arises to fill in for the lack of absolute "knowledge." Every subculture with a set of beliefs clamors to have the last word on the subject, claiming themselves guardians of the Truth. Many different factions are willing to war over their inventions, but no one is willing to confess that they simply don't know what the truth is.

We delude ourselves that we want to implant honesty in our children; what we really want is to imbue them with our particular kind of dishonesty, with our culture's dishonesty.

Sidney Harris

6:36 Everything we invent in this way and live as if it were real or true will determine our experience of life, and even our ideas about death. It's difficult to grasp that our beliefs and assumptions have such influence. To recognize this, one would first have to forgo attachment to his or her own personal opinions and admit that the ideas at issue are beliefs rather than the truth. Acknowledging this point is scary for anyone. It opens the door to doubts, and few people can tolerate the possibility of their whole belief system unraveling.

6:37 Keeping that in mind, it becomes easier to understand how difficult it is for us to question any of our beliefs, no matter how subtle or seemingly inconsequential they may be. We're quite willing instead to accept the consequences. We'll shoulder all the woes of the world so long as they fit in with our way of holding reality.

6:38 As you can imagine, there are many kinds of beliefs and assumptions that warrant scrutiny—not only your personally indoctrinated beliefs accumulated over a lifetime, but shared human assumptions that don't just influence your perceptions of self and life, they create your perceptions of self and life. This can be hard to fathom.

6:39 Clearly, this is a big and deeply layered subject. In working our way toward understanding, we need to proceed in steps that will probably seem much more like leaps. To start us off, one largely unquestioned assumption is that not-knowing is bad and to be avoided. In this work that notion must go.

To Know or Not to Know

6:40 The issue here isn't whether not-knowing should be allowed to occur—it already does. Our challenge is the ineffective relationship we have to its occurrence. Even using the term "not-knowing," we are drawn to hold it as a negative. Although we have no appropriate term for this state, this tendency of language indicates cultural values and is not necessarily an adequate expression of what's there.

6:41 Not-knowing is itself. It is primary. Before knowing can happen, or does happen, there must first be a space for it, a state that is not filled up with "knowing." In our culture that doesn't matter—we avoid not-knowing. We avoid the appearance of it, the awareness of it, the existence of it as a primary state of being.

6:42 You and I continually experience not-knowing, but our attention is on what we know and perceive, so we don't discern—and don't want to discern—the presence of the state of not-knowing. Although not-knowing is the "source" of knowing and is indispensable for learning and creativity, it remains a virtually unrecognized principle in our world. Instead, when we are confronted with an experience of not-knowing we see it as a malady.

6:43 Not-knowing isn't just acceptable, it's "so"; it's true. In every moment of every day there is much that is unknown to us, and beyond specific things not known, we abide in a constant state of not-knowing, which resides as the silent base of our entire experience. What is always and constantly true is that at some point our knowledge and our perceptions stop—we run out of knowing and experiencing and it goes no further. Past this place we have no idea, no perception, and no knowledge, but this is not usually acknowledged.

6:44 The very act and nature of knowing means that there must be not-knowing. It is a basic and natural part of our awareness. Not-knowing is a constant, ever-present aspect of "being." Knowing stuff doesn't change that or diminish that in any way.

6:45 Without reference to knowing, and so without a "not," it would just be that fundamental experience, perhaps something akin to openness, or nothing, or freedom. It would be like a clear space or a blank canvas: the basis for what is to come.

I think 99 times and find nothing. I stop thinking, swim in silence, and the truth comes to me.

Albert Einstein

6:46 **Exercise: Not-Knowing What's There**

Right now, look at some object—a chair, the wall, a tree. As you look at it, not-know what it is even though you perceive it. You may know its name, but what is it really, beyond your relation to it and independent of its name or use?

At first you may not have a knack for perceiving in this way. As you work at it, however, and begin to experience not-knowing as a reality rather than as a thought, you will become more adept at it. Remember, you're not trying to "pretend" anything. It is a fact that you don't actually know what the real nature or essence of anything is. Simply get in touch with that fact, and wonder: what is it?

As you do, you may notice an increase in the quality and depth of your perception. Before your eyes the focal object can become more present and perhaps vivid, even if more open and unknown. If such a shift in the fullness and aliveness of your perceptions occurs it is because you begin to move "dead" concept—accepting the obvious as fact—out of the way and replace it with an open wondering.

What I mean by "dead" concept is taking for granted that the name or label of the thing is the same as the thing. When that's done we move attention quickly on to other matters. The moment we "know" what something is by naming it, it immediately becomes a taken-for-granted distinction. This distinction is inherent in the identification or name of the thing and makes it a "one" or a "that," and so a done deal, without requiring any further focus on the object, and certainly without any wonder or investigation.

Test this out by simply knowing what it is and take it for granted—it's a table or chair, or whatever. Notice what happens. Notice it becomes simply that thing and requires no more attention or wonder.

Now, again not-know what it really is. Work on experiencing genuine not-knowing, even as you struggle to perceive or know what is really there. Notice what occurs in your awareness.

In this way you should begin to grasp that not-knowing isn't just a subject for inquiry, it is also the first step of ANY true inquiry.

6:47 Once you recognize within your own experience that you in fact don't know what anything is, then you can start to openly wonder what the nature of existence really is. Once you wonder, real questioning can begin. Answers may come and go. With true questioning, however, nothing will suffice but a genuine, personal insight into the matter.

6:48 In our work on transcending life and death, not-knowing plays a central role. It's not just that we don't actually know what life and death are, but by turning our backs on this core aspect of our very person we shut ourselves off from what is an immutable and authentic aspect of ourselves, one that is beyond concept and belief.

6:49 Instead, consider not-knowing as a doorway to your absolute nature, as well as the tip of the iceberg of the foundational "nothing" upon which reality is possible and created. This not-knowing—or perhaps you might relate to it better as that aspect of your experience that is silent and still—isn't about what you know or don't know, it is the state that exists prior to all experience.

6:50 **Guided Meditation: Not-Knowing Reality**

Right now, look out at the perceived world. Unusual as it might seem, imagine this not-knowing "place" is the foundation for the very existence of the space and objects you see. It may take some doing to shift to such an unprecedented perspective, and probably seems inane and impossible, but do it anyway.

You perceive a world around you and within you, but this is not a direct encounter. While you are perceiving, start to get that whatever is ultimately true about existence is not found in your perceptions. Allow yourself to not-know what is here, and consider that somehow this not-knowing is the source of the world you perceive. Do your best to make this real for yourself.

6:51 Applying this ability to your work on life and death, notice that this not-knowing, nothingness, or silence doesn't come or go and is a constant of existence. If it also indicates that aspect of yourself that can't die—because it is independent of or prior to life activities—then it would be useful to access this nature. To move in that direction, start by entering not-knowing, abiding in the silence that is always a constant aspect of your experience. Consider this a possible doorway into the nature of existence and contemplate from there.

Living as a Conceptual-Self

6:52 What do knowledge-oriented humans do with our inherent inability to answer a question so important as "What am I" or "What is life?" We invent things, of course. Since we could first form the question, we've been devising theories about what it means to be a self, where a self comes from, where it resides in the body, and where it goes when the body dies. All manner of beliefs have been created, but the fact remains that almost no one actually knows the real nature of these most essential aspects of life and existence.

6:53 We've long assumed that our "being" is somehow related to our "perceptive-experience." But what if the perception of being and the nature of being are mutually exclusive? What if we simply don't know what we really are? That idea doesn't sit well with us. In the meantime, we tend to just embrace some belief or other.

6:54 Neither religion nor psychology—not even philosophy—are appropriate here. Whether or not these embody any truth is beside the point. For us, the ideas behind them will always remain hearsay and so cannot reach the depth of experience or consciousness needed for this pursuit. Instead, what we're after here is a direct no-frills personal experience of whatever is true about life and death.

6:55 Our task is to grasp what something is, not just what we think or feel or hope about it. We could say we need to look "beyond the limits" of our beliefs and knowledge. But "beyond" sounds even further away, and what we want is in a different direction, closer to us somehow. In order to experience what's so, we need to comprehend what's prior to all our beliefs and knowledge.

6:56 Knowledge, beliefs, and answers are merely concepts, no matter how seriously you take them. Our most grounded observation—one that is hard to dismiss—is that you are a body, you are a sack of cells. These are divided into many different groups of specialized cells that do particular jobs to serve the whole organism. One of these jobs is found in the specialized brain cells that produce concepts. This conceptual activity is where we seem to reside, isn't it?

6:57 Certainly the only indication that you exist as an inner self-awareness is the manifestation of conceptual activities that suggest something or someone exists because of these activities. When we see ripples in a pond, we imagine that some stone must have hit the water to create ripples. Even if we don't see the stone, but only the effect it had on the water, we assume some object caused the ripples. Seen or unseen, however, we never think to call the stone "water." And in our case, we find only ripples while the stone remains a mystery.

6:58 Our assumption here gets us into trouble when we assume that this entity, like the stone, is an object or exists in some form that is simply unknown or unperceived. Why isn't this entity simply attributed to the body? Because we relate to concept and awareness as activities of the self, and we don't imagine something physical is capable of producing such immaterial actions. Therefore, we assume that the source must be of a nature similar to the conceptual activities themselves, or of a nature that is prior to them, and objects seem incapable of such activities.

6:59 You think there is a source-self behind your perceptive-experience causing conceptual activities. But you can't find this source-self. Consider that's because you aren't located there or anywhere, you aren't an immaterial mind-object of some kind separate from the body.

6:60 The only place where you can experience and perceive is where you can experience and perceive. Therefore, what you conceive and perceive completely determines reality for you. You experience these activities but not the source of them, assuming the source is located behind the activities. But perhaps no source self-object exists, and the assuming, perceiving, and conceiving makes it seem like it does.

6:61 Because it is inconceivable to you that your nature is not an object or substance of any kind, you invent a distinction of being an immaterial self-object. This is assumed to be the source of your self-awareness, what you think of as the real-you behind the scenes. This insistence that you exist in some form, no matter how ethereal it may be, is an obstacle to becoming conscious of your nature. In the meantime, life is lived through the activities of a conceptual-self, and yet, this self is an invention built upon many layers of assumptions.

Freedom from Assumptions

6:62 Since in our world not-knowing is bad, and two things we don't know are what we are and what life is, we develop an adversarial relationship to this fact, dampening our willingness to confront it. Instead, we rely on hearsay, beliefs, and social perspectives to tell us what we and life are or should be. As such, many deeply held overlooked assumptions form the foundation of our experience of self and life.

6:63 One of our more difficult tasks in this work is making a connection between assumptions and the effects these assumptions have on creating the reality in which we live. Even when we make some progress with this, too often it remains an intellectual connection, and this does little to eliminate it. Unless we can unearth the assumptions that create our self-experience we can't let go of them, and letting go of them is necessary to transcend life and death.

6:64 Instead, we continue to hold fast to assumptions much like a monkey who, grasping a piece of fruit inside a narrow-neck bottle, remains imprisoned because he won't let go of the fruit. It's not that he's so greedy or stupid, it's that he doesn't grasp the connection between holding onto the fruit and his inability to escape the bottle. We are very much like that. Once we realize within our own experience the relationship between assumptions to which we cling and our conceptually dominated experience, we can let these assumptions go. Prior to realizing this relationship, however, we will remain "monkeys trapped in a bottle."

6:65 The first thing we need to do to get free is become conscious of what we're assuming. This has to be done through personal contemplation. Taking a look at some candidates can warm us up to the task and provide some directions in which to look.

6:66 What are the core assumptions that dominate our self-experience? Whatever they are, they won't appear as mere ideas but will seem to be perceptions of reality. They won't offer themselves up easily to scrutiny. Our first encounter with such assumptions would have to be seen as unconventional, since they'll likely go against the grain of accepted truisms. Given this, they may also be difficult to understand, and so we should be patient as our consideration unfolds.

6:67 Intellectual attempts to conjure up possible assumptions can provide material for further contemplation, but that alone is not likely to lead to insight. A conscious experience of the assumption at its source will always be different from the thought about what it might be. If we want it to make a difference, we need a real experiential recognition of the assumptions that are actively operating in our own mind and experience.

6:68 We have already touched on many deep assumptions about the nature of reality. It is these kinds of existential assumptions that blind us to the realities of life and death, but there are quite a few more that need our attention. To grasp them as forming our reality, however, we must create an open and contemplative listening as we move through various assumptions. Since they are so foundational to our taken-for-granted experience, they may well seem abstract or hard to pin down. They usually act in a part of the mind that is not readily accessed.

6:69 Generally, this depth of thought is only discussed in such environs as a philosophy class, and it is taken seriously only as long as our fascination for interesting ideas lasts. Yet assumptions that are at the root of such conditions as feeling separate and isolated, incomplete and longing for what's missing, being disconnected from the nature of life and death, are not merely a matter for metaphysical discussion. They are a serious part of the foundation for our daily thinking and perceptions.

6:70 We must be willing to discover and confess ideas and beliefs that run contrary to social acceptance, and even contrary to what we may personally want or believe. The only thing it needs to be is true—whether we like it or not is irrelevant. This doesn't necessarily mean true in an ultimate sense—which itself is difficult to grasp even though, for this work, it is essential—but also what is actually occurring, such as something found to be in fact assumed though we were unaware of this condition and perhaps believed it to be otherwise. It may be that we believe the emperor has clothes, but once it's pointed out that he does not, we mustn't insist that he does regardless of our fear of disfavor. We can see that personal beliefs can only get in the way. It is the truth we are after.

6:71 Normally, it is very hard to get people to grasp this, since they are overflowing with opinions and views. I am guessing, however, that the prospect of death makes it easier to get people's attention, as well as increases their willingness to admit that only the truth will suffice. You can't fuck around with death, and clearly your desires and opinions on the matter are irrelevant.

6:72 Regardless of any individual assumptions we may dig out, shared assumptions revolve around believing ourselves to be an individual self-awareness, living as an intangible self-object in a private inner world. In simple terms: once we've mistaken ourselves for something not real, shit happens. The particular twists and turns aren't nearly as important as the fact we are trying to survive as this self, and yet this self itself is not real.

The true value of a human being can be found in the degree to which he has attained liberation from the self.

Albert Einstein

6:73 What cements us to a life drama is thinking our self-experience is real, and taking ourselves and our drama seriously. Keeping this in mind assists us in not getting lost in the maze through which we may enter as we try to sort out some of these assumptions. The connection between the assumption and its influence on our lives needs to be clearly seen. But, like being in a maze, it may more easily be seen by backing up far enough to see it as part of a whole pattern.

6:74 As the story unfolds, the relationship between various beliefs, assumptions, and the experience these produce should begin to become clear. The complexity and obscured nature of this subject require a much greater depth of contemplation about what's discussed, but we can begin to sort out some of this right now. There are generally two domains of assumptions, existential and social. The overlap between the two is huge, they influence each other a great deal. Existential assumptions form the foundation upon which all social assumptions are built, but social assumptions generate what seem to be existential matters, even though they are not, and the social domain is where we live, creating our experience of self and life. We will first focus on the social and work our way more and more into the existential.

6:75 Although we'll briefly look at various possibilities, the real work will continue to rely solely on your own contemplation. To start us off and set down some groundwork, let's take a look into our core self-experience of being incomplete. Our sense of being incomplete is what generally drives most of our overall life pursuits, even if only in the background. This sense of being incomplete shows up in such experiences as feeling alone, and like something is missing or wrong within our very existence, fueling our efforts to attain something we think will make us whole and happy.

6:76 Although this chapter deals with real and important assumptions that keep us running on the wheel and caught in unnecessary suffering, I consider it a rather superficial layer to what we are tackling here. Many readers, however, may see it as deep subject matter difficult to understand or transcend. But that might be because it is a new study for them, and the fact that these attachments are strong. Some attachments might be challenging to eliminate, but to transcend our distress about being somehow incomplete we need to give them up. Although being successful with this work will make a huge difference in our life experience, we are still quite a ways from the deeper assumptions that keep us stuck in life and afraid of death. So, after tackling and getting free of these dynamics, in progressing chapters we will eventually work our way toward how this condition might relate to transcending life and death.

Being Incomplete

6:77 As mentioned, one of our tasks is to be complete with life so that we can better let go of it. Therefore, one area for us to investigate is why we're not already complete. From time to time, most people run into a core feeling of lacking something essential. It is the sense that something is missing or not right in one's self or life. It sometimes arises as a feeling that something is personally wrong or "broken" with oneself deep down, or as if there is a void that needs to be filled, and that obtaining whatever is missing would make one feel whole and happy. I'm referring to this condition as being incomplete. Although this subject has been addressed elsewhere, I want to revisit it here, grounding us in this normally overlooked experience so we are not overly abstract in our approach to deeper matters.

6:78 **Guided Meditation: Incomplete Meditation**

Put your attention on your most intimate sense of yourself. Can you find any feeling within your "internal state" that you might call empty or incomplete, as if something is wrong with you or missing in your life? What is that like for you? When you run into feelings like this, what do you usually call them? How do you explain them or deal with them?

When you isolate a feeling of being incomplete, does it seem to have a specific cause, or is it always there? If it seems to have a specific cause, can you recall whether it was absent before that cause? Is it possible that the feeling was present already, and that you felt some relief when an apparent cause is identified so you could embark on a resolution?

What, if anything, seems to "fill" this emptiness? What do you think you need to attain or achieve in order to be complete? What do you pursue in life along these lines?

Look into the issue of feeling incomplete and see what you can find in your own experience and life. Don't stop on the surface. Look deeper and ask yourself: what's at the heart of this feeling? Sit for a while and dwell on any sense of being incomplete or insufficient in some way.

6:79 Accompanying this sense, or included in it, is always a feeling of isolation and separation—the sense that you are alone, even in a crowd. Most of us are not happy being alone, but neither are we completely happy in our relationship with others. Both seem to hold a "promise" that remains unfulfilled. We find some sense of hope in the beginnings of fulfillment—either trying to be at peace within or fulfilled by relationship—but this always degrades into vague feelings of disappointment because it never goes all the way.

6:80 We then tend to assume that real fulfillment is simply out of reach, either temporarily or permanently depending on our personal history and programming. But none of us questions the foundation of our relationship to this matter. We don't notice that overlooked assumptions may be the source of both our desire for fulfillment and our failure to achieve it.

6:81 What could this sense of being incomplete be founded on? Every negative exists in contrast to a positive alternative. If these negative feelings are occurring, we must believe that some other, more positive feelings should be true instead. Certainly, we must presume that our experience and selves could and should be some other way.

6:82 It's likely we assume we're not as we should be, if for no other reason than we confuse our sense being with an incomplete and deficient conceptual-self. Observing that we identify ourselves as something other than our true nature is a start, but what else do we assume to be true of ourselves or reality that leads to feelings of being incomplete and meaningless, alone and separate?

6:83 Incomplete occurs in relation to two possibilities, fact and fiction. In simple terms, we feel empty in relation to the fact that we *are* empty, which is to say, we are missing an experience of our nature and the real nature of life and death—we are ignorant. We also feel empty in relation to cultural misunderstandings—or fiction. This "fictitious" emptiness may feel like a real condition but is founded on false notions, on the belief that something should be present that is not, or that something shouldn't be present that is. This includes the likely fact that we have never "completed" our self-concept, we haven't accomplished the ideal self we imagine we should be, and so must feel as if something is undone, missing, or insufficient. Both fact and fiction feed each other, and the result is a powerful background sense that I'm calling feeling incomplete.

Chasing After Fulfillment

6:84 One assumption that feeds this unhappy sense is the presumption of fulfillment. We presume that we should be fulfilled, even deserve to be fulfilled. We also assume we know how this should take place, and that attaining some ideal will provide a sense of fulfillment and happiness. When asked, however, most people really have no concrete idea how they could attain fulfillment beyond a fuzzy notion of obtaining what they desire.

6:85 Anyone who has gotten past the initial delight at attaining some desire can attest that deep fulfillment and happiness are not forthcoming, or at least not for long. We can observe that after fulfilling any number of desires, the need for fulfillment remains an issue. Still we assume that somehow we deserve to obtain what we want—that we deserve to feel good, get our way, and have our every desire realized—and then we'd be happy. Although it may seem like it, happiness never was the goal of our efforts. Self-persistence is our goal. This is an important distinction.

6:86 Although everyone says in earnest that he or she wants to be happy, this statement really means: "I want to have what I want, and to not have what I don't want." For most of us these seem like the same goal, so what's the problem? The thing is that wanting and not wanting is really a statement of self-survival, not happiness. There is a reason this dynamic goes unnoticed for what it is.

6:87 As a metaphor we could say we are like a mouse running inside a wheel. What keeps us moving is the allure of some tasty cheese—the myth of obtainable "survival-happiness"—just outside the wheel. The "cheese" is only there to get us to run, it is not there for us to obtain. Unfortunately for us, we don't know that. Since we don't seem to be closing the gap, we run all the harder chasing this cheese—the promise of happiness or resolution.

6:88 If we didn't believe we were entitled to the cheese, or we knew we will never get the cheese, we'd stop running. But our wheel and our running and what we perceive as our particular needs are a large part of what makes us "this particular one, living this particular life." In the overall scheme of a self surviving, it's imperative that we remain ignorant of what's true and what's only an illusion. If we were to grasp this dynamic for what it is, this self we've become confused with might lose all its steam to pursue what in the end are false goals.

6:89 Since we assume that getting what we want should naturally come about, but doesn't, we can see the many ways in which struggle becomes a constant activity, and a lack of fulfillment, both shallow and deep, can't help but work its way into our ongoing experience. Chasing unattainable fulfillment is but one of the ingredients in the cheese that our mouse so diligently runs after. We think that life is in the running, and death is what happens when the running stops. Yet, if we're just running after imagined cheese never attained, aren't we wasting our lives with meaningless activities until death puts an end to it? This fruitless pursuit is often found in chasing ideals.

Pursuing Ideals

6:90 What if ideals never were meant to be attained? Sounds silly, doesn't it? "Of course they are meant to be attained; it is only ourselves that are lacking." Perhaps not. Perhaps, in fact, there is nothing lacking within ourselves at all.

6:91 If an ideal was not meant to be attained, in other words, "lacked the possibility of realization," which is one of the definitions of an ideal, then what good is it, and why does it exist? An ideal, in this context, is created to serve the function of providing the hope of personal fulfillment, of attaining happiness and completion—but this is an illusion, an idea or concept based on wishes and hopes founded on the desire to fix a malady that the ideal really has nothing to do with and can't resolve.

6:92 In any case, notice it's not working. Ever wonder why? We can see once again that the analogy of chasing an unattainable cheese fits here perfectly.

6:93 Why is chasing after ideals never going to "complete" you? I go into this in detail in other books, but the short version boils down to this: the desire to attain some ideal is based on your sense of lack within. No attainment from without, or anything adopted or attained by you—and more than likely pretended—can fix or change what's within. Only becoming completely OK with you as a being in this moment can eliminate this sense of being incomplete. Not some imagined future attainment.

6:94 The mass of beliefs and images we have that act as "ideals" are wired into our thinking, self-image, and self-concept. They act on us without any conscious effort on our part. We understand this better by recognizing that many patterns in our thinking are devoted to what we are not. An ideal is not something observed, but something imagined and idealized.

6:95 Being wed to so many imagined ideals, we can't help but experience a huge sense of lack. We can't help but compare and contrast what isn't—fantasies of our future destiny, images of how we should be or how things should turn out, beliefs about what life should be like, standards to which we should measure up, and so on—with what "is," or at least "is perceived," and we find the "is" lacking. By extension, we find ourselves and lives lacking.

6:96 We remain separated from this cheese never meant to be attained and suffer in our ignorance and struggle. We are stuck with these beliefs, leaving us bereft of the qualities that suggest we are already what we should be. An "ideal" is largely used as something to indicate what we are not. At best it provides a distraction with the false hope of resolution. At worst, it's something we use to beat ourselves up with because we find ourselves and our lives continuously lacking, and we may well embark on fruitless pursuits of resolution doomed to failure.

6:97 It will take some contemplative efforts to discover all your ideals. The doorway to such a practice is a non-judgmental feeling-sensitivity to your innermost notions about yourself. The point here is that comparing yourself to ideals can't help but contribute to your nagging sense of being incomplete. Stop it.

6:98 Consider, if you live constantly awaiting future attainments to make you complete and happy, you can never be complete or happy. Given this future mythical resolution will never happen, throughout your whole life you will fail to be complete and to live fully, until death does part you from the effort. Think about it.

6:99 **Guided Meditation: Freedom from Ideals**

Look into any ideals you have, in whatever form you have them.

What do you hold should be the outcome of your life?

What destiny do you think you should attain?

What do you think would fulfill you if you could attain it?

What should you be like, what is a perfect you?

What sits in the background and goes mostly unacknowledged as what you don't have in life, or what you aren't, even if this is not glamorous or all that clear? Dig into it.

Notice you compare your current experience to these ideas, and this makes your current experience of self and life less.

Also, notice that all of these are imagined concepts, they are only figments of mind. Stop insisting they are needed and they aren't needed. Stop comparing yourself to them and you aren't less than or missing anything.

Consider these ideas and ideals to be just "cheese" you are running after, never to be attained. What happens to your experience when you acknowledge that possibility?

Now consider, no matter what happens in your life, it will all die when you do. How does that change your view of these ideals?

Right now, stop comparing any ideal to your current experience. Eliminate all notions and ideas of something you must attain in order to be happy. When you do that do you experience being complete and whole the way you are? Consider that without such concepts acting on your self-experience, you are already complete.

6:100 Inherent in the drive to attain ideals is a need for meaning. It's not hard to see how this need might be another contributor to feeling incomplete.

A Need for Meaning

6:101 If we presume that we should inherently have meaning, we would naturally expect meaning to fill our experience of self and life. Without meaning, why do we exist, what is life for? A life or self devoid of meaning is regarded as depressing, therefore as something to seriously be avoided. Let's look anyway.

6:102 Imagine that your existence is itself—that your actual "being" exists for itself. This might be said like "you are because you are" or "you exist because you exist." The only way something has meaning or value is in relation to something else.

6:103 If we ask, "What does an apple mean?" what are we asking? We find we are stopped short. We need to ask what do we mean by "What does an apple mean?" Unless we are referring to something other than the existence of the apple, the question doesn't make sense. This is because an apple doesn't "mean" anything just "being" an apple.

6:104 What does a person mean? What do you mean? Just like the apple, these questions have no relevance. We don't mean anything by just being. In order to determine our meaning, we have to look at our relationship to our community, or our value or usefulness in relation to something else.

6:105 For example, an apple is valuable to us as a food item, it is valuable to the apple tree as a reproductive organ, and if we used the apple as a ball, it would be useful for playing catch. But what does the apple mean? Unless we apply some meaning to the apple's existence, we cannot really determine such a thing. If we can't say what kind of tool it could be used for, what function it might serve, or what destiny we can imagine for it—all of which are relations of the apple to something else, such as to ourselves, the tree, a game, or an ideal—we can find no meaning whatsoever. The apple simply exists.

Without relationship or comparison, without ascribing a use or value, there is no inherent meaning in the apple all by itself. It is simply being an apple—it has no meaning.

6:106 When we apply meaning to the apple we miss the experience of the apple just being an apple. Meaning is a secondary application. Does the apple deserve "apple rights"? Does it deserve fulfillment, or to feel good, or to have its way? Obviously it would be impossible to tell what that could be, but even if we could, it would be ridiculous to assume that apples deserve anything beyond being an apple. It is equally absurd to presume that we deserve anything, or require value just in the course of "being." "Being" has no meaning. It just "is." Therefore, we have no inherent meaning; we simply are.

6:107 To our ears this might sound like a negative, but it isn't negative at all. "Meaninglessness" here doesn't mean "less meaning" or "negative meaning." Meaningless means "without meaning." It is "no" meaning. Therefore, we are inherently free of meaning.

6:108 Realizing this should immediately end our struggle for meaning. Do you grasp how that works? It might sound depressing to hear that you have no meaning or worth, but the good news is that, although you have no worth, you absolutely cannot be worthless. Since value is a function of use, it is artificially applied to things; it is secondary and not inherent in anything. This asserts that it is impossible for anyone to be inherently worthless.

6:109 It also means that one cannot have value. The whole issue of value and worth, of meaning and significance, is a social issue. It is not applicable to "being." One simply is what one is. Without artificial comparisons you are independent of value and meaning. Better or worse cannot apply to "is." Think about it. Better or worse than what? More or less valuable than what? You see that unless you compare your mere existence to something else, or to an ideal, such assessments have no meaning.

6:110 Would you cease to exist if everyone thought you were worthless? Would you begin to exist if everyone thought you were great? Of course not. Did you exist before you had any notion of good or bad, self-consciousness, knowledge, worth, or any judgments whatsoever? Of course you did. So obviously you aren't any of it. Your "being" exists as itself, for itself. The rest is secondary.

6:111 The point is that feeling incomplete because you can't find meaning is a mistake. If there is no meaning to "being," then no meaning can ever be found. This is not cause for depression, it is simply the truth. Instead of having a negative relationship to this condition, you can find reason to celebrate the freedom it affords.

6:112 It is the same basic dynamic that we saw occurring with not-knowing. Whenever we designate some inherent condition of our own being as a negative, we are compelled to deny and resist that condition—separating us from a genuine experience of our own existence. In this way, we experience it as a malady that needs fixing. But it isn't a malady. It's what "is."

Not Knowing and Being Incomplete

6:113 We've seen that whenever we look deep within, we can always find a sense of not-knowing in one form or another. However it appears, the bottom line is that our experience doesn't include a direct knowledge of the most fundamental aspects of existence, including ours. Given our shared assumption that this somehow points to a defect, we naturally feel discomfort and perhaps even a bit of panic when we encounter it. Since this condition is seen as an existential malady that must be resolved, our solution is believed to exist outside ourselves and our current condition. Therefore, in this way, we see ourselves as incomplete as we are.

6:114 As must be obvious by now, not-knowing is a normal aspect of being human. Whenever we set up antagonistic relationships to our own natural condition, we will continue to run into problems. Because we actually don't know how we came to be, what we really are, or what life is, we are drawn to make stuff up. Most of our shared world is invented, but almost no one recognizes this even though we all participate within it. It's difficult to recognize this dynamic for what it is. Because we live primarily within an invented reality, we fail to see that we are still ignorant of what's fundamentally true about our existence.

6:115 We are clear that we exist, we just don't know how we came to exist or the ultimate nature of existence. Given these remain unanswered questions, we are bound to sense a profound ignorance at the deepest levels of our consciousness. This ignorance evokes a sense of disconnection from the very root of our existence, and so adds to our sense of being incomplete. Doesn't it seem strange that our everyday experience should seem separate from the deepest aspects of ourselves and reality?

6:116 Contrary to our culturally popular assumption that asserting an opinion or taking on a particular belief about these ultimate matters will somehow resolve one's place in the universe, in fact the opposite is true. Standing on the artificial ground of hearsay or opinion—no matter how seriously or reverently it's done—actually places us in a position of pretense. It forces us to ignore our ignorance and binds us to a conceptual overlay that might seem like a ship come to our rescue, but is no such thing.

6:117 As long as we can get our minds to believe some given answer in all seriousness, we might be able to fool our sensibilities and psychology into perceiving reality as being consistent with such beliefs. But if we question the truth in any way, our lack of personal and authentic experience at the root of self and reality will emerge, and we are likely to feel lacking or defective. In truth we are neither lacking nor defective; we are simply ignorant.

Chapter Seven

OUR EXPERIENCE OF EXISTENCE

Our Fall from Grace

7:1 We've touched on what seems like an inherent part of our existence: feeling alone and isolated. But what does it mean to be existentially alone? It means that this aloneness exists simply because you exist. You exist as a distinction that is set off from all that it's not—which is what makes a self a discrete entity—and this creates a core sense of being separate and isolated. Because this self—which is primarily identified as an inner self-awareness—is conceptual in nature and lacks any objective solidity, your sense of disconnection from reality is enhanced. You tend to overlook the source of this universal human condition and suffer as if it is an undeserved affliction that perhaps you alone endure.

7:2 Since we seem to live within our own private internal world, a sense of isolation is to be expected. From time to time, we may share our experiences with others and value their company, but some deep aspect of our being never seems to be touched by them, or rarely in any case. We've already discussed the origins of this condition. Among other contributors, our sense of disconnection is created by our lack of direct personal experience when it comes to the nature of our own existence. One thing everyone fails to grasp, however, is that our very self-experience is created by making the distinction of self and not-self.

You creates not-you, not-you creates you.

7:3 Remember, the inside and outside of a circle are created in the same moment; if the circle isn't drawn, there is no inside or outside and so no separation. It is the same with you. Don't create a distinction between you and not-you and there is no you, and no separation. This might be better understood through the use of the Lucifer myth.

7:4 A myth of long ago tells us of a fallen angel, Lucifer, whose statement to God went something like: "I'd rather rule in hell than serve in heaven." My understanding of this myth is that Lucifer is the self—that it points to an illusion within, an activity to which our original being falls prey, separating us from what's real and true. The hell in which we rule is our own self-mind. The heaven we refuse to serve is the real nature of being, the absolute truth.

7:5 It is within our own self-mind that we seem to have free reign. Here we can adulterate or distort whatever we wish. We can choose what to accept and what to reject, what to believe and what to disbelieve. It is within our own mind that we can lie, pretend, misrepresent, ignore, imagine, and more. It is here that we have our opinions and pass our judgments. We can reorient data, rearrange facts, and disregard the truth if we so desire. We can alter our perceptions and recreate our memories. It is here that we reside as a self-overlord. This is where it appears as though we rule.

7:6 We can do all this, but we can't create a sense of being connected. Our "rule" requires a separation between what we experience in our own self-mind or cognizant awareness, and our experience of others and reality—as well as a separation between us and the absolute truth. Although we seem to be the self-overlord, in truth we suffer the consequences of this illusion, and so our little fiefdom also becomes our prison. We spend our time serving a false master and struggling against meaningless foes. This is the world of the self.

7:7 On the other hand, if we were not dominated by ignorance of any kind and did not identify with the distinction of a separate self, then we would have no choice but to succumb to an experience of being at one with the truth and reality. Without self, there is no separation.

7:8 Regardless of how this illusion of self-rule came to pass or what we may be able to do about it, the fact remains that currently we find ourselves within an awareness that is separate and introverted. At our core we suffer a sense of "existential aloneness"—an experience that we are separate and alone simply in the act of existing. This is a result of experiencing ourselves as a separate self-awareness, and this awareness is, by definition, isolated. Connected or not connected, this is the one that will die.

7:9 Assumptions may be conceptual, but simply because something is a concept doesn't mean it is without power. Our core concepts have great power and influence on our lives. They can very easily be perceived as real and solid aspects of life. All these self and life "experiences" are rooted in the conceptual realm, yet their force in our lives is undeniable. They simply aren't real or necessary, and they aren't etched in stone.

Why are you unhappy?
Because 99.9 percent of everything you
do is for yourself–and there isn't one.
Wei Wu Wei

Our Social Reality

7:10 As with every aspect of self, the issue of our social-self-survival has many layers to it. As "social creatures" it's clear that our social concerns take up the greatest portion of our energy, especially with all the machinations that frequently accompany our interactions with other people. Even so, the domain of what I'm calling "social survival" is much broader than we might suppose. It is the largest and most continuously attended domain of self-survival.

7:11 You should understand that I'm not talking about the way you behave at parties or how popular you might be, although those are social elements. What I'm calling your "social" experience is active even when there's no one for miles around. The mere existence of another person—whether in front of you or only in your mind—creates an entire world. Creating the distinction of sentient self and sentient other instantly creates a social domain.

7:12 A social context is responsible for so much that usually goes unnoticed. The act of comparing yourself to others—which creates ideas such as being a good or bad person, being superior or worthless, and so on—can only occur in a social context. The existence of a social world generates realms such as communication, manipulation, judgment, sexuality, empathy, and argument. Without "other," we wouldn't have concepts such as value, self-worth, individuality, beauty, deceit, honesty, agreement, or accountability; nor would we experience reactions like hurt feelings, intimidation, pride, love, embarrassment, loneliness, hate, or shame. Try to think this through and grasp the reality of all this.

7:13 A social reality is the source of language, family, religion, politics, the media, community, culture, entertainment, education, fashion, status, employment, government, subcultures, music, law, and on and on. All these activities exist solely because the social domain exists. Imagine what life would be like without any of those domains of experience.

7:14 Our social survival is the source of every concern regarding self-image, self-consciousness, and self-esteem, and these issues don't pause for us. In fact, most of our thoughts and feelings are socially oriented, since they arise and exist in relationship to other people—specifically or in the abstract.

Even when we are quite alone, how often do we think with pleasure or pain of what others think of us.

Charles Darwin

7:15 Our overall experience of life is shaped in reference to others and the community we inhabit. Even in the life of a hermit, most conceptual activities are devoted to the social self. In fact, without others, he could not even be "a hermit." When there is no one around, our continuous sense of self in relationship to other selves remains an inescapable aspect of our self-awareness. We engage a constant stream of internal dialogue, and the existence of language is solely a function of a social context—remember, social reality is created simply through the distinction of self and other, and that distinction doesn't go away just because there is no one around.

7:16 This whole domain is central to our lives, and yet we are rarely able to comprehend the enormity of its effect on our experience. The very fact and experience of you as a sentient self exists only because of a social context. At this point we're just trying to ground this domain in specifics, but as we proceed we will need to grasp it as an existential matter. As we continue with our considerations I want you to keep working on becoming free of the social world and finding an experience that exists completely independent from a social context.

Proof of Our Own Existence?

7:17 Everyone has heard the phrase from Descartes: *Cogito, ergo sum,* or "I think; therefore I am." The most common interpretation is that it asserts "beingness," the proof of which is our thinking: if I think, I must exist. And yet few people have any idea what it took for Descartes to arrive at such a simple statement. Perhaps a quick look might be useful.

7:18 His work in this area related to doubt—he began a practice of doubting everything. But being unable to doubt the very act of doubting revealed something beyond doubt. In such a realization one becomes aware of the existence of the source condition that is doing the negating or doubting. In other words, the first thing is always what is occurring as itself. It is simply what "is." An assessment or action is always secondary.

The thought of an apple is not an apple, but it is a thought.

7:19 What's most intriguing about this subject, however, is the speed with which people grab onto a statement that is rarely understood but seems to confirm one's existence. Why do you think we adopt and assert such a thing so readily? "I think; therefore I am." It is frequently said with a certain degree of pride in the background—right next to the doubt that presses such an assertion to the fore. Could it be that we aren't so certain?

7:20 Yes, it could. We're not certain. Strange thing to say, isn't it? But true nevertheless. "I think; therefore I am." Why do we feel so drawn to such a statement? Why is it so well-known and popular? Could it be because it is one of the few assertions that flat-out suggests proof of our own existence? For most of us it is completely superficial, in no way suggesting a direct experience or insight. Yet it still seems to validate the fact that we must exist, that we are real. After all, we do think. Is this proof that we indeed exist? What a close one! We were almost caught doubting whether we are real or not.

7:21 The depth of our "self" doubt is not something fully acknowledged. All sorts of beliefs can divert us from such a discomforting and unconventional notion. Yet somewhere deep inside and rarely visited, we doubt ourselves. At some point, everyone confesses some sense of inauthenticity and ignorance. After all, for all you know, you may be the only one that doesn't really know who you are or what life is all about. This generates a feeling of insecurity and uncertainty. Riding on the crest of this doubt are tendencies to pretend, misrepresent, embellish, fake, believe, and so on—no matter how sophisticated their presentation. In simple terms, we doubt that what we experience as ourselves is genuine or real.

7:22 No one was given the authoritative manual regarding life and how to live it. We are personally quite blank on that important subject. We may have learned a great deal, and adopted many beliefs and viewpoints, but this does not diminish our ability to notice that originally and fundamentally we are ignorant, and that everything currently getting us through life began as external to us. This isn't a very comforting observation. It suggests that we don't inherently have what it takes to handle the tasks of life, or to know what life is all about. We seem to have to get these crucial skills and knowledge elsewhere—they don't come with the package at birth.

Self-Survival and Death

7:23 Regardless of the circumstances that invite our fear of death, no fear would arise if we weren't committed to pursue self-persistence or life. If we could free ourselves from self-survival, we would free ourselves from the angst of death.

No self and other, no life or death.

7:24 Such a statement might still sound far-fetched or nonsensical. After all, the most important and cherished impulse of being alive is the desire to persist. Without such an impulse, we assume that we would not live very long, since the forces of nature would soon overwhelm and destroy us. This might be true, but regardless, our reflexive drive to survive is the source of our resistance to death, and so we need to do more work to understand how this is so.

7:25 It is clear in the most obvious forms of physical danger, such as being attacked by a grizzly bear, that our fear is directly related to our concerns for self-survival. We can see that all our fear just prior to the attack exists within our own mind—seeing this monstrous creature charging our way will likely evoke a great deal of fear and anxiety. Yet if we didn't give a fig about whether we lived or died, this fear would not exist.

7:26 When the bear comes chomping down on our body, certainly we can expect a significant degree of pain, and yet without any fear being triggered by imagining the dismal forecast of the end of our life, there is only pain.

Although this might well be very uncomfortable, we are not suffering our "death," only some pain. Most people don't realize how much more painful physical pain becomes when we add our emotional and mental suffering to it.

7:27 Even this physical pain, viewed deeply enough as a preference for certain sensations over others, would disappear if we could manage to achieve a state of having no preference for or aversion to any sensation or experience whatsoever. Imagine doing that. Imagine what you would experience if you had no preference or aversion to any sensation or experience no matter what it was.

7:28 Because preference and aversion only exist to assist in our survival, it is possible to not create the painful mental and emotional reactions evoked by such circumstances as being mauled, and it is also possible to not create pain in relation to the physical sensations of being mauled. So we can see that it may be possible to not "suffer" even the most brutal form of physical death. Such a possibility depends on giving up the desire and attachment to persist in any way at all, and eliminating at the core all preference or aversion for one experience over another.

7:29 If we can't imagine experiencing this principle in such an extreme circumstance it's because we are still stuck in a context of self-survival and remain blind to any reality outside that context. If freedom from concern for our physical death would end suffering related to physical danger, then freedom from concerns over conceptual or "egoic" death should do the same. It does. We need to be willing to challenge assumptions that are as close to our hearts as our very selves and our lives.

7:30 Moreover, we suffer from the ignored knowledge that in our struggle to survive we will, in the end, fail. The main assumption that results in this struggle, and its failure, is the assumption of self and other. We presume that we need a self and self needs to survive. We do not, and it does not. Let go of this self-idea and we transcend life and death.

Three Categories of Existence

7:31 Let's hone in and clarify what it is we actually fear losing in death. We can divide our experience of life and existence into three distinctions to help clarify what we're talking about when referring to our concerns about dying. These are: objective reality, biological life, and social life. Existence and non-existence occur in all these domains, but, curiously, it is only the last of them where death becomes a problem.

Let's divide our reality into three categories:

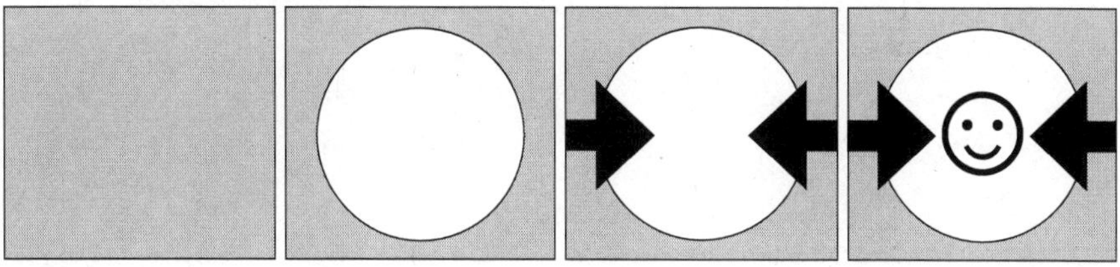

Objective Reality
The world of objects.

Biological Life
Active resistance to dissolution, identifying with a separate "living" object.

Social Life
The distinction of sentient self and sentient others = a social context.

Our Life
We experience being an individual sentient entity, a self-awareness. This is what we relate to that will die.

Objective Reality

7:32 Objective reality is the world of objects. Here being one way or another is irrelevant, existing or not existing is the same, being a solid rock or having it turn to dust means nothing. If we could somehow solely exist here, life and death would not be an issue. There would be no self, and no awareness because all that exists here are objects.

7:33 What's also considered true here is that nothing ultimately comes or goes, it just changes form. So whatever form arises is irrelevant. Applied to you as an object, you are meaningless and your existence or non-existence doesn't matter, and as an object alone you have no perception or self-awareness. Here, you can't care about life or death, since there is none. Do you get that?

Biological Life

7:34 Biological life, on the other hand, actively resists dissolution. That is the nature of life. Yet as merely life itself—as we can see in most creatures—there is no idea of life or of death. Life isn't thought about, it just occurs. When death comes, it is just death. If we could exist here, life would be what it is and death would not be known or an aspect of our experience, it would only occur when it occurred. Death only becomes a problem when there is some self-awareness component. Only when we make a distinction that there is an entity that will be lost is there a problem or reaction to death.

Social Life

7:35 Creating a domain of "conscious-entities"—*ergo* sentient self and other—generates a social life. But if there were detachment here, then any conscious-entity coming or going would be meaningless in itself. It only becomes an issue when we identify as one of the conscious-entities, and so become invested in the survival of that particular entity. But once we create the distinction of self, this is where our experience of self-existence exists. Having a life that we can lose only occurs here, death is only feared here. So it is actually being a social self where, for us, life and death exist.

7:36 You may not want the object of your body to be destroyed, or the biological aspect of your body to fail, but you don't want these things only because then you as a conscious-awareness will cease. It is this socially created "entity," which happens to depend on the objective-biological, that is the subject slated for death.

7:37 Your life experience is social, you exist as an individual only because of others. Your self-awareness only exists because of the social domain. In other words, you exist as a conscious-entity only because of the context of conscious-entities, meaning there must be other conscious-entities. What you identify as an individual self-awareness is where death matters. This constant effort to persist as a sentient self produces a lot of internal effort and social toil, which shows up in both the minutiae of life and the dramas of life. Regardless of the drama, it's the social domain, with its creation of an individual conscious-entity, where concerns occur about life and death. Begin to let that sink in.

What Is a Social Context?

7:38 How much of your self-awareness is social? As far as the life and death of yourself is concerned, all of it! This might be hard to grasp because you perceive objects all over the place and they aren't social, and it appears that the biological is independent of social concerns in and of itself. Yet, when you look deeply into your experience you begin to see how much your entire sense of self and life is dependent on a social context. Let's see how this is so.

7:39 Start with the fact that there are obviously many social components to your experience. Certainly, going to parties, hanging out with friends, relating to family are easily seen as social events. One thing people tend to miss, however, is how all-encompassing a social context is on their entire self-experience. When you hear the word "social," again, you are likely to think of interacting with others, but this is only one activity that acts itself out in our social reality.

7:40 As we've seen, civilization, personal worth, meaning, status, communication, being seen, accepted and valued, being thought well of, being remembered, even being left alone—all only exist in a social context. Much is social that is not seen as such. We might imagine that social activity is restricted to something like chatting with friends, but look further. Notice the Japanese custom of *seppuku*—killing oneself because of disgrace or dishonor—is strictly a social act; obviously their social existence was seen as more important and essential than physical survival.

7:41 We can see that our relationships with others are central to our experience of life and ourselves, but perhaps we miss the fact that self is the foundation for every perceptive-experience we have. Therefore, whatever form our self-experience takes will influence our entire field of perception and certainly our perspectives on life and reality. If our experience of being a self is found within or created by a social context, then that will be what our perceptions relate to.

7:42 Notice that "having a life" for you probably refers to your social world. When you recall your life and life history, what comes to mind? Mostly your social life, yes? And if you think of some purely physical scene, isn't this scene important for how it relates to social values and what it means to people? A beautiful waterfall, a stunning sunset, are likely only beautiful and stunning—and remembered—because of shared social values and aesthetics. Even being alone is social—you can't be alone without the possibility and existence of others not being present. All self-concerns, life plans, being worthwhile, accomplishing stuff, being depressed, etc., exist solely within a social context, which means they exist because there is a world of self and others.

7:43 Even when we aren't relating to another person, we most often have a social context influencing our experience. If we watch our relating to objects, for example, we can see how often and in what ways we still hold objects as somehow part of our social world. When we trip on a rock and then angrily kick it away as if to punish it, isn't this relating to the rock as if it's a creature? We might think a stormy sea is out to get us, or that calm waters are welcoming and benign. In such ways, we begin to see that our experience of even the physical often relates abstractly to a social context.

7:44 When we are muttering or making other sounds while alone, at first this seems non-social, but look closely. How many of these emanations relate to the existence of others even if not present—to unconsciously want sympathy or empathy, to show irritation, or some such? Probably all of them. These sounds are only meaningful in terms of a social context. When an infant cries, although he may not have been very socialized yet, his cries are obviously related to others, most often the mother, so we see the social component is already baked into the cake at birth. We begin to see that almost everything we do and think is social, even when we don't notice this relationship.

7:45 For example, for us sex is social. We think it is only biological, but for us it is really a social affair, and the biological outcome is a side-effect. Just stacking up all the clearly social aspects to sex—the flirting and seduction, getting to know someone, working out how and where to go about it, feelings of acceptance or rejection, performance, approval, interaction, emotions, what it means, and so on—can easily be seen as social. But it goes further than that. Even rabbits having sex could be considered a social event. Why? Such a basic biological act seems devoid of anything we might call society. True, but whenever there is an "other" in relation to a "you" this is a social context. Can you see how broad the scope is of what I'm referring to as social?

7:46 With a little attention, we also begin to notice that most of our emotions and reactions are socially related—embarrassment, guilt, love, lust, and so on. These are all social emotions—meaning they only exist, and can't exist without, a world of sentient self and other. But we might imagine we can have more primal emotions such as fear, anger, or desire without them being related to others. Even if we can have reactions such as fear and desire independent of a social context, we should acknowledge that at their root these only occur conceptually. Why does that matter in this case?

7:47 I know most people won't understand how human emotions are created, but you can find more information about this domain in *The Book of Not Knowing,* Chapter Twenty-Three, to help clarify what I'm asserting here. But why is it important to grasp that these reactions are conceptually produced? Because concept is a function of mind, and mind, in this case, determines our interpretation of experience, including that of self and life. If conceptual activity produces our experience of self, then self is completely wed to that ongoing activity, and as we've seen self is the source for all emotions, isn't it? Since the self is primarily a social event, and is itself created conceptually, then all emotions will be generated by and related to this social self. A bit of a convoluted explanation perhaps, but it will untangle more as we proceed through the book.

7:48 When it comes to our desire for life and our fear of death, a rather sophisticated conceptual domain and conceptual identity need to take place. This is a long story that we don't need to fully understand at this point. Yet, we should begin to see that human conceptual capacities are primarily developed within a social context. Of course, if I'm right that it's our socially created self-awareness that is worried about life and death, then it really doesn't matter if some feelings can exist independent of a social formulation. Still, it's somewhat complicated, so let's play it out a bit.

7:49 If you were in the middle of outer space without a soul around, you might imagine there would be no social component. Yet, in your experience the fact you are alone and there isn't anyone around are social concerns. Your fear of dying out there alone is a social fear, not just a biological one. Social means relating to other creatures, primarily other human selves like you.

7:50 As with the circle, where the inside and outside are created at the same time, this is exactly the same with the self. When we create a self we have immediately created a not-self, and once the distinction of sentience is made, then the distinction of a sentient self (conscious-entity) creates the distinction of other sentient selves in the same moment. They are in fact inseparable. They create each other.

7:51 Notice that perceptive-experience is dominated by the distinction you make of you and not-you. It is only within your self-awareness that the distinction of you and not-you is created. Without this distinction, and so assumed separation, there would be no experience of you or of not-you. I know it may seem like you merely perceive the fact of you and not-you, but think about it. If you didn't make this distinction, you could not interpret anything as being you or as being not-you.

7:52 As we saw, when we go beyond the distinction of self and not-self as merely objects and create the context of sentience, self and other selves become new distinctions within experience. This means we now experience self as a conscious-entity, and we experience the existence of other conscious-entities with which we can now interact, and this act creates a social context. Remember, everything perceived is automatically interpreted, *ergo* "known," as it relates to the self and self-survival. If the self that is experienced as ourselves is a socially created self-awareness, this social-self dominates our experience of reality. Recall the assertions in the "Three Categories of Existence" (diagram above): it is only the socially created sentient-self that is concerned with dying. A social context dominates our experience far more than we know.

7:53 That the mere existence of the distinction of self and other creates a social context might still seem difficult to grasp. But remember, we are talking about our experience, not the "fact" of objective reality. We are concerned with our life and death, and this relates to our "self" awareness, not really to any abstract notion about a reality beyond our experience. In Part II I am trying to ground our understanding of a social context in specifics so we can see it as real and occurring, as well as expand this understanding to realize it involves far more than we have previously thought.

7:54 Consider, there are tons of inanimate objects all around, yet when you die do you think you will miss them at all? Not likely. As you die you will probably miss other "you's," since the fabric of your self-experience is founded on others. The social reality is what dominates your mind and internal state, and so your attention and actions. You might be beginning to see how your experience of life revolves around self and others, but still wonder, how does death relate to this distinction?

How Social Relates to Death

7:55 When we grasp that language, and so our internal dialogue, is solely based on the existence of others—and therefore is always and only socially occurring—we get that using an internal dialogue as our primary form of "thinking" is a function of a social context. Consider how much your self-awareness involves your private inner world and your internal dialogue. How much of your life do you live there? Such an inner world and inner person can't exist without the distinction of a sentient self and other.

7:56 Study your experience. How much of it involves language, internal dialogue, ambition, meaning, a life story, conceptual-emotional activities that go on in your private inner world, and so on? All these exist solely within a social context. Your inner self-awareness and mind reside within these activities. Notice that every time you speak to yourself or think using the internal dialogue you are relating to others—and see that the internal dialogue is a cornerstone for your thinking.

7:57 Notice that the activities occurring within your own mind, feelings, and perceptive-experiences are founded on a social context with or without people being actively around. Even if you were a hermit and never saw another person, if you are talking to yourself—and who doesn't do that pretty much incessantly?—you are generating social content and so living within a social context. Therefore, it should start to become clear that your very experience of being a self is socially dominated.

7:58 Your experience lives or dies in relation to others. You are a self only in relation to other selves. Your self-experience—the very one that will die—exists in a social context. This might still be hard to fully grasp, so let's ground this assertion in an example using something you experience all the time.

7:59 Right now try to stop your internal dialogue. Take a minute or two to be without any internal dialogue at all, not even in the background. *Do* the exercise, don't just think about doing it. Doing it gives you a very different experience than the one you imagine you would have thinking about doing it. When you are done with that, come back to the book.

7:60 Why is it so hard for you to stop your internal dialogue, even temporarily as an exercise? Because this activity is generating an experience of relationship—*ergo* self and other—and therefore it is maintaining a sense of self. This self doesn't want to let that go. Language is totally a function of self and other, without which it cannot exist. If this self-sense is created through the distinction of self and other and maintained by activities such as the internal dialogue and other mind-activities, then clearly your self-awareness is socially created.

7:61 To help clarify the world that is created by a social context, imagine you are suddenly living in a world that consists of only objects—no others exist anywhere. At first in your imagination you might think you would be lonely and miss others, but now imagine there never were any others, or even any other creatures of any kind. You can't miss what never existed. What would your experience be like?

7:62 It's hard to imagine such a world because so much in your experience is determined by and dependent on others that it is overlooked and simply taken for granted. But work on it. In a world of only objects where no others ever existed, grasp that you can't have any internal dialogue, since language could not exist. That alone would transform your experience in a big way, but it wouldn't be the only change. In such a world, there is so much you would not have in your experience.

7:63 To hammer this home, go through every example you can think of that could not exist in your experience in such a world. You could not have a self-concept or identity, or self-anything, really. You could not be embarrassed or in love, you could not wonder what people think of you, you could not judge anyone, even yourself. You would have no issues about searching for meaning or self-worth. You would have no "mind"—much of which lives in your internal dialogue—and much more would also be absent. Your self-experience would be pretty much unrecognizable. Think about it, and work hard until you can create an experience of a world where there is no sentient self or other, just objects.

7:64 Now, after such a huge shift in your world, do you think dying would be much of a leap from where you are in this solely object-filled world? Without a social context, you couldn't even die alone! And dying would have no meaning or even be known for what it is. Are you starting to see how much of your entire experience exists in a social context?

7:65 Isn't it this self-awareness—the so-called "conscious-entity" that you think you are—what you don't want to die? This very self and self-experience can only exist through the distinction of self and other. Certainly, the biological seems independent from social aspects, and yet how much of your bodily experience do you constantly relate to others? All your concerns with body image and how you look are solely social functions. How many of your bodily functions do you keep hidden from others (defecating, periods, rashes, etc.)? Except for the mere fact of your body, providing perceptions and physical survival, what is your relationship to the body?

7:66 Unless you identify yourself *as* your body, the body is something you "have" and in which you live. It is necessary in order to have perceptive organs and so perceptive faculties, and for relating to the environment through physical actions. Yet, humanity's accepted assumption and experience of self have been split off from the body.

7:67 Primarily what we identify as ourselves isn't the body but an unseen entity living in a private inner-self-world founded upon concepts and assumptions. This is the one we identify with and live *as* our "selves," and what our attention is wed to as the experience of our lives. This is also what we don't want to die. The only reason we care if our body dies is because then *we* die.

7:68 If the body died and we still existed in some form or other, this would be a big change but not a death. This is why religions of all kinds offer the notion of life after death. Yet this is just a conceptual myth to mollify people's fears of death and to enroll them into that religion. Why do life-after-death fantasies exist? So we can believe that we will remain within a social existence in some form after death.

7:69 Dying is one of the few things that is actually not social. It is leaving others completely, because we die alone, and in death self and other cease to exist. Of course, when alive we shower even death with all kinds of social stuff. We imagine life after death, erect objects to house the dead, have funerals, engage in many superstitions, and so on. But all those activities are social, and done for the living not the dead.

7:70 Remember, when you die, you die alone, all by yourself. Again, what overlooked experience and assumption does this reveal? It points to the fact that your entire self-experience is already alone. Throughout life you're alone. You live in a private inner-self-world, and this is experienced as isolated and separate—and this is the very experience that is concerned with dying.

7:71 Your body is not really alone. It is an object always surrounded by other objects, and all objects share three-dimensional space and so are not really isolated. Although all objects are separate from other objects, would there be any sense of you being isolated and alone if you were just a body? You experience being isolated, alone, and separate only because no other "conscious-entity" can join you within the space where you seem to exist, your private inner-world. So, contrary to what may seem apparent, the body is not really the source of your sense of being existentially alone.

7:72 Your experience of being an inner self-awareness—held as some kind of ethereal unfound self-object—is what generates the sense of being existentially alone, and except for the promise of real connections rarely made, this condition is constant. The fact that you are fundamentally and existentially alone is felt as a malady that should be overcome. So, you struggle with taking care of this individual and separate self, while trying to remedy the sense of being alone and isolated.

7:73 Isn't it ironic that the very act of creating the distinction of self and other—and so the possibility of relationship—generates an experience of being separate and alone, leading to an obsession to resolve this malady by trying to connect with others or accomplish some attainment that is only meaningful in a social context? Without this distinction we don't need connection; with it we are endlessly attempting to remedy the apparent malady created by the distinction itself. Kind of ironic, isn't it?

You and Not-You

7:74 Are you beginning to see that your inner self-experience exists as conceptual and social? Notice that the vast majority of your experience occurs solely within your own mind, and the rest of your experience—which relates to an objective world—is influenced and dominated by your mind. Yet, you may misunderstand the implications of this fact. If you're in a rush to believe that you create your entire experience, you may miss the fact that not-you has a significant say in the reality you experience.

7:75 The objective aspect that is not dominated by your mind is what in fact you can't control. You have no choice but to succumb to the fact that a tree is not a car and a car is not water. You interpret them and can judge them, you give value to or ignore them, but you can't change the fact they are not only of your mind.

7:76 This reveals that in the distinction of self and not-self, the not-self has a say in the reality you experience—even though it is all interpreted by you. The dynamic between you and other creates a social world—the world within which your self-obsessed experience lives—but this world exists within a larger reality of you and not-you, or you and the objective world.

7:77 Our concern with death lives within the experience of being a separate inner self and this is a social creation—without a social context no such self-awareness can exist. This self-awareness may not be an objective reality, but it is the experience within which we live, and it is this self-experience that is dedicated to living life and avoiding death. The perception of an objective reality is the foundation of our world, but it is not the same as our self-awareness. The nature of self is conceptual, and as we've seen, our experience of self and life is built upon many deep existential assumptions. It will take work to dig all these out.

7:78 The task of experiencing the real nature of life and death requires that we recognize and detach ourselves from any and every concept we have about who we are—even the subtle and hidden ones. This can be as immense and difficult a task as it is a worthy one. As we continue to tackle this notion of conceptual-social domination, let's take a more grounded look at how it operates in our daily lives. Proceeding in steps and stages, we can begin to uncover and detach ourselves from the dominance of and confusion with the conceptual and social domains and return our consciousness to a more genuine sense of what's true prior to those activities.

Chapter Eight

SOUND AND FURY

8:1 When we step back and look impersonally at life we see a lot of drama that really goes nowhere and means nothing. Consider what Shakespeare was saying when he wrote that life is "full of sound and fury, signifying nothing." I have mentioned that I think William may have had some degree of enlightenment, as his perspective on life seems viable only from a detached viewpoint. This may be possible without enlightenment but is more likely with. Consider his quote about the very nature of life and a person's role in it:

> Life's but a walking shadow; a poor player,
> that struts and frets his hour upon the stage,
> and then is heard no more; it is a tale
> told by an idiot, full of sound and fury,
> signifying nothing.

8:2 Consider yours and everyone's life in this light. It is all meaningless drama that just seems important in the context of being a self. But outside that context it can easily be seen as sound and fury signifying nothing.

8:3 Once, as I was flying over a city, I looked down and saw many rows of thousands of houses lined up next to each other. In each of those houses lived people, and every one of those people had a life that they lived as if it were real and important. They devoted daily efforts to acting out their vision of the life they thought they must live. Each may be different one from the other, but all were acting out the same basic drama of life, and each lived in relation to a story told about their lives. Beyond the mere physical aspects of survival (which are most often very simple and basic), none of these life efforts are necessary or real in that they don't contain any inherent meaning beyond the story told by each person, and this story is strictly conceptual—a made-up figment of mind.

8:4 Unless someone identifies with and gives meaning to their story, it is just a meaningless story—even though it may be taken very seriously. As in a novel, the story might contain all sorts of woes and aspirations, adventures and doldrums, and as the reader you might feel invested in it and its outcome. But once you put down the book you see it is just a story that is unnecessary and unreal. So it is with your life story. The only reason you take it so seriously is it's all you have, and it is *your* story.

8:5 Sound and fury doesn't just apply to the turmoil that plagues us from time to time, it also applies to familiar states and routines. To be clear, even such states as being bored and lonely are part of the drama. The more mundane states are simply different forms of social drama. Although perhaps we see them as less energetic, or low key, or routine, they are also really just part of the sound and fury.

8:6 As well, engaging in theatrics over the lack of meaning in life—getting depressed about it, whining about it, or taking up some negative attitude about this fact—is also more drama that is itself hollow and misdirected. People can flip between these two, getting caught up inside life's dramas or getting depressed by the meaninglessness of life. But both are sound and fury, and neither is appropriate for our work here.

8:7 Let's look again at William's quote concerning life and death and expand it to include what was said previously, but try to take negativity out of it—which might be challenging since the play's character (Macbeth) was rather disturbed at the time:

Tomorrow, and tomorrow, and tomorrow,
creeps in this petty pace from day to day,
to the last syllable of recorded time;
and all our yesterdays have lighted fools
the way to dusty death. Out, out, brief candle!
Life's but a walking shadow; a poor player,
that struts and frets his hour upon the stage,
and then is heard no more; it is a tale
told by an idiot, full of sound and fury,
signifying nothing.

8:8 Can you see everyone's life, including yours, in this light? Does this sound depressing or negative? Consider it is neither. It is an observation of the reality of a self and a life when you stop taking it personally, seeing instead the illusion of taking the drama seriously, including the ultimate end that is death.

8:9 Of course, relating to this reality means turning our backs on the established insular life views to which we normally cling to avoid confronting the naked aspect of death and how it shines a harsh light on the meaningless drama of life. There is a reason we get completely caught up in this life-drama and take it very seriously. We take it seriously because of the principle behind our very persistence—self-survival. We fail to notice, however, that no matter what we do, in the end we will fail to persist.

Life is a tragedy when seen in close-up,
but a comedy in long-shot.
Charlie Chaplin

8:10 Let's start looking more into this domain that we take so seriously. Perhaps we can see it more clearly by making a distinction between what is genuine in our experience and what are just fabricated wheels spinning away. When we recognize the huge amount of our experience that we might call "false" we can more readily let it go. But it is good to grasp that what we consider fundamentally real will also die, so we will need to find a way to let that go as well. Let's start with what is clearly unreal and unnecessary.

He who would distinguish the true from the false
must have an adequate idea of
what is true and false.
Baruch Spinoza

Ineffective Remedies

8:11 Within the sound and fury, it's not uncommon for people to feel dissatisfied with a life or self that seems meaningless, worthless, isolated, or missing something important. From this underlying condition many attempts are made to remedy our sense of malady and lack. Some of these "solutions" come from the community, such as religions, spiritual movements, or other shared belief systems. Some are found within the individual as a collection of beliefs, opinions, assumptions, or fantasies.

8:12 These remedies might seem promising for a time. Yet all are only additions, something placed on top of what's inherently present. They do nothing to clarify the real nature of what's there. Further, this whole dynamic represents just the tip of an iceberg. By engaging in such "solutions" we further reinforce the creation of a conceptual-self from which to relate. This self is always in some way artificial.

8:13 We need to realize that the solutions we've adopted are based on shared assumptions and therefore do not and cannot resolve our deep sense of being incomplete. The only way to do that is to get we are already complete, or experience directly what we really are. Adding beliefs and convictions, or going through the rituals of life that promise resolution but can't deliver, are futile activities. This is like someone trapped in a burning building piling papers up all around to save himself. It ain't going to work.

8:14 Directly experiencing what's already so is a very simple act. Yet so much seems to stand in the way of becoming conscious of our nature. it appears to become a complex task. The complexity lies in our conceptual identity distracting our attention, but our "nature" is already simply so. If we could toss out all that isn't us, perhaps we'd be left with an experience of who we really are.

8:15 How can we better recognize assumptions buried within the mass of taken-for-granted information that comprises our selves and our knowledge? We begin by creating the ability to do so. This requires a number of skills, such as a deeper honesty than our cultural norm, a new level of self-discovery, and a degree of openness that will enable us to think beyond our assumptions. The main obstacle to increased consciousness is assuming reality is how we think it is and perceive it to be. This keeps any truth outside of this experience inaccessible.

Self as Mind

8:16 Generally, "self" and "mind" are held as one and the same. It's an easy assumption to make—what else would we suppose? In our awareness, we make an important distinction between what is "me" and what is "not-me." Within the "me" distinction, we observe an endless stream of mental content that is exclusive to our particular selves—our memories, perceptions, fantasies, thoughts, emotions, sensations, and our very sense of awareness—what we call our minds. All this activity is held together, given continuity, and made usable in large measure through the ongoing stories we tell ourselves in which each of us is the central character. We live our lives inside its plot, and this endless internal narrative simultaneously frames, reflects, and creates the reality in which we live.

8:17 Where does all this come from? Our selves, obviously. But what and where is the one that generates all this mind activity? We're not very clear on that subject, but we've got some entertaining notions about it. It's not hard to imagine that in some uninspected place in our mind or inner awareness, there resides the genuine and pure root that is our "real" self. We might suppose that, simply through existential mechanics, this real self must remain "backstage"—always out of sight, but still managing the whole show like some Wizard of Oz. Although some of this may seem to be self-evident, it's really all assumption and conjecture. We don't actually experience this "real self" behind the scenes, we just assume it's there.

8:18 The original function of mind is to do a job, the essence of which is to keep you alive and successfully being you. This involves the problem-solving function of the brain, finding solutions to challenges and managing a relationship with whatever's encountered. Toward that end, it also creates your story lines and maintains the continuity of your character and identity. It works pretty well, doesn't it?

8:19 Of course, this same "mind" must also protect, maintain, and perpetuate itself—if it gets lost or damaged, it can't do its job. The mind unceasingly promotes the interests of itself in the name of the one who "possesses" it, and all its mental-emotional activity is calculated to get this self-mind through life.

8:20 This is all well and good, but it seems that the conceptual activity that is created to serve the body and life has become an abstraction called the self. We become identified with our conceptual activities as if they are independent of our organic physical life, and so become attached to our beliefs, to our roles and traits, and to the strategies needed for maintaining all this. We rarely acknowledge that all our mental, emotional, and perceptual activities are processes created to serve a specific purpose. We're so busy identifying with mind's conceptual mechanisms that we lose touch with what's real. It's not hard to see, then, how self becomes confused with mind—and identifying with some immaterial source that is receiving perceptions and producing conceptual activities.

8:21 Inevitably, the presence of mental activity is identified within one's awareness as the self—and so we become identified as an immaterial conscious-entity. We consider our thoughts and emotions to be aspects of ourselves, and we hold our awareness and intellect as though they *are* our selves. Yet, none of this may be true at all. In the meantime we live and exist as if we are a conceptual-self.

Conceptual Influence

8:22 Your beliefs and assumptions have a strong influence on your experience. Since accepted concepts and beliefs are usually just "lived from" rather than inspected, it can be difficult to see their real influence. Take a moment and do the following exercise to see if you can get a better hit on some of this influence.

8:23 **Guided Meditation: The Influence of Beliefs**

What do you believe about yourself, life, and death? Try to notice all the various beliefs you have, from significant to minor.

Also bring to mind those beliefs you have but tend not to notice because they are taken for granted, or are in the background, or overlooked. If you've never done this before, take some time and look into it.

Now, choose one significant belief you have and ask yourself: How does this belief influence my experience or perception of the world? Try to catch how something you believe influences your experience and, to some degree, even the way you perceive things.

Now I want you to eliminate that belief, at least temporarily. Just clear it out completely. Make sure it isn't operating even in the background, and then see what shifts in your experience.

Once you've made this shift, bring back the belief and see even more clearly the influence it has on your experience.

Now make up a new belief. If you don't already, you could create a belief in God, or perhaps that you are god; you could create a belief that you are a spirit from another reality, or that you are wrong about everything you know. As you make up a new belief, just for fun pretend to really believe it.

What happens to your experience? Stay with it for a while. What changes when you do?

Consider how many beliefs and assumptions you have, and imagine each of these influencing your experience and self-awareness in some way, often quite significantly. Try to imagine, or better yet experience, how much all your beliefs constantly influence your experience of life, self, world, and reality.

Now, consider eliminating all beliefs and assumptions. Don't worry about the challenges that might arise because of it, simply do it, and see what experience you have when you do.

8:24 You should see that the influence of beliefs and assumptions on your experience is staggering. Beyond such influence, however, there are many other conceptual influences on your experience and your perceptions. To better see this influence let's do another exercise.

8:25 **Head-Turning Exercise**

Right now take a moment to turn your head from side to side, looking left and then right. What perception gives you the impression that you're moving your head? You can feel your head turning, and your visual field changes, seeing what's to your left and your right.

Now close your eyes and do it again, and notice that you can only feel your head moving. But do you also have an image of your head moving, as though you can "see" your head moving or what it looks like as it moves?

That image is a concept, not a perception. Since you can't actually see your head moving, you are translating the feeling-sensations into an image and conceptually adding this to your "perception."

Can you see that this is actually a concept and not a perception?

8:26 We mix such images and other conceptual contributions with our perceptive-experience all the time. But we don't notice that they aren't actually perceptions, they are conceptual in nature. Just as beliefs do, all our conceptual activities—thoughts, ideas, speculations, images, values, and much more—influence our sense of reality without our knowing it. Consider how the sensation of turning your head is augmented with a conceptual "image" of that activity. That same interconnectedness between concept and perception is how our beliefs and assumptions become fused to our perceptions.

8:27 If our goal is to know what's true, such a dynamic would obviously need to be sorted out. Since beliefs, assumptions, programming, and conclusions are all based on "imagined truths," their influence on our perceptions can only muddy the waters.

8:28 **Guided Meditation: Conceptual Self-Awareness**

Right now put your attention on your inner self-awareness, what you experience and live as yourself—that which is not your body. As you focus on this experience, get how much of it is conceptual. Notice conceptual influences that you previously thought were just perceptions or observations but are actually added by your mind.

Can you find anything in your experience of your self-awareness—living in a private inner world—that is not conceptual or influenced by concept? Keep contemplating this and digging into it, and try to grasp that your self-awareness may be entirely conceptually based.

8:29 Concept obviously dominates our minds and selves, but it also dominates what we perceive as the objective world. Beyond our conceptual additions (interpreting, assessing, judging, labelling, associating, and so on) to what we objectively perceive, grasp that all perceptive-experience is not actually the subject itself. Instead, it is an indirect activity that is conceptually interpreted and, therefore, is not an experience of what's there. Such understanding changes how we hold objects, and even how we experience what we perceive.

8:30 You likely missed what was just said, so let's look at it again. If what you perceive is not what's there—is not the real nature of existence—then what you perceive and know as reality is in fact not reality. It is an activity within reality that produces a phenomenon carved out of perception by a self-mind and organism to serve a purpose for this particular and very limited aspect of existence. But this doesn't at all reflect the real nature of existence.

8:31 So what's to prevent you from calling that a fabrication, an illusion, a limited activity that produces a specific and biased phenomenon? What is its purpose, and what produces this phenomenon? I have asserted that self-survival is the purpose for and generator of this activity. Even though it dominates everything we know and perceive, neither self nor survival is the whole story about existence, even though it seems like it is. But this is extremely difficult to fully grasp. So, let's look into it a bit more.

Reality versus "The Bull"

8:32 Our self-orientation and survival mechanisms don't just influence what we perceive, they completely dominate as well as create what we perceive. Our entire perceptive-experience and conceptual world are designed commensurate with the principle and phenomenon of self. We perceive everything in relation to ourselves, no matter how minor the event or object or even how altruistic the viewer.

8:33 Our perception is a "for-me" experience. That is the purpose of our interpretations—molding our perceptions to relate whatever is encountered to ourselves and our needs. Yet, self is a very limited and biased event, it is not all that is, nor is it aware of the nature of its own existence or of all existence. It only exists within the distinction of self and not-self. And as we've seen, our "selves" are highly conceptual fabrications. All that we perceive is configured in relation to this self-fabrication. That immediately makes our perceptions biased and distorted to fit a purpose.

8:34 This automatic function is so flawlessly designed that it leaves no holes. It constitutes our entire world—what is perceived, thought, and felt. That's the job of self-perception. Its job is not to experience or know what is absolutely true, only what is relatively assessed and how that relates to us in particular. Because of this we survive and enjoy a life lived successfully, but we are also stuck in our created perceptive limitations, binding us to self-referencing experiences rather than an open investigation of what's true. Try to experience this in your own case.

8:35 Although people can get this intellectually or abstractly, it's still quite difficult to realize the full scope of the principle and reality of survival. It is no less than life itself and every aspect of our perceived reality. Some of you may have heard of the centuries-old Zen pictures and poetic commentary regarding Ten Bulls or Oxen. These depictions suggest stages on the road to grasping something important in Zen. Originally the complete set of pictures numbered eight. These eight all relate to a Bull—Searching for the Bull, Discovering the Bull's Footprints, Perceiving the Bull, Catching the Bull, Taming the Bull, Riding the Bull Home, Transcending the Bull, and Both Bull and Self Transcended. So what is this Bull?

8:36 Obviously, it's a reference to something that ancient Zen masters saw as seemingly central to an awakening consciousness. What could this be? Some have speculated that this Bull represents the eternal-life principle, our primordial nature, the ground of existence, and so on. Consider the possibility that "the Bull" is the entire field of experience, our entire perceived reality and the persistence of one's self and life—in other words, the self-principle, or self-survival.

8:37 The application or superimposition of a world of self-experience and perceived relativity over and against what's True is so overwhelming and completely taken for granted that it isn't at all seen for what it is. We live inside this field—manifesting through mind and perceptive-experience—and thus we assume that it is simply a reflection of reality. Hearing about the possibility that it's not, however, may set us on a course to look for this "Bull." But we can't find it anywhere because at first we fail to grasp that we are inside it and *are* it and that it is everything we perceive, including ourselves. When we do grasp this reality, we begin to find it everywhere.

It's not like finding Waldo, it's the whole damn picture. Can you find it?

8:38 The Bull is your self, it is life, and it is the "genius" of a physical world and our existence within it. Often missed, however, is the fact that none of this is the true nature of anything. Simply being a person and a self creates a personal perspective and set of influencing beliefs and assumptions that obscure the Truth, but the Bull goes far beyond such obfuscation.

8:39 As we've seen, the creation of the self as sentient also creates other sentient selves, and the distinction of a self and not-self determines our perception of objective reality. As we progress, in later chapters, we will see that the very foundation of this perception is pure bias, because a set of universally shared existential assumptions detach it from any consciousness of the true nature of existence. This perceptive-experience, although functional and serving a purpose, is not true—in other words, does not represent the real existential nature of existence.

8:40 It's hard to grasp that what you're thinking and perceiving right now is this very activity of survival (or Bull), and not your real nature. Try to at least get some sense of this fact. Because your experience is exclusively self-referential and "relative," you have no way within perceived experience to access the absolute nature of existence. Further, given the mix of domains and levels of self-survival that you engage, it is nearly impossible to even accurately assess an unaltered and unbiased relative condition of life.

8:41 For example, your social survival puts many reactions and concerns in the way of assessing matters strictly in terms of physical survival, and your beliefs distort and obscure what might otherwise be an unbiased view of conditions. Your jumble of self-concerns and agendas get in the way of any clear perception of what's there, and your emotional or personal reactions to stimuli blind you to any factually based interpretation of what's occurring. These are all "relative"—not absolute—relations to what's "factually" true. If you have such a hard time grasping what's simply objectively true, how on earth do you think you can grasp what's absolutely true using the same methods for experiencing things?

8:42 Indeed, our whole perceptive-experience is basically a "radar" picture of a relative world carved out of objective distinctions that serve self's purpose, upon which is added a largely "subjective" projection superimposed on this indirect phenomenon. This entire subjective and indirect activity or phenomenon isn't seen for what it is, and so we miss the fact that the world we perceive is not the world that is there. All of this makes the Bull obscure, but once found, it is unavoidable. We realize that it encompasses not just our entire inner world but our outer world as well, comprising the function and content of every perceptive-experience we have of everything.

8:43 Controlling this activity appears nearly impossible because not only is it the sole activity we know, it is necessary for our survival, and we're completely aligned with and committed to that purpose. It is our selves and our lives, and we have no desire to give up either. What's important is important because of the needs and concerns of the self. What seems real seems real because of the fact of being a person.

8:44 Still, if we manage to transcend our automatic attachment to the distinctions of self and life, we can start to see this Bull as an activity we are doing and begin the work of taking control. With an "inhuman" commitment and struggle, we might manage to "tame" the Bull. When this activity no longer runs us then our experience is seen as generated rather than something to be endured.

8:45 Consciously grasping this activity enables us to transcend the Bull. Once we're no longer pushed and pulled around by the whims and drives of the Bull (which is of our own making), we become free of it and ourselves. The whole foundation of survival is based on the self, therefore, getting rid of the self and not-self distinction changes everything. Directly experiencing our very nature and the nature of life, we transcend both Bull and self, and perhaps become conscious of the absolute nature of existence.

8:46 **Bull Guided Meditation**

Right now sit with your attention on the perceptive-experience of you and life—your entire experience of existence. Get it as a whole. Stay there. Don't focus on any one perception or idea or sense, include it all in your attention. Just be with the experience of reality right now and grasp it as a whole. Dwell on this experience.

Now, work hard to "get over yourself." Don't make "you" an aspect of reality at all. Dispense with the distinction and so the experience of you and not-you. Once this is established, what is experienced?

Grasp that all perceptive-experience is simply a phenomenon of survival. It is indirect and biased, it is just doing a job and not reflecting reality. Eliminate dependency on and a blind belief in perception itself.

Can you find anything in the awareness and perception of reality that is completely free of this "Bull" or the domination of self and survival? Work to become conscious of what is prior to and independent of this perceived reality.

...what you and other creatures see now—as mountains, rivers, and lands—all this I say is the result of an original fault of sight—of the "cataract" as it were on the true power of sight which I possess. If then this ordinary power of sight be, as it were, a cataract on the eye of my true sight, it follows as a matter of course, that the pure mind of my true knowledge in seeing all these unreal associations is not afflicted with this imperfection.

Gautama Buddha

Self Isn't an Object

8:47 Clearly, dying isn't in the plan for survival. Yet, as we just saw, our entire perceptive-experience is created by and for survival. One thing that is missed by using that word, however, is that everything we experience is survival. Survival is the principle of life, so substitute the word "life" if that helps. This means that, for us, everything known, experienced, or perceived is a function of and created by life, and the operating principle of life is survival. As we've seen, life, or survival, crafts and determines all perceptive-experience, thoughts, feelings, and everything else that constitutes our world and our relationship to it.

8:48 One reason I use the word "survival" more commonly than I use the word "life" is I need for you to see your perceptive-experience of life as something you are doing, not something that is a given or done to you. Being outside your scope of control and ownership, life is seen as something in which you find yourself, and so as independent from yourself. It is what keeps you alive, without which you die. You seem to exist within it and because of it. So, the word "life" doesn't evoke the sense of ownership and participation that "survival" does. Even though survival also seems outside your control and something that dominates you, it does contain an element of personal participation and action.

8:49 Whether or not you are the source of anything is a tricky matter that skirts paradox. Although life seems beyond you, at the same time your entire perceptive-experience of the world and of life is within you. This is what you live and relate to as real, even though it is actually a function of yourself and is something you are doing. So the word "survival" puts this activity in your lap as something you are up to—even if it is beyond your ability to fully consciously grasp how this is so. Again, if something is created to serve a purpose, it is not inherently real, it is an activity being done. If you are doing something, you can also stop doing it.

8:50 All that being said, a social context is what primarily dominates our experience of life, and clearly the social domain is collectively of our own making. Remember, as discussed in the section "I Is Us" (in Chapter Six), our shared social reality only lives within us, without which it doesn't exist. If each individual doesn't "do" or "create" that reality and so perceive it, it doesn't exist. Since our social life is the primary focus for us, our social-self is the one we care about when we die. We don't really care about objects, and although it may sound strange, the fact that we will lose objective existence isn't really our concern.

8:51 Our concerns don't reside in objects except how these objects relate to our social circumstance or physical survival. We really don't care about objects when it comes to death. Objects exist in the "not-me" domain, and our concerns are on the "me" part of that distinction. Beyond providing the "place" in which we exist, the only aspect of objective existence that we care about is when it helps or interferes with our lives in some way. The physical aspects necessary for biological life might seem prior to social survival, but remember, we care about physical survival only because it is necessary for our self-awareness or conscious-entity to exist.

8:52 Do you think you'll miss the table when you die? How about the chair? Maybe a rock, a car, a shirt? It isn't hard to see that even if these things are important to you in life, they sure aren't in death. They don't go with you any more than others do, but you care about losing self and other, not objects.

8:53 Even losing the only object you have, your body, isn't your real concern, is it? As pointed out earlier, if you still existed after your body died, would you really care? Perhaps you'd care some because you've become attached to and identified with your body, but this would not be a death, it would be a traumatic change. That's quite a different matter.

8:54 If your self-awareness lived on after death, you might miss the body; but whatever form your self-awareness took at that time would be your "body," so to speak—just like currently your self-awareness assumes the form of an invisible inner self-object. Again, if your self-awareness remained and continued, losing your body would not be a death, just a dramatic change in perceived circumstance. This desired outcome feeds the offerings of most religions.

8:55 If you suddenly lost all ability to move your body, would you cease to exist? No, you would be exactly the same but without an ability you previously had. If you lost any of the perceptive senses provided by the body, the same thing is true—you still exist but without that sense. The point is, objects are not really your concern when it comes to death, you just miss this point because you live in an objectively perceived world and with the fact that when the body dies so do you. But have you ever asked: why is that? Such a question will be addressed later, once we've tackled and transcended many more existential assumptions, but it doesn't hurt to start considering it now.

8:56 When you die it doesn't matter if you lived in a mansion or a shack or were homeless. Those only matter, if they do, while you're alive and only because of social relations and values. At death they don't make any difference. We might think that a homeless person dying alone in the gutter is extremely sad, as opposed to someone dying in their bed with loved ones all around. But that is clearly a social concern. For the dead person, the experience of dying might have been different, but being dead is the same.

8:57 We've seen that the operating principle of life is survival, but we may overlook the fact that what we devote our energies to depends on what we identify with. Our social-self may be deeper than we think. It might be a central or perhaps an essential part of our development as a person. It also may not be what we think it is.

8:58 Consider that there are reports in more than one case of experiments done, for various reasons, on a number of newborn infants in which the babies were taken care of—with humans providing all their biological needs—but were deprived of social interaction and any further human contact. As a result, all these babies died, even though there was nothing physically wrong with them. It seems, at a very core level, biology isn't enough.

8:59 Without a social element it appears there may be no impulse to continue living, and apparently this is determined prior to even having encountered or developed a real social experience. This clearly suggests there is a huge difference between life as a biological event and life as a social event, at least for humans.

8:60 Beyond the basics of physical persistence, our social development becomes quite complex. We begin to see that death is really a social matter, not merely a physical one. We should acknowledge this insight and approach our considerations accordingly.

Existential Self Assumptions

8:61 When self becomes confused with mind, and mind becomes seen as the self, the mind's self-serving activities end up creating an experience of reality that is entirely self-referential. Remember, mind—which also dominates perceptive-experience—has no interest in what's true. That's not its job. Instead, its job is to keep the body and self alive while maintaining an identifiable self-awareness—which requires creating and identifying with mental-emotional activities.

8:62 You're still alive and you're still you, so your mind has done its job. Mind will naturally protect and promote all the beliefs and assumptions behind the activities that keep you that way. Some of these assumptions are existential, meaning they seem to be about the very nature and existence of your self.

8:63 Unless you think to question the validity of the assumptions behind all this, they will simply appear as reality to you. Previously, in the section "I Is Us" (Chapter Six), we looked at some shared assumptions that probably seemed for all the world as just observations of reality. Obviously by calling them assumptions I'm suggesting they aren't true, that they aren't real in the sense that they are activities we invent or do, and therefore they can be done away with. Yet this fact can be difficult to entertain, let alone experience, so it may take some time to sink in. Let's look at a few other likely overlooked assumptions about the nature of yourself that also probably go unchallenged:

- You are located as an uninspected self-object that lives as separate and alone in a private inner world.
- You exist as a self-awareness, a conscious-entity.
- You are incomplete trying to resolve what's missing within.
- You live as if you're a character and a person.
- You think you need to connect with others in order to be complete.
- You locate yourself at the source of perceptive faculties.
- You use the internal dialogue as your main form of thinking.
- You probably believe that mind and body are independent from one another.
- You assume there is something you need to obtain in order to be happy.
- You assume you need to exist.
- And, whatever else is assumed and lived.

8:64 Again, the items on the above short list likely appear as just conditions of your existence, but they aren't. They are foundational assumptions that form the fundamental building blocks of the "experience" of your existence. Even though they seem to be observable realities, they are actually all conceptually created. What does that tell you about their nature and realness?

8:65 They are taken for granted as if real and existential truths of your existence. But if they aren't, then what is? Freeing yourself of the roots and branches of the conceptual-self might lead to a more genuine insight into your nature.

8:66 The existential aspects of our experience are so thoroughly accepted and taken for granted that they are never challenged or inspected. They simply rest in the background as the reality in which we live. From this foundation, a conceptual-self is built and forms who we think we are. This self-experience elicits a great deal of activity in order to manage life, and patterns from these efforts in turn form our personality and character traits, thus defining our experience of being a person.

8:67 In this way, existential assumptions determine our sense of self and our experience of life. As seen, for example, we have a drive to fulfill our lives in some way, to attain something missing. What we think is missing and what might fill it are both generated solely through concept. When we neglect to challenge our beliefs, assumptions, and "selves," we fail to grasp that their natures are conceptual—*ergo,* they are simply figments of mind that don't need to exist. If we devote our life energies and efforts to dynamics that may be circular and never-ending, we will fail to be complete with life as is.

8:68 As stated, when it comes to our self-experience, one of our goals is to be complete with life. Therefore, we might ask: why aren't we complete already? Obviously, we aren't, and in a big way. Again, generally this is because of self-survival, but specifically it has everything to do with existential assumptions and the mental activities we engage because of them.

8:69 As long as something is identified *as* the self or *of* the self, our minds will maintain and defend it. It's not exactly a life-and-death struggle to maintain our character traits, and yet the drive to do so is so strong it may as well be. This effort often involves trying to achieve stuff we think will resolve us based on who we think we are. Yet, no amount of altering the activities of mind or behavior will change the fact that if we don't know who we are, then we don't know who we are.

8:70 One thing to grasp at this point is that the moment you pin yourself down to something perceived, it's not you anymore—it's something perceived. Just so, when you hold yourself to be some concept, it is not you—it is something conceived. The foundational existential assumptions about your very existence, and the concepts and beliefs that form your character and personality, create and dominate your self-awareness. Getting free of all these concepts is a significant task but will certainly lead to unprecedented insights.

The Great Way is not difficult for those who have no preferences. When love and hate are both absent everything becomes clear and undisguised. Make the smallest distinction however and heaven and earth are set infinitely apart.

Seng-T'san

Chapter Nine

FORMULATING OUR WORLD AND CREATING OUR DILEMMA

9:1 At this point, you might be wondering why I don't just get to the point and tell you the answer to transcending life and death. Yet, I'm also sure you don't really think that such a shift in consciousness is easy, or that an "answer" does anything at all toward that end. I caution you not to assume you know what I'm doing or why. There is no answer we're moving toward, only a leap in consciousness. That's what we're preparing to do—but you don't have to wait, do it now. Along those lines, without deep insight into your experience of life, you don't stand a chance at transcending it. So hang in there.

9:2 There is much more to unpack, and sometimes it may seem repetitive or to jump from subject to subject. Yet, as an analogy used in a previous book, think of it as climbing a mountain using a switchback trail. To get to the top you will often see similar views you saw on the way up, but in each case it will be from a different perspective than before based on the work and insights gleaned up to that point. Over time, through this work, a much deeper and unconventional consciousness should unfold, which will be needed in order to tackle this unprecedented subject. Remember, keep contemplating all this and having experiential insights as we go. Onward and upward.

Being Born—and Creating Self

9:3 Let's go over some of the basics again. We've seen that self and other create each other, and that our self-awareness is dominated by conceptual inventions and existential assumptions. Transcending life and death requires we deeply understand and experience for real the nature of this reality. Self and other must exist in order for language, connection, interaction, individuality, self-identity, and more to exist, and these need to exist to create the experience we have of our self-awareness. You only exist because of not-you, and you become an individual person through the inventions that are created within a social world—which can only arise when we make the distinction of self and other.

9:4 Let's look freshly into the basic origins of some of our most taken-for-granted and central experiences to see how this self-awareness is created. Since what will die is this very self-awareness, we should work hard to know what that is and how it was created, and to discover its nature.

9:5 To understand more deeply the incalculable contribution that overlooked shared conceptual inventions make to the human experience, we should go back to birth. As adults we assume that everything we experience is simply a reflection of what's obviously there, and so we have little or no ability to recognize the origins of our experience, and further, fail to grasp the conceptual reality that is created along with such inventions as language. To overcome this impediment, make a focused effort to imagine what it was like to be an infant.

9:6 **Guided Meditation: Creating Sentience**

Empty your mind, and imagine you are an infant right now. As best you can, create an experience where there is no language, no "other," and no "mind." Imagine an experience absent of these and many other related distinctions you take for granted in your current experience. Imagine that your perceptions are almost non-existent and very unformed. You can vaguely make out some visual phenomena and you perceive unidentified sensations and sounds, but that's about it.

It may be difficult to imagine this, but you've made shifts in your experience before—such as turning off internal dialogue, even if only for a moment, or becoming more present in the silent-stillness of not-knowing. Although what I'm asking you to do now is more profound than those, start with your ability to make a shift and try to create a rather "blank slate" in your imagined experience.

As this infant, imagine your experience of others is only as "animated objects." You don't see a "person," and there is no such thing as mind or sentient beings. As you develop you will be working out very, very basic perceptions and learning how to recognize objects—that aren't really objects yet, but merely perceptive phenomena—and do simple movements. Later, you'll learn to relate these movements to what's perceived. Although there is a lot of learning going on for you, it occurs in a very different world than the one you currently inhabit.

Now imagine that as you become a baby, through some leap in consciousness, you create the context of language. Now, all the antics and sounds of the animated objects are seen as "expressions" and not just noise. You don't know what's being said yet, but you know that something is being done that is different from and other than perceiving mere objects. How is such a leap possible?

At some point, you make a distinction that there is an object (body) associated with your experience and grasp that it is separate from other objects. Beyond experiencing two objects, however, a new distinction arises that self and other are conscious-entities. This is an all-important distinction. Try to grasp the "reality" that must be created for these new distinctions to be perceived.

You go from just trying to work out basic perceptive distinctions of objects and movement to a whole new world that includes others and sentience. By creating a context that allows for the possibility of language, you find that it instantly becomes possible to communicate with others, which isn't possible unless the other is seen as a sentient being that can be communicated with.

For another to be seen as sentient, one's self must also be seen as sentient—which is to say the distinction of sentience must be created and applied. If it is applied to another it will be applied to the self because that distinction is attributing to a creature the ability to perceive and feel—to be aware of one's own perceptive-experience. Once this distinction is made, if that aspect is now recognized it will be recognized in both self and other. Do you get that sentience in self and other are created at the same time? Do you see that a context has to be created that includes the distinction of self and other as sentient before language can become possible?

Consider that without seeing others as sentient and inventing language, you not only can't talk to yourself, you have nothing in your experience that indicates a "thinking being," no "inner self" isolated from the rest of your experience—which, as an infant, is primarily body and objects.

Now eliminate sentience, thinking, mind, and inner-self, to be like an infant, and soak in an experience of such a simple being.

We consider the self to be the source
of our awareness,
where awareness originates.
It might be true instead that self
originates from awareness.

The Book of Not Knowing

Being a Body

9:7 Continuing to use our infant consideration, let's look into what it is to experience being a body. We can well imagine that the infant and even the baby doesn't know it is a body. They are aware of sensations and sights and sounds, but how could they have the notion these are attributed to being a body? For example, they don't automatically relate the sensation that generates moving a hand to the sight of a hand moving; these are two independent perceptions.

9:8 It would take time to make such connections, such as: "When this sensation is felt, that sight occurs," then perhaps, "Oh, this sensation generates that movement," and so on. This would apply to many, many connections and conclusions with all kinds of perceptions. Consider that our current experience of being a body isn't a given but is dependent on a lot of learning, making many conceptual connections.

9:9 People often think they are a body or associated with a body but don't inspect what this actually means. We might think we reside within the body, but that is referring to us as an inner self-awareness. On the other hand, being a body rather than being an internal awareness, or some such, is very different from what most people think.

9:10 As a body, the perceived world exists all around with little or no reference to the body itself. There is no "inside" hiding from the "outside." What's there is a perceived world without the distinction of an inner perceiver, an inner self-awareness. Instead of being an inner-self-object, the body becomes the self-object, and so what's perceived is perceived from the body outward.

9:11 Except for a general feeling-sensation associated with the body, the perceptive organs all relate to what's outside the body. Besides determining simple objective relationships—like I'm here, it's there—what's perceived isn't related to the perceiver, it is simply "that," without much self-referencing. Where would you find yourself as an internal person when all that exists is body and world? You wouldn't.

9:12 **Guided Meditation: Eliminating the Inner Self by Shifting to Being the Body**

Take a moment and make a shift so that instead of holding yourself as inside your body, you experience simply being the body itself. Doing that, the body becomes the self-object, and nothing else is added to that or substitutes for it. You hold yourself as the body itself. In this way, you will place all your focus entirely outside the body.

This is not about feeling the body or focusing on the body, that is its own activity. In being the body you are that and only that, without any attention given to inspecting it. Instead, you are living *as* the body—just like currently you live as an inner conscious-entity.

Perceive the world from the body out, without giving any thought or attention to being some entity within. Stop believing or accepting as true that you live within, and instead experience yourself as being only a body.

In so doing, except for a background feeling-sense of the body, your perceptive-experience resides solely outside your body, as if your awareness and consciousness are located outside and all around your body. Eliminate the notion of the inner-self-object, and simply experience being the body as the object of self, and so experience that your perceptive-awareness is focused outside the body. What happens when you make this shift?

9:13 Using this shift in your perspective—without taking for granted an assumed and imagined private inner-self—notice that in simply being a body there is no experience of an inner self-object. Also notice that perception doesn't mean there is an experience of someone located behind the perceptive organs—that is an added assumption. Being "conscious" of the results of a perceptive phenomenon doesn't require a location, but if one were assigned, in this case, it would simply be the body itself.

9:14 By experiencing "being a body"—making the body the self-object and nothing else—it becomes clear that any notion of a "perceiver" behind the perception doesn't need to exist, and a location for the one perceiving isn't a given either. For example, before infants will react to an object flying toward them, they must have some experience of impact. They might bump their head, or their brother hits them in the head with a toy fire truck, or some such, and after a few of these kinds of experiences, they begin to make an association between the visual perception of an object speeding toward them and the pain of impact. Prior to those first instructive encounters, however, the perception of the incoming object is rather meaningless and not something to fear.

9:15 Along with such new perceptive-experiences and conclusions, we can imagine that the baby now develops a different relation to their body-self as being located at the source of perception. Still, this is only a bodily location and doesn't create that inner sense of an ethereal "source" self-object that we currently identify with. How does that come about?

Creating an Inner-Self Separate from the Body

9:16 In just being a body you are stripped of so much nonsense and conceptual activity. You are freed from the sense of being an inner-self—which, remember, is the experienced distinction related to being alive and dying. So, to better transcend this "inner-self-sense," let's look at how it might come to pass.

9:17 We have seen that everything is always about you. No matter whether you are a worthless turd or a god, completely selfish or enlightened, a happy person or a miserable wretch, what do all these have in common? You! This tends to be overlooked. We just accept this condition as reality. But it's not inevitable.

9:18 Imagine that self is generated by the universe swirling into a collection of matter becoming an animal—like milk forming clouds in one's coffee.

From this, the human brain creates abstract activities called concepts, and through these concepts imagines a self. Yet, throughout history, this self hasn't always been seen as the same distinction.

9:19 Over time it seems humanity has gone down the road of creating smaller and more ethereal distinctions of what a self is. At first perhaps the self was simply the distinction of a body separate from other bodies or objects. Eventually a new distinction was created, and we started to think of ourselves as a "person," and not just a body. Fun fact, the origins of "person" are found in ancient Greek plays where a person or persona was a character in a play; this suggests being a "person" wasn't always the case.

9:20 From here at some point we became a mind and then an immaterial inner self. We've already seen, to some degree, how this might have happened. Eventually we moved more toward being a source self (something behind the scenes of what we experience) and then perhaps a soul, a higher self, or some such. Do you see this trend moves increasingly toward being less related to the physical and more toward a smaller and more separate self?

9:21 Because we fail to find this self directly, we keep inventing new possibilities for it, becoming smaller and more abstract as we go. We can see that this direction is becoming less and less objective and more detached and ethereal. Why do we think this is useful or a good direction in which to go?

9:22 Consider, it's not. It is an abstract pursuit that just leads to more complications and imagination, but not to more consciousness. So in our work here, we need to put mind and body, self and object, back together. Once this is done, we can stop speculating about what a self might be—like trying to find Waldo—and more realistically ask: What is it?

9:23 Be open to the possibility that your body is actually the only object related to the creation of the idea of a self, that no inner self-object actually exists. Again, entertain the possibility that "you" are a function of the brain generating a rather new (on the evolutionary scale) powerful "problem solving" and imaginative capacity, and this activity creates a new world of possibilities.

9:24 This imaginative problem-solving function learns to create abstract thought and solve problems that aren't there. One central idea that arises from this ability is that there must be a source to these conceptual activities that isn't physical, and this generates the notion of an abstract inner self-object, the substance of which is cognitive-awareness. From this "ability" a new assumption and conclusion is made that this source is a "self" that exists independent from the physical world.

9:25 When sentience is created as a distinction, the self becomes identified as a separate inner object in relation to other sentient selves assumed to also be inner objects. But sentience can't be found as an object, it is only gleaned through the activities of the body. Therefore sentience seems to reside within the bodies that "house" it. So a conclusion is made that my self is over here inside the object of my body, and your self is over there inside the object of your body.

9:26 To be clear, I'm suggesting that no such self exists. Instead, it is just a function of a body with a brain generating abstract complex conceptual activities concluding that these activities are separate from and independent of the body itself. It is a distinction, an activity, not an existential reality, as we think. Once this is done, however, a non-physical self is born.

You Depends on Other

9:27 When a separate self is created, an identity needs to take place. How is this done? Again, imagine that as you grow, beyond learning how to work and manage a body, the largest percentage of your development is determined by relating to the existence of others. Although you tend to hold your "self" as a separate and independent entity, the truth is that your very sense of self is created as well as crafted in relation to others. Remember, the act of creating a "self" awareness creates the domain of "other" in the same moment. Get this as a present experience, and not just as hearsay.

9:28 Beyond the original creation of the distinction of self and other, over time you crafted everything you experience as yourself in relation to what you experience as others. Everything you experience as a self is related to your experience of others and not-self. In other words, if you gather and define everything that is not-you, you will also be revealing the outlines of your self.

9:29 This will take some work to grasp, that's why I keep revisiting it. It's true generally, as in your mere existence is dependent on the existence of not-you. But also specifically for each aspect of your self-experience. Choose anything that is characteristic of your person, or that defines you in some way, and notice how it relates to and is compared with others or not-you—each defines the other.

9:30 For example, you can't be a grumpy old man without the existence of others who are not grumpy or old or a man. You can't be characterized as one who is selfish unless there are others who are characterized as not selfish, and so on. Do you see that every self-characteristic is generated in relation to what it is not? If one didn't exist, neither would the other.

9:31 Once again these assertions require unprecedented existential insights in order to grasp them. Just hearing about them or even accepting them as fact isn't enough. You have to experience them. You need to have an insight into this asserted reality, one that steps outside the taken-for-granted world in which you live. Such insight will blow your mind because it is very much not the norm and will deeply change your experience of and perspective on these matters. Without such existential and experiential insights, however, these words will simply remain on the page.

9:32 We've seen that creating the distinction of conscious-entities produces a vast new social world. As this social world is created, a new form of self is also developed, defining oneself as a particular sentient being separate from all others. Without these conceptual-perceptive distinctions such a world would not exist.

9:33 Notice that you experience a you and a not-you in the objective world—so a table and another person are both seen as not-you. But look further: when you experience the distinction of sentience, you have created a new domain independent from tables or inanimate objects. This sentient you and other is where a social self and identity are created, and where your self-awareness exists. Can you see that within this new domain a "you" will be formed that is always in relation to and relating to other you's? Here you will make many more new distinctions within this new social context.

9:34 With the development of language—and so the possibility of connecting with or sharing our experience with others—we correspondingly create the internal dialogue that forms the centerpiece of what we commonly regard as our thinking. From this experience, we come to make a distinction of an internal state or "mind," as well as conclude that we are at the source of our perceptions; and since the internal dialogue is a matter of recreating the sound of our own voice we locate this sense between the ears, just like we locate the source of our sight behind the eyes. When these conclusions are drawn we then identify with this activity as being the location of an inner unseen self-object.

9:35 The creation of this inner-self is pivotal to a sense of being isolated and separate. It also provides the ability to live within a private inner world where so much mischief occurs, such as allowing a disconnect between our experience and our expressions—consider the consequences that this alone produces. Going beyond such consequences, experience the reality that is created by creating an inner-self separate from the body and physical reality. Despite the fact that it is actually unnecessary and not ultimately true, the distinction of this inner-self and sentient other is far more important and key to our experience of life than we have imagined heretofore.

9:36 For example, although you suppose that you're talking to yourself and that it is a volitional and willful act, when asked to stop all internal dialogue you find it much harder than you had imagined. Why? Because you aren't really talking to yourself. You are actually talking to "other." Since your inner-self-existence is created by a conceptually generated social world, maintaining a relationship in your mind between you and other is essential. No other, no you—sound a bit like death?

9:37 Therefore, within your self-awareness you keep an ongoing internal dialogue—or some other form of language—running that demands the distinction of self and other be made and present. An internal dialogue requires the existence of self and other because language solely exists as a function of this distinction. This conceptually produced activity keeps your inner-self-sense present by constantly relating to others in the abstract, thus conceptually generating and maintaining an active sense of self and mind. This is why stopping the internal dialogue is so difficult—but it is not impossible. [For a more in-depth look into this dynamic, see Chapter Four in *The Genius of Being*.]

Creating a Social Life

9:38 After the creation of self and other as sentient entities—allowing for the invention of language—the stage is set for the generation of a social world. People take their social world very seriously. It appears to exist all around them and usually occupies the biggest slice of their attention and energy. Although it seems to simply and objectively exist, the fact is this social reality—important as it may be to us—is an invention, and so as an inherent or objective reality it is an illusion. It only exists as a mental invention that is superimposed upon what's perceived. People tend to know this in the abstract but not to any experiential depth.

9:39 When I refer to some matter being an illusion in this context, I'm pointing to the fact that it is an invented conceptual activity and not an intrinsic or existential reality that occurs on its own. It's more like something exists only because we *think* it exists. Simply getting the imaginary nature of such experience helps free us from it, allowing us to recognize the illusionary nature of these inventions even as we continue to participate within them.

9:40 Think about it. Where does the seemingly tangible reality of your "social world" live? It seems as though it just exists on its own, and you are required to find your place within it and relate to it appropriately. This is only because there are a lot more others than you, so this reality is heavily weighted outside of you alone. Yet society is composed entirely of concepts and activities. The only objects present are bodies, and bodies alone aren't enough to create a social world.

9:41 Obviously, our social reality exists within the same context that creates self, other, and language. This social reality is composed of taken-for-granted and shared beliefs and agreements. These kinds of agreements and assumptions may be necessary for creating a civilization, but they exist without any substance whatsoever.

9:42 Whenever you step out into the world, what occurs in your experience beyond the perception of your surroundings? If others are nearby or expected, the feeling of your environment changes somewhat, doesn't it? What is this feeling about? Is there some fear or excitement involved, perhaps some sense of possibility or unease? Does a sense arise of the need to attend to social management in some way? Notice that a seemingly tangible world emerges, layered with significance and meaning.

9:43 When an interaction occurs with another, what governs the form it takes? Doesn't what you think of them, and what you think they think of you, determine the experience you have of any encounter? The whole matter of self-image is related to your thoughts about the way you are viewed. When another is around, or just in your thoughts, your feeling-reactions to whatever you imagine is occurring within their mind determines your experience of the relationship, doesn't it?

9:44 These reactions and actions are produced solely by your own thoughts, judgments, and assessments, arising reflexively and held to be simply a reflection of what's there. But they aren't a reflection of what's there. They are actually just imagined by you. Take a look—where and how do these assessments arise?

9:45 When you judge someone, where does that take place? When you determine what another is thinking or what the meaning is behind what's said or done, again, where does that take place? Notice these are all imagined by you, they are not actually objectively experienced. Yet these imaginations have the power to dictate your interactions with another person and with people in general.

9:46 What may be even more dominant in any particular interaction is the superimposed framework of a social world that is conceived by you. This structure is at once both cultural and personal. It contains values and etiquette, standards and protocols, models for behavior, shared assumptions and beliefs, and the social meaning of everything perceived, as well as your personal agenda and history. It is the framework by which you will judge any encounter, and the social reality within which you live. It's hard to see the social world for what it is because you live inside it, and therefore it remains as unseen as water to a fish. Often overlooked is that it also determines a great deal of your experience of your self.

9:47 As we've seen, a new world is created simply through making a distinction of sentience in self and other and inventing language. This immediately creates a social context in which to hold the new distinctions that arise from "perceiving" a world of sentient beings that can connect in some way. Whatever content is created produces the framework for our social world. Once produced, however, it appears as an immutable experience because this very experience depends upon the foundation that creates it. Although completely invented, participating in some form of a social world isn't really a choice because a social context is what determines your very existence as a self-awareness. Starting to see the connections?

9:48 When someone considers opting out of the "bindings" of society, what often comes up is some notion of rejecting social mores, of being "outside" social convention, being a rebel or recluse, and so on. Actually, these positions are all existing features of our social conventions. An aspect of the social world in which we live is to consider such matters, and to decide how much and in what ways to fit in. Yet, the illusion is the existence of a social world itself, not just what's in it.

9:49 Invention or not, jettisoning the social world isn't really an option if we are going to live as a social being. To do so would mean eliminating language and culture, agreements and social interaction. If you did manage to drop all social reality, you would not be able to interact with humans; you'd be more like an animal that would either be shot or tagged and released back into the wild. You couldn't participate in a modern human world at all. But consider that upon death this world will automatically end, so you need to transcend this world while living within it.

9:50 To socially interact with others, you have no choice but to work within a social context and shared conceptual inventions. The accepted forms for communication and the agreed-upon methods for relating have to be taken into account, because relationship isn't about you, it's about you and others. To bridge the gap between the two requires some way to do so.

9:51 It's a bit like wanting to talk to someone on the phone but without the necessary phones, wires, or cell towers to connect, you couldn't do it. There could be any number of inventions to create and connect phones, but once the inventing is done, you must use whatever has been agreed upon and built or you cannot engage in a call. Insisting on having your own unique phone that is a carrot, separate from any form of connection, won't work—you'll never talk to anyone. What's socially established has been learned and shared by everyone for the most part. That is the starting point for any interaction, but it doesn't have to be the end.

9:52 For example, this book and communication exist within a social context. Without it we couldn't communicate and consider any matter. This communication can only take place within an invented social world and language, even though the subject matter presses us to consider realities outside the very world we are experiencing at the moment.

9:53 A new possibility of freedom arises when you grasp that the social world is an invention rather than a reality. In life you may have to operate within the parameters of a social structure, but the reality of your nature does not, and in death cannot. A consciousness free of any social influence provides the capacity to see social life for what it is, but it can be difficult to grasp this possibility. Perhaps a place to start is to work on it.

9:54 **Guided Meditation: Prior to the Social-Self**

Once again, imagine being an infant, this time still in the womb. Whether or not this state is completely absent of any social reality is irrelevant, just imagining such a relatively "empty" fetal state helps provide a springboard from which to grasp the existential nature of experience without a social world. So, do your best to experience what it would be like to still be a newly formed infant.

Isolated within the womb, you clearly wouldn't have any social concerns or angst, and you wouldn't worry about what people did or felt or thought. There would be no morality, no culture, no beliefs, and no society of any kind. You wouldn't worry what people thought about you because "other" wouldn't exist for you, nor would even the idea of being seen.

Try to eliminate all these elements during your contemplation, keeping in mind that even a rudimentary social order is still a social order. Work to imagine an experience where there isn't any social world at all.

9:55 If you can temporarily free yourself from a social context, and so from the plethora of assumptions and distinctions that make up a social world, you are better equipped to experience the real nature of this invention—it's all concept. Actions taken relating to these concepts may be objective, but since they are founded on what we could call "false" perceptions, they are not necessary. The point is, a social world is conceptually invented, therefore, whether it persists or not is irrelevant.

9:56 Since our whole social reality is an invention, this also means your self is an invention. Once we can begin to get beyond the illusion of our social experience, we have a better perspective from which to look into the illusion of every other "life" experience.

9:57 Toward that end, have you noticed that there doesn't have to be anyone else actually present for "other-related" struggles to go on? You have self-image concerns when you're alone not only because you are always in relationship to others, but also because your supposedly objective "perceptions" of life are actually highly subjective and so don't require the presence of another person. You can easily evoke mental-emotional activities related to others just by having an idea or memory, thinking about yourself, talking to yourself, or even looking in the mirror.

9:58 Given we feel somehow less than, broken, disconnected, or wrong in some way, we struggle to resolve this condition. We most often seek out resolutions to such maladies in our social world, missing the fact that the social world is what created these supposed maladies in the first place. Perhaps by looking into this imagined condition—even though it feels very real and important—as well as the assumptions that found not only it but our attempts to fix it, we might find a way to free our consciousness from this whole mess.

Chapter Ten
PROBLEMS AND RESOLUTIONS

Being Existentially Alone

10:1 We need to continue to acknowledge and soak in the reality that our fundamental experience is one of being an inner self-object—because it's only going to get worse from here, folks. As we've seen, here, our most basic experience and awareness is one of being existentially alone. This means that as a self we are isolated and exist in a condition that is separate from everything else and especially from all others. Why is it important to acknowledge this? Because it's the one we identify with, and so it is the one that will die.

10:2 The construction of this experience has roots in our self-condition and sometimes shows up in our experience as loneliness. To set the stage to better understand this condition, let's begin by pulling from my book *Ending Unnecessary Suffering,* speaking about loneliness:

10:3 *Loneliness* [an excerpt]

> Loneliness is one of the more core conditions for pretty much everybody, although it is most often buried under all of life's distractions—anything that keeps the mind busy and occupied. Yet, there are occasions when we confront our loneliness, and sometimes conditions press us into an experience of loneliness, especially during periods where others are absent from our lives.

Clearly, this reveals you are imagining that your happiness is dependent on some experience other than what you have, and that this can only be produced by others and not you. In contrast, your current experience of living life by yourself is seen as lacking.

The foundation that sets the stage for such suffering stems from the fact that you live in a private-inner-world that only you experience, and this is held as the place where you reside. But no one else can ever also reside in this "place." So, you will always be alone there, and the only avenue to connect with another private-inner-world is through communication. Here you might be able to develop a sense of connection. But this can't be done without others, and so you feel you need others, and often a special other, in order to be intimately connected.

When this isn't happening, you can easily feel alone, isolated, and lonely. Acknowledging that such a deep connection with another is usually rather rare means most of the time you live on an island of separation. With or without people, to avoid suffering loneliness you probably feel the need to be distracted, to have something fill your mind and experience so you don't have to face the deep loneliness that you feel just being a self.

Clearly you aren't okay with being alone. You aren't okay with merely "being," and you need some form of distraction from this condition. It seems that your mere existence as a being is incomplete and you need the imagined "promise" that someone or others can somehow complete your experience.

Did you follow that? Let's go over it again. The core concept is that you aren't okay just being you and you need others to complete you in order to make you happy. Since you live in an existentially isolated private-inner-world the only avenue to connect to another is through communication. And you need others for that. So, in this way, living as an incomplete self causes loneliness.

Your experience of loneliness requires imagining another possible world that you don't have. I know it might seem like you have no choice about it, as if it is just a fact of circumstance—and what makes it even worse, this notion is supported by the culture in which you live. Yet, try to grasp where that "fact" lives. It lives solely in your imagination, and what you say this condition means to you. You are alone, and you imagine not being alone would be a more satisfying experience.

In contrast to an imagined circumstance, you see your current experience as negative and unacceptable. You desire or long for something that you don't have. Again, you assess that you, by yourself, are not good enough, are not complete without someone else to validate you. Your self-experience is felt to be lacking and incomplete. Therefore, you judge your current "imagined" experience as negative and painful.

Why do I say current "imagined" experience? Certainly, if it is your experience you aren't imagining it but experiencing it, right? Actually, not really. What you currently experience is your body and what you perceive as occurring both physically and conceptually. But there is no loneliness there. The loneliness is added, through imagining comparisons to what you don't have but think you need, and so what is currently experienced is given a negative meaning. This is added and it is imagined. Stop imagining this added layer to your experience and it doesn't exist.

Again, I acknowledge that since we are social animals, and have also developed an overactive ability to imagine all sorts of stuff, that this change of mind could seem difficult. I know for the vast majority of people that it is a difficult challenge to overcome, because we think such experiences as loneliness are inevitable, a fact that we must suffer. So, it is easy to overlook the power we have to simply not compare what is factually occurring with this imagined experience that is not occurring.

But, hard as it is to accept, a deep loneliness tends to be a core experience for most humans even when it is overridden with distractions. When your attention is being filled with active life-activities you won't notice the loneliness aspect. But it is still a dynamic that should be dealt with. It will come around to bite you in the ass at some point, especially as you get older.

It is useful to work on "completing" yourself, by grasping that you are already complete and whole and that your experience is all that is needed, no matter what it is. This goes a long way toward ending this malady.

10:4 Beyond and consistent with overcoming our experience of loneliness, we need to grasp how this is related to death. Obviously, being existentially alone, and so an isolated and separate self, is the condition of our experience. This is important to us because it not only is the one who is going to die, it creates the condition that generates the angst about losing this one.

10:5 Consider that this separate-self becoming non-existent is what we call death. But imagine if you deeply experienced being one with or connected to all others and reality—and so not separate or isolated—would it matter very much that you lost your separateness? The end of that separation would be a rather minor issue, wouldn't it? This may sound weird since it seems our individual separate self is just a fact of the universe, and so we don't have any choice about its life or death. But that may not be true.

10:6 If it's the isolated nature that we would miss, what does that say? Certainly we cling to this sense because it is all we have, it is what we experience as our existence. Yet, this might also be an illusion. Obviously I'm suggesting that we may not be separate, that this isolation is something that occurs within our conceptual-experience but may not be the ultimate truth of our nature. If we experienced ourselves as not separate, then if this separate one dies, is that a problem? We see dying is only really a problem from the perspective of this unfound self-object, which, hard as it is to accept, only exists as an assumption.

The fundamental delusion of humanity is to suppose that I am here and you are out there.

Yasutani Roshi

10:7 In our world, the self is all we have—if we lose that, we lose all. We lose all because everything is perceived via the existence of ourselves, and our central role in the universe is to interpret everything in relation to us. If we lose that, we lose the whole world that we experience. So challenging this taken-for-granted and seemingly obvious experience—that we are an isolated existentially alone entity—would be a radical divergence from our solid life experience. But consider it, and put it on the back burner for now. We will get to it later.

10:8 Not realizing a real connection with others, or a completeness in ourselves, throughout our lives we long for this separation to get handled, but never attain it. We remain alone. Any other possibility is just intellectual imagining, and this is not at all grounded enough to tackle matters such as life and death. Instead, we have to grasp how the social self is central to and dominates our experience of life, and transcend this illusion by becoming directly conscious of the true nature of existence in a deep way.

10:9 Your self-awareness exists solely within the social domain. You are separate because you distinguish your self from others, you exist as a conscious-entity only because of other conscious-entities. As an inner self-object—although unseen and unfound—you live as if you are an aware object, and this awareness-object can die.

10:10 Isn't it strange that the conclusion of being self-aware is based on the assumption that this self-awareness is also objectively separate? Alone, as either an object or a concept, death isn't an issue—as already discussed. They have to work in tandem and combine—holding yourself as a conceptual-object that exists in a social context—for death to become an issue. Although this conceptual self-object really doesn't amount to a hill of beans, this is the self we experience being and fear losing.

10:11 Try to identify the very experience you live inside of, and get where this self-awareness lives. Consider that who you are prior to any social context is very different than who you live as. It is who you live as that is concerned with dying.

10:12 What composes our social self-experience is rather complex. It is made up of many assumptions that act as cotter pins to our fundamental view of life. We don't really need to go into every single belief, concept, assumption, or perspective, however, to know that life is full of a lot of social drama regardless of source.

10:13 What may be a little harder to see is that although it seems like it's full of significance, it's all just a meaningless story being given meaning—sound and fury signifying nothing. Seeing it this way helps reduce our resistance to losing it. We are also beginning to see that we really never get away from the social reality that creates our self-experience.

Even Privacy Is Social

10:14 Consider that even privacy is a social function. When you are physically alone, when you get away into your private place, your sanctuary, no matter where it is or how it occurs—your house, your room, a hotel room, a hidden place in the forest, your tent, wherever—how does this privacy relate to others? How is your sanctuary a function of a social context?

10:15 You can see, of course, that the very nature of privacy depends on the possibility of being exposed to or surrounded by others. Therefore, others are the main factor in being private or sequestered. Yet, go further.

10:16 When you are in a space all by yourself, what do you feel, what do you think? Notice these personal activities relate directly to the absence of others and the fact that you are freed from the demands of others, as well as being protected from them, and so on. Do these conditions influence your experience? Of course they do.

10:17 Take a look. What occurs in your mind and behavior that is different from when you are around others? What do you feel that is different? Can you get that these thoughts and feelings are relating directly to others and their absence—and not just their absence but your freedom from them? So, this experience is clearly a part of a social context.

Can you see past the social enough to know that you can't see past the social?

The Promise of "Out There"

10:18 Given that our experience of being separate and alone is seen as a malady, we are drawn to search for a solution to this condition. Where do we attempt to find a remedy for this sense of being incomplete? Obviously, by attaining something that we don't have, and this has to be something separate from us and our experience—because if it were within us already we would have no malady—and so it must be something in the world "out there."

10:19 In your imagination, how do you perceive "out there"? As the next adventure to entertain you? A possible solution to your problems? A scary event that might hurt you? It promises all these things, as well as boredom, repetition, and the unexpected. But what is really "out there"? No matter what it is, it is only more perceptive-experience—whether it's good or bad depends on you.

10:20 The promise of "out there" is bolstered by the fact we've had good and satisfying experiences before. We might have fallen in love, or had a fun adventure, maybe encountered interesting people or ideas, and so on. Because of these it seems that if we could only find the permanent circumstance that makes us feel good all the time, we could resolve our sense that something is missing or that we are lacking.

10:21 Yet, ask yourself: Has it worked so far? Of course not. But you may assume that's just because you aren't good at finding the right golden circumstance, or you haven't found or attained enough of it, or some such. Think that is true? No, it isn't. Yet, truly grasping this can elude you, because this draw is strong and seems viable. But this draw is based on an illusion.

10:22 No matter what the imagined solution is, it is never a solution to anything existential about yourself. It can never change your sense of separation and isolation because it can never exist in the place where you experience this malady—your private inner world. At most, it can only distract you for a time.

10:23 Did you get that? Nothing "out there" will ever be "in here," will it? So, whatever it is, the most it can do is affect your experience in some way. It can't change the fact you live as an isolated inner-self, or somehow make you complete. Can you see that nothing external to you—which is the definition of "out there"—can ever resolve what is created within you and by you, no matter what it is?

10:24 We might think something external to us can fix us because we have experienced a disease that a medication cured, or hunger that eating handled, or engaged many other remedies to change our experience in some way. But those kinds of solutions are actually external to us, they are not inherent or existential, they are also temporary. Clearly, they can't "fix" the sense of separation and isolation we experience as the condition of our private inner self-world.

10:25 No circumstance can ever fix you or make you complete. Only you can. It is your own mind that creates a sense of being incomplete—feeling like something is missing within you or is wrong with you. No outside force can change that in any way. When you grasp that, you should also get that there is nothing out there—no distraction, accomplishment, attainment, circumstance, experience, drug, group, or belief system—that will ever make you whole and "complete." Being complete, and so without something missing or in need of a remedy for an unreal malady, is a matter of consciousness, not attainment.

10:26 In addition to the basic condition that is felt as being separate and isolated—and so feeling some need for inner company or oneness or some such—there are often unrecognized assumptions about yourself that you are broken in some way, that you are inherently flawed, worthless, incapable, wrong, or what have you. These certainly don't help create a sense of you being complete and OK as you are.

10:27 Without any of the usually unrecognized conceptual contributions that send ripples through the pond, you are actually already inherently complete. Think about it. Why would you be born as a mistake, a broken object that needs something in the universe it doesn't have to make it whole? The universe is already what it is, everything that exists exists as it is. An object can only be broken or have something missing if you think it does; you have to compare it to its former shape or to another object or an imagined object that is different in order to assess something is missing or broken. Is this the case for you? Are you a broken object or a mistake?

Remember the three-legged dog;
it's happy and complete regardless
that it's missing a leg.

10:28 Or perhaps you are a concept. How can a concept be broken or missing something? It can't, it is what it is. It might be ineffective or mistaken if it's relating to something objective. But it is what it is. Unless you have the concept that you are incomplete in some way, you aren't. So as an object or a concept or even a conceptual-object, you can't be incomplete or broken, and there is nothing out there that you need in order to be you. You are already you!

Here and Now Is Not There and Then

10:29 What's also true is that the promise of "out there" is always conceptual. It is something you are imagining. Take a look. When you encounter something, it's not imagined or in the future anymore but is something you are experiencing for better or worse. Even when encountered, however, it is still external to you. In the end, whether encountered or imagined, it is simply more sound and fury. But can you grasp this enough to permanently let go of the myth of "out there"?

10:30 You can see this is difficult because your mind will continue with its quest for resolution, and resolution has to have some solution. If the solution is not here and now, then it must be out there and in the future. But completion has to be here and now, because completion is about what-is—your present experience in this and every moment.

10:31 Being complete means there is no resolution still to be had or to search after. Chasing resolution means you feel incomplete, that something is wrong with you or missing in you that needs to be attained. When you are complete all that you need and "are" is here and now. This *here and now* can't be in contrast to some *there and then,* since that would elicit a comparison to an imagined promise not present, and you're likely to be in conflict once again.

10:32 Since this domain of "out there" occurs solely inside your mind, even attempting resolution through an inner attainment—such as through meditation or adopting some self-improvement ideas, or whatever—is still distinct from you and not a permanent fix to your condition of being isolated and incomplete. Without understanding how and where you create being incomplete, such "inner" efforts will only be a distraction or offer temporary relief. They will not provide a real freedom from the myth that attaining some promised resolution through changes in circumstance will fix you, especially since such inner efforts will undoubtedly be based on the same imagined promise of resolution.

10:33 Just like attaining something objective, altering your subjective experience is still just a change in experience, not a real change in your self-condition or what your mind is doing that creates this malady. There is nothing wrong with and much benefit to such practices as meditating to quiet and calm the mind, but like any other distraction or change of state it is only temporary. Becoming conscious of what's true is very different from altering your state or experience by trying to find some resolution to what ails you. Endlessly searching keeps your attention always looking elsewhere, whether within or without.

10:34 As long as you imagine there is something around the bend that will make you whole and satisfy your needs, you can never be complete and whole where you stand. In life, there is no problem seeing what's around the next bend if you want, but this can be done without thinking it will fix you in some way. When you give up the idea and drive to find something not present, you can be complete and whole and satisfied with where you are, no matter where that is. This is very different from the imagined promise that something somewhere "out there" represents the solution to your personal problems. Realize that in death there is no next bend, and so such an option isn't possible.

As long as we have some definite idea or hope about the future, we cannot really be serious with the moment that exists right now.
Suzuki Roshi

10:35 How long can we continue to search for the next new thing, or try to attain that which is missing? The world of imagined promises is infinite, it will never end. This means such activities can constantly and endlessly be created. We can fruitlessly chase after the cheese of resolution our whole lives until death puts an end to it. But along the way we are never deeply satisfied, happy, or complete now.

10:36 Curiously, the infinite nature of this process leads us back to the absolute. Are you conscious of the relationship between infinity and the absolute nature of existence? Most people aren't. But it doesn't matter. To tackle the real nature of death this realization may make a difference, but for letting go of imagined promises it doesn't.

10:37 Again, completion in this matter has to be here and now, and the here and now can't be in contrast to a there and then. In fact, when it comes to life and death, ultimately the nature of here and now has to be understood as nowhere, and this nowhere must encompass both here and there. (Fun fact: putting the words *now* and *here* together makes it "nowhere.") Only the absolute can do that—that's where our infinity realization becomes useful. By grasping this "Nothing-Infinite" consciousness—which is the same as your true nature—you can put this struggle to rest. But you don't need to grasp the absolute to be complete within your experience here and now, just stop creating the concepts that keep telling you that you are incomplete.

10:38 Remember, the only reason the drive to pursue a resolution is so steadfast and engrained in you is because you are committed to self-survival on a primal level, and so you divide up experience into good and bad, better or worse, and try to attain the good and avoid the bad. Since you experience being isolated and alone as a malady, *ergo* bad—and likely have existential self-assumptions such as being broken, worthless, wrong, or what have you—this creates the impulse to find a resolution to fix what's wrong. Your endless desire to achieve a final positive self-experience is driven by self-survival. Yet you will never be complete with what-is by chasing after myths. Since you are considering death, or the end of the self, survival can't be the operating principle for your consideration.

10:39 Clearly death is outside of survival, because you don't survive. So in order to transcend life and death, and move your experience of life into the same place as an experience of no-life, you have to become free not only of a social context dominating your experience but also of self-survival dominating your experience. In this way, you can be complete within life now, no matter what experience is arising.

10:40 As you can see by now, this is a long story, so hang in there. Understanding all the elements that make such a shift real and possible can only unfold over time, but you will need to connect the dots in the end. The root cause of the sense that something needs to be attained in order to become whole, as well as the need to resolve your sense of isolation and separation, live within the many mistaken assumptions you have of self and life, and these are both deep and abundant.

10:41 One of the distinctions that keeps us off kilter in life is the search for meaning and the fear of meaninglessness. So, let's look again at meaning, since it is a core element that generates our needs and struggles, and is central to feeling incomplete. We have addressed meaning and meaninglessness some, but there is more to get about this reality.

Meaningless Doesn't Mean Anything

10:42 Earlier we touched on the idea that life and self are inherently meaningless, and that's likely one idea that still doesn't sit well. We are troubled by such questions whenever they come up—the meaning of life, the significance or worth of ourselves, what existence is all about. Our desire for answers might lead us to some doctrine or personal conclusions, and these could suffice for a time, but the real questions will continue unabated in the background despite any viable-sounding "ideas" that come our way.

10:43 Forsaking all ready-made conclusions reveals our discomfort with confronting the reality that inherently we have no genuine answers and find no intrinsic meaning to our existence. Our inability to assert from our core the meaning of self and life suggests that we might be looking in the wrong place or for the wrong thing. Perhaps this occurs because where we need to look is not only unacceptable to the human mind but also very difficult to grasp.

10:44 Meaninglessness is intolerable to the self-mind. It is resisted, ignored, suppressed, overcome, and denied. Rather than confront this meaninglessness head-on, we're apt to seek some kind of consoling beliefs that will help us "find" meaning or will "provide" meaning.

10:45 Life, self, and the universe are all absolutely meaningless. And the fact that it all doesn't mean anything doesn't mean anything! Notice that, despite the word within the word, "meaninglessness" does not denote less meaning. It refers instead to NO meaning. Meaninglessness is not a negative or bad thing, since that connotation would itself be meaningful. Negative has meaning! Without meaning added, what-is is simply what it is, however it is perceived to be.

10:46 So "meaningless" simply indicates a condition of being without meaning. We ourselves are meaningless. "Being" cannot be either inauthentic or worthless, since to "be" is itself and has no meaning. It is an authentic event because it is the first event, it is the mere existence of something.

10:47 As seen, the truth is you cannot be worthless because you have no worth to begin with. Being exists prior to worth or value, which are always applied to things, they are never inherent. Understanding this might help in overcoming a resistance to the idea of being without meaning. But merely hearing about it isn't enough; what's needed is to experience it.

10:48 Meaninglessness needs to be grasped as a fundamental truth of your existence because meaning keeps you bound to and blindly involved in the drama of life, preventing you from getting free of it. Entertain the thought that death also has no meaning. Clearly it is only because of your self that death means anything. Perhaps it could be said that the truth of existence transcends meaning. At least that sounds better, doesn't it?

10:49 Grasping the meaninglessness of life and death can only be done directly. A deep and direct conscious experience of this kind may still not seem possible. This could be because, as a culture, we've restricted such a search to the domain of hearsay. In other words, we assume that the only option open to us is to believe something about it, which rules out the possibility of a personal direct consciousness or even profound insight.

10:50 Yet, you should be able to see that the whole domain of meaning is a product of the mind, it is solely generated from what you think. If you want to be meaningful then think you are meaningful—just make it up—since that's where meaning happens. Instead, you compare yourself to others, social values, ideals, and so on, trying to assess your own meaning or value. When you fall short or appear less than whatever you are comparing yourself to, you feel meaningless or worthless. From here, you're likely to desperately seek some distraction or attainment in the hopes of feeling good again. But it is an endless cycle. Better to get off the wheel altogether and learn to incorporate the truth that your existence has no meaning, and that's OK.

10:51 Besides the fact that you and life are meaningless, the main takeaway here should be understanding that meaningless doesn't mean anything. Life is independent of meaning, or prior to meaning. The meaning of both life and self is generated by a mind dominated by a social context, and without such conceptual activity there is no meaning.

10:52 Remember, and bring into your experience right now, the fact that meaning is created by relating everything to yourself. Grasp that if you relate everything perceived to yourself in order to create its meaning, then yourself (as the source of the perceiving) can have no meaning—unless you relate the idea of yourself to something else. It's similar to how the eye can't see itself because it is the source of the seeing. If you create meaning—if you are the source of assigning meaning—then you yourself can have none. Get it? Contemplate this until you can experience what's being said. It probably won't be easy, but if you work on it, you can get it as an experience.

10:53 Since our experience of life exists in a social domain—which we're beginning to see encompasses far more than we usually think—meaning is a cornerstone of our experience. To see life in a context that can relate to death well, we have to understand how a social context dominates our experience. The concept and angst of having a life that we can lose only occurs within the social distinction of self and other, death is only imagined and feared here, and this whole domain is wed to meaning. Our job is to transcend this domain and so experience being independent from a social context and all the content it produces.

Your Role in Life

10:54 Before we look into transcending a social context, let's take a moment to focus on one way of looking at the reality of your self-awareness. As seen, one of the first and most significant distinctions you make among all this perceived phenomena is the distinction called "you." When tackling the issue of life, the focus quickly turns to "your" life. And yet what is this "you" that seems to be alive? What is your relationship to life? Is this "you" instinctually produced? What is your function as this internal-entity-that-is-aware? What is your job?

10:55 Let's dive in here by considering that as a body you are a collaborative bunch of cells. Every organ and system of your body is made up of cells mindlessly functioning in concert toward particular ends that collectively produce and maintain life. All these individual activities create an animal—an assemblage of individual and specialized cells mindlessly living on their own.

10:56 You probably identify quite strongly with the body. It is what objectively exists, and is your main claim and proof of existence. But this has to remain as if a "self-evident" belief because you aren't conscious of even one of the roughly 37 trillion cells that constitute your body. Do you know each or any red blood cell personally? Do you experience whizzing around inside tubes? No. You, as a conscious entity, have no consciousness of the activity occurring within any mitochondria. You have no awareness of your kidneys working, or your lymphatic system, or any of a huge number of activities that right now are keeping you alive.

10:57 So how can you say you are "that" when you don't find yourself there? How could you find yourself there if you aren't conscious of or even perceiving any of it except from the "outside," so to speak—knowing such things about the body only through what's learned as abstract concepts? If you believe that this sense of "you" is a body that is virtually unknown to you, then you are rather like a rock that also has no experience of itself. And yet, you probably identify with a self-awareness, a so-called conscious entity.

10:58 So where is this self-aware-you located? Are you your foot? If your foot were cut off, would you disappear? Except for the distress and loss you may experience, you as an aware and perceiving entity would not change at all. "You" aren't involved with any of the micro-activities or systems that comprise your body. You don't even know what's happening with them, save for some signal sent to the brain whenever a body part is in trouble. What you identify as your self relative to the body is an end product of brain activity, sort of like passing gas is an end product of the digestive process.

10:59 If this is so, then what is your job relative to the body? Isn't it to manage the organism's gross maintenance and its relationship to the environment? Watch yourself. You scratch, why? You eat and find a place to defecate. You plan, do work, find mates, socialize. Why? Watch everything you do. Why adjust your body as you sit? Because that's your job, isn't it? That's what you're charged to do, to solve problems and manage life.

10:60 In order to handle this animal's overall physical survival, you find shelter, avoid too much heat or cold, and so on. But because you've developed all sorts of ideas, beliefs, assumptions, and knowledge—since you also identify with and find your self-experience as a conceptual social creature—you're charged with maintaining an immense conceptual and social world as well. Further scrutiny, however, reveals you really aren't any more conscious of the foundation of your conceptual activities than you are of your body, you just act on the end results of these activities. As a willful entity, you are driven to achieve instinctual goals, programmed goals, and conceptual goals. Whether relating to the physical or conceptual, your job is to manage the perceived environment, both inside and out.

10:61 Regarding biological life, your "self" may be just a function, like an organ, serving a purpose. Although ignorant of anything beyond the scope of your cognition, your self's purpose is to figure out how to manage life, how to survive given what you perceive as the conditions of each moment. Through your body's perceptive faculties and conceptual ability, you locate yourself as some "inside" awareness-activity that is identified with the job of life management.

10:62 This job seems to be centered within your mind, so you naturally assume that you reside within or perhaps are a mind. It appears that this "aware-you" exists and grows as a result of learning, more than it does as a result of instinct, doesn't it? Your heart beats without your knowledge or the need for you to do anything, and you breathe just fine even while asleep. The "you" as a function of your brain needs to sleep in order to release toxins and re-shrink the brain. The rest of your body doesn't stop functioning, only you do. In fact, unless this you-entity disappears pretty much each day for several hours, the body will die. You must go, so the body can live. Interesting observation, isn't it?

10:63 Think about it. What are you to this collection of cells? Since your job is to direct which perceptions are acted upon and how, you're not much more than a switchboard operator! Really just another "mindless" function. The need for survival in a world of creatures and elements—as perceived by specialized cells that form eyes, ears, nose, skin, etc.—has produced a sophisticated switchboard operator function with an instinctive caretaker role.

10:64 This managerial job is one of handling survival by directing the collection of cells to do this or that—whatever can be managed by your will. Experience the implications and reality of this with each action and thought and feeling you have. This you that you identify with turns out to be like a burp, just another function of a specific collective life struggle. What is the real nature of this burp?

10:65 If this problem-solver and switchboard operator is all that you identify with and experience as yourself, then, when the body dies, you die, because this job is terminated along with the organism. On the other hand, if you manifest as but are in fact not this switchboard operator, then perhaps you won't die when the body dies—you'll just lose your job. ☺

10:66 Beyond your rather simple physical role regarding your body and biological life, however, everything else is social, isn't it? Again, the only reason you really care that the body dies is because then you—as a conscious-entity produced by brain activities—die. If you are a switchboard operator for the body, as well as an abstract problem-solving self-awareness that is created and exists as a social entity, then this is your role in life and what dies at death.

10:67 You cannot help but confuse the nature of your existence with the job that you do, or exist for, but perhaps your true nature is not limited to this role or job and so not limited to life and death. As a belief or fantasy, this does nothing to change your condition because you only find such existence in what you're conscious of, not what you believe or even perceive. Your mission—should you choose to accept it—is to discover what's true.

Life Outside a Social Context

10:68 Since all of this life and death and "being incomplete" business is conceptually and socially constructed, what would it be like to experience life outside any social context? Remember, a social reality is created simply by creating sentient self and other. Your self-experience exists because of this distinction. Therefore, a social context exists without others being physically around, it exists in the very experience you have of being a self-awareness. No other, no self. So you can see your existence is dependent on maintaining the experience of others and not-you.

10:69 Now that we are immersed within and sensitive to our world of social existence, let's begin to work on getting beyond it. Consider what life would be like without a social context. Once again, we might imagine we would be alone and lonely, having no contact or interaction with others. But we must remember that this is still an experience within a social context. You can't be alone unless others exist and are absent.

10:70 If we consider what would be experienced without any social context at all, not even as a possibility, we see that our experience would have no others existing even as a concept. Without others there is no social context and so there is also no self. When this is the case, if something still exists, it isn't alone or lonely, it just is. End of story. What such an experience might be like could be rather unimaginable at this point, but start to move in that direction as best you can.

10:71 No matter what such an experience turns out to be, there would be no contrast to another possible experience that includes others, language, communication, connection, and so on. Without a social context these possibilities could not exist and we would not miss them at all. Although eliminating a social context eliminates self and other, our current experience tends to be stuck in this isolated separate self that we live within. So, let's continue to work on being complete within that condition before we try to get out of it.

10:72 **Guided Meditation: Eliminating the Struggle to Connect**

Notice you've been plagued with a sense of self-isolation throughout your life. Find this sense and notice your desire to remedy it, to feel complete and connected. Dwell on this experience of being alone and separate. Can you find a desire to remedy this isolation?

Consider that being existentially alone is not something to resist or struggle against. It is your present experience of existence. Since it is your experience of existence, perhaps it is even a doorway through which you can search for your true nature once you stop resisting the seeming reality of that experience.

Now, can you let go of the idea of and need for a remedy? Can you be OK just being an isolated entity without any social concerns? Can you allow yourself to be, to exist as-is, rather than resist this condition as a desperate malady to be fixed?

Notice what comes up once you've made this shift in perspective. Perhaps silence, or a simple sense of being without parameters or location. Maybe you fail to be complete and some social-mental activity arises again, such as longing for connection and belonging. Notice whatever comes up and let it be. Then return to this original state of separation and isolation without resistance or judgment, without comparison or the desire for it to be otherwise.

Be without even a hint of needing anything "out there" that might improve your experience. Do your best to experience being complete as this existentially alone entity by dropping the idea of being alone. Concentrate instead on just being.

10:73 We can see that even when we accept our experience as-is without the existence of or comparison to others, we may still return to this nagging sense that there should be something more to life, that there must be something "out there" that we should have or attain or experience. Embrace the possibility that this is only a construct of mind. Instead, get that your experience is all that *is* experienced and all that *can be* experienced—because it *is* what's experienced and there's nothing other than what "is" that can *be*—and there is nothing missing or out there that needs to be attained.

10:74 Of course, we have had perceptive-experiences that awe us with beauty or excitement, insight or pleasure. From this memory, we can easily imagine that when such stimulating experiences aren't happening, they could and perhaps should be happening and so we want to seek them out. This gives us the impression that our experience could be better than it is. What are we missing with this reasonable conclusion?

10:75 Perhaps what is missed is the fact that no matter what experience is possible, it is not going to fix you and it is not something you need. Want proof you don't need it? Get that you exist right now without it, and you're doing just fine. It will always be that way. As long as you are a self, there will be good and bad experiences. No matter how many new good experiences you accumulate there will also be bad ones, and try as you might the most delightful or fulfilling experience fails to remain, just as it fails to change your condition, it only temporarily changes your experience. As it has always been, no experience can change the fact of your isolated existence, or of feeling incomplete, they can only distract you from this condition.

10:76 As with the promise and draw of "out there," perceiving stuff does not change your condition. By definition whatever is perceived is not the perceiver, and is merely encountered. Therefore, it can't change or complete you because such resolution must be done by you where you experience *being*. Remember, your experience of self resides within a private inner world, and that isn't "out there," is it? Being at the effect of circumstance doesn't change you or your apparent condition, it just changes your perceptive-experience, and only for the time the circumstance influences your experience or distracts your attention.

10:77 Further, you likely miss the fact that the division of better or worse, good and bad, is a function of survival, created solely in relation to your particular self. It is completely subjective. Remember, this self can only exist in relation to not-self. Because of your need to survive, good and bad will be determined by the experience of this separate self, since you automatically relate everything perceived to this self. So no attainment or any experience will ever change that. Get it? No experience will ever realize the promise of attaining something not-you that will resolve or complete you. It can't happen! I will keep saying that, but only you can get if it's real or not.

10:78 The truth is you are already complete when you stop thinking you aren't. You are not broken or in need of any circumstance to fix you, you are perfect as you are and nothing can change that. Stop thinking something is wrong with you and nothing is wrong with you. Please understand, I'm not trying to flatter you or bolster your morale. I'm simply asserting what's true. Such statements are not about your ego or self-importance or fantasies, which are just versions of the same mental activity that produces the suffering of feeling incomplete in the first place. I'm suggesting you should transcend all that bullshit, and this is a completely different experience than the norm.

10:79 Again, since we are considering death, or the end of the self, survival can't be the operating principle for our pursuit. Eliminating all social context, we are freed of the need to resolve or fix ourselves. Then, we exist without any comparison or need for attainment, without any promise of something not present that suggests a sense of completion. Without social goals, ideas, and ideals, we are already complete—we are just existing as-is. There is nothing else that needs to be. We are rather like the three-legged dog, happy as-is without the slightest disturbance caused by thinking we aren't what we should be.

Getting Beyond Self

10:80 Besides changing our minds, one of our goals needs to be to transcend the distinction and so experience of self and other altogether, becoming conscious of the source that itself isn't an experience at all, and isn't limited to a self and its interpretations. Toward that end, we should first transcend social dominance.

10:81 Now, here's the thing, after tackling and eliminating the domain of a conceptual self and the domain of the social self, we really have nothing left that is ourselves—except perhaps the body. But that isn't what we're worried about dying, really.... We are worried about our conceptual-social-self dying. The body still remains as an object after we are gone, and disintegrates slowly, having returned to simply being an object without a survival component.

10:82 Of course, when we try to stay with a sense of self that is without any social concept—grasping that our whole self-awareness is built on social concepts—we may still have a sense of being a separate and isolated entity, and as we've seen, we resist this isolated condition. But what if this very resisted experience is next to the core of what we really are, a condition that transcends life and death?

10:83 You may simply not be conscious of it yet because you are wed to a conceptual social-self and so can't see what lies outside this experience. If you take your separate entity out of a social context, it is not separate or alone! It is what it is. What is that? You have to eliminate the social context—meaning you have to eliminate the distinction of self and other—to find out.

10:84 Such consciousness is hard to come by because our whole experience of being and of life is built on this distinction. But this will all cease to exist at some point. We see that one of the main features of death for a self is the loss of other. You die alone. If you could let go of other and self you might be free of death as an end to you because in a significant way you will have already ended.

10:85 But this is quite difficult because you strive to survive as a matter of default. You are obsessed with yourself—even though you are only a figment of mind, you remain ignorant of this reality and imagine you are real and necessary. In every moment you are always the central feature of experience, and one way or another everything relates to you. Therefore, the force of self-survival tends to push any confrontation with death out of the picture.

10:86 We need to fully understand and embrace survival to be able to look past the forces that keep us unable to confront our own end and so fully grasp our present reality. Although our self-awareness resides within a social context, we can be conscious without this context. And although our perceptive organs reside in the body, we can be conscious without the biological. With such freed-up consciousness, perhaps we are on the doorstep of the real nature of existence.

10:87 So now, experience what exists without any social context at all—no self and other, no being alone, no need for anything to complete you, no social world of any kind. Get to the core of your existence, independent of the self-awareness that was created by a social context. Without the distinction of self and other, what do you experience?

10:88 **Guided Meditation: Beyond Self**

As a practice, stop dwelling on your self. Get that in every moment you are always obsessed with your self, it is the central principle of all your experience.

Now, get over yourself, stop focusing on and reinforcing your attention on yourself.

Consider: How can the limitations of a self be the real nature of consciousness?

Try to become conscious prior to or absent of the distinction of self and not-self. What is this consciousness? It might be virtually impossible to imagine, but work toward such consciousness as best you can.

I do not fear death.
I had been dead for billions and billions of years
before I was born,
and I had not suffered the slightest
inconvenience from it.

Mark Twain

Chapter Eleven

STUCK IN IGNORANCE

Unacknowledged Blinders

11:1 Let's acknowledge that our entire experience exists between the bookends of birth and death. Before birth we are completely ignorant of any existence or reality, and after death we are also completely ignorant. We have no knowledge or experience at all of what exists before or after these boundaries. We have all kinds of excuses, justifications, and positions about this total absence of knowledge, but none change the fact that we are completely ignorant, and we ignore this ignorance.

11:2 Your entire experience exists between the lines without going beyond either side. Death is ignored completely, before birth is equally unknown, and birth is chalked up to mystery. Still, we have lots of ways to shut down any attempt at knowing about or approaching the reality of death. For example:

- It's a depressing subject, best not to think about it.
- We can't do anything about it, better to ignore it.
- Since we can't do anything about it, it's better to focus on life while we have it.

- Since we're going to die, life is meaningless and acknowledging this makes us nihilistic.
- We won't really die, we will go to heaven or be reborn.
- It's never really going to happen, it's always in a future that will never arrive.
- And so on.

11:3 No matter what we come up with, the reality is we are completely ignorant of existence before birth and after death. Everything for us, all of our experience and our lives are lived inside these bookends without any consciousness of what is beyond either side. Doesn't this say something about the limitations of our experience and consciousness? What is the reality or nature of existence outside our limited experience?

So Far

11:4 We are still laying the groundwork for our work on understanding and transcending life and death. As you can see, there is much of which to become conscious and to confront in order to set the stage to go deeper. You might be thinking we have already gone pretty damn deep! True, but we still have a lot more to do. Hang in there. Each of these assertions contributes to understanding a foundation that is sophisticated and deep enough to attempt actually attaining this consciousness, and not just hearing about it.

11:5 Getting past the limits of birth and death demands a completely different approach than your current thinking and perceiving allow. You have to be able to think outside the world within which you live and become conscious of what's true beyond your self and perceptions. But remember, this is all an ongoing contemplation. Have you had insights and experiential breakthroughs with these (often repeated) assertions yet? If not, do that now; if so, deepen what you have. Let's briefly touch on some of the highlights again so you can see what you truly experience and what you have just read about.

11:6 After tackling and eliminating the domain of a conceptual-self and the domain of the social-self, we have a hard time finding anything left that is ourselves. Still, we insist we must exist. But what if our experience of being is just a by-product of brain activity generated as a function of survival? If we let go of this activity, is there anything left that is consciousness?

11:7 We've seen that when we work to experience a sense of self that is without concept or social context, we imagine we'd be a separate isolated entity. Yet, we further see this separate and isolated experience is still conceptual and social, it is just absent of the presence of others and greatly reduced in its conceptualization. Stripped of as much social mind as we can manage, we are perhaps left with a primary and primal sense of being. Yet, we don't experience what is prior to or beyond this sense.

11:8 Remember, we need to transcend survival to be able to look past the forces that keep us unable to confront our own end and truly grasp our present reality. This is quite difficult because we are committed to survival and primarily the survival of the self as a "sentient inner self-object," which we've discovered is a social creation.

11:9 The terror of not existing seems very real. But why? Why are you attached to the sound and fury that acts itself out as a life, and to a mere blip in the universe that thinks it needs to persist? Because it is all you have, and your entire experience is centered on you and your separate existence assuming it is vital and needs to survive.

11:10 You only think you are separate because of the distinction of self and not-self, which creates your sense of existence. Consider that without the conceptually created distinction of self and other, you aren't separate; and at the heart of your existence you may not be a self. Entertain the possibility of getting rid of the distinction of self and other, and going further to eliminate you and not-you. If you do that, then what consciousness remains?

Our life is shaped by our mind;
we become what we think.
Gautama Buddha

Our Inability to Confront Death

11:11 The chances are incredibly high that you failed to achieve the above consciousness. The chances are that you even failed to grasp what is really being suggested or asked. So, let's back up again and push into subjects that are more accessible—even if they tend to be overlooked.

11:12 From this effort you might be better able to push the envelope a bit more when it comes to a deeper consciousness. By being exposed to all the considerations addressed up to this point, you are enabled to see upcoming assertions in a different light and so can grasp them more deeply than you would have without this background. To begin, let's address how your experience and mind automatically reject death.

11:13 Our experience of death is normally just ignored. But when we look at it, it's impressive how incapable people are at confronting death. Everyone has some ideas about death—they fear it or think they've come to grips with it, but mostly they ignore it. This relationship to death, however, is strictly conceptual. People are actually incapable of really comprehending death or even thinking about it as a reality.

11:14 **Guided Meditation: Short Death**

Try it now. Imagine your own death—not a fantasy of you surviving in some fashion or being reborn, but actually dying, no more you.

Let go of all fantasies and religious beliefs, and any consoling thoughts about what such a contemplation might do for you.

> Make the end of you present and real. Keep your attention on the fact of your own death, of no-you in this very moment. Get that it really will happen! Stay with it for as long as you can.

11:15 How long could you really keep attention focused on death, on no-you? You not only find it difficult to do, but probably in a matter of seconds or minutes your mind will slip off the subject as a reality. Death is anti-self. No more self, at all. How can a self imagine this? How can a self confront it? It is no-self, and that is antithetical to the very heart and soul of *being* a self.

11:16 Death isn't a process or even your destruction. It is *no you*. That is a different matter than "dying." Since a self can't fathom or effectively "think" of no-self, death is not something we confront successfully. Managing to transcend the primal fear of no "you," however, is central to increasing consciousness, because no matter what you become conscious of, unless it is exactly what you experience now, your current self-experience is challenged.

11:17 Can you even imagine an experience of no-you? Notice that every experience you have or can have is inherently based on you. Remember, you are the primary feature in all experience.

11:18 This may be why all sorts of "survival-in-some-form" scenarios have been created throughout human history. The mere idea that all your efforts to survive, to attain, to resolve, to grow, to build, and so on are meaningless struggles that will fail in the end is unthinkable. It invalidates your very existence as a self, so some other notion is needed to fill that space. No matter what it is, it has to be better than fruitlessly striving in a meaningless life ending in non-existence, doesn't it?

11:19 Indulging a drama that what I'm saying is in any way negative, however, is still not grasping the matter. Developing an ability to confront death may be something we can put to good use in our contemplations. If an unconscious aversion is an automatic human relationship to death, we can see that such an ignoring-force might well apply itself broadly, such as when attempting to let go of any self-aspect or contemplating beyond our plans and desires for an imagined future.

11:20 This ignoring-force is the power behind our inability to get past assumptions and beliefs, to get past our perspective and experience. This common automatic ignoring-disposition is the main obstacle to having experiential insights, breakthroughs, and enlightenments. So, perhaps embracing dissolution, and empowering the ability to let go of our selves, knowledge, and viewpoint, has an upside, even before death.

11:21 Face it, you will lose yourself sooner or later. Even if you continue to live for a time, you will get old and die. You'll either let go of everything or have it taken from you. Dwell on your inability to confront or even recognize the reality of death, and notice how it can't really sink in. Even when you acknowledge that it is a fact that will happen, it's always "later" and is ignored as a reality in the present. Try to grasp that right now no-you is a reality that will occur and in a finite period of time, not an infinite later.

11:22 See if you can come to grips with the fact you will lose everything—everything you cherish, everything you have, everything you are. Once you get that, notice it puts the meaning of those things in a different context.

11:23 Just as we have no experience of creating our own existence, we also have no genuine experience of what death is. We're left with an enormous unknown in our lives, a gaping hole in our consciousness that we might feel compelled to fill by adopting belief systems or religions claiming knowledge about such things. The truth is, however, that we don't know, and the search for a real consciousness about the nature of death is not advanced by covering up that fact with comforting beliefs.

11:24 Usually, when people think they're confronting the reality of death, it is still only an imagined concept, and often of dying, not of death. Death is really just the flip side of birth. It isn't difficult to notice that we have no idea how we came to be. Somehow we became conscious of "existing," but prior to that we are completely blank—save for stories and concepts about how human life comes to pass, which does nothing to fill in the complete absence of a personal experience or consciousness in the matter, any more than believing a stork brings a baby into existence.

11:25 We accept that as an infant we indeed existed, and yet the self that we experience being now didn't seem to exist then, did it? What was our experience before we became self-aware? We don't know because we have no memory of it. But it does suggest that what we experience as our self-existence now was built and created conceptually, and that life and even some form of experience can exist independent of a self-awareness.

11:26 Although we haven't died yet, a real experience of our own existence being finite is supported by the fact that we don't know how we came to exist. If we can "start," we can "stop." If we can be created, we can be destroyed. Except for the fact that we somehow started existing and will someday stop existing, we have no genuine experience of the nature of death, and don't know any more about it than we do about birth. Therefore, when we consider death, we are left with nothing but imagination.

11:27 Still, the idea of dying brings dismay to the self since clearly it is the end to self-survival. Obviously, an end to life is a failure of self to survive, so the "destiny" of our lifelong self-survival drive is inevitable failure. Unless we invent fantasies about life after death, or imagine that somehow the self persists and only the body dies, we are left with simply no more self.

11:28 But why do we imagine this self will persist when it didn't exist before we started experiencing being self-aware? Of course, because we are stuck in survival and can't fathom or even entertain the obvious fact that this self came and will go. We fail to grasp that this self is an illusion, a temporary activity formed to do a job and not a permanent aspect of the universe. Therefore it will not remain.

11:29 What does remain is the Absolute, and it "remains" because it never lived or persisted as anything. Does that sound like the self? Does that sound like you? Of course not.

11:30 But don't then mistake this for imagining you must be something else or elsewhere. The nature of existence is actually absolute, but this is not what you identify with or experience as "you" at all. Unless you become conscious of that which doesn't live or die, you will suffer death as the annihilation of your self. Even if you do become conscious you will still suffer the death of your self, because yourself doesn't survive death. Yet you can be conscious of the nature that is already free of life and death.

11:31 The implication that increased consciousness could result in a more "positive" possibility may sound like just more hopeful airy-fairy rhetoric, but keep in mind that this is the reason absolutes have so often been co-opted by belief systems in the first place. Your job is not to believe anything but to become conscious of what's true. In short, the observation here is that the self-mind can't comprehend either the absolute truth or the death of the self, but it is possible to grasp a consciousness that is beyond yourself and your mind.

11:32 I push some points repeatedly because they so easily go in one ear and out the other without us stopping to really soak in the reality of it. Keep trying to experience what's true about death, and confront the present reality of it even as your mind continues to dodge the matter (returning to ignoring it), and grasp why this is so. Since the matter keeps slipping away, we will approach it in a few different ways, delving into more detail as we go. I will keep flipping back and forth between discussing life as it's lived and pressing toward a new and unprecedented depth of consciousness.

Embracing Not-Knowing

11:33 There are any number of intriguing belief systems—spiritual, philosophical, even scientific viewpoints—that we can adopt to try to change the way we experience life or death. But for the most part, after our initial infatuation subsides, the fact that they come from an external source and require a belief in what others say begins to erode any deep sense of validity. We don't feel completely authentic in this way since we have not experienced for ourselves the truth of the matter.

11:34 In contrast, notice that we are completely and undeniably certain that we don't know. This not-knowing is *ours*, and it's deeply personal. It is valid and requires no belief or hearsay. We can "stand" in Not-Knowing fully and without doubt. Strange as it may seem, from here we can more powerfully and genuinely pursue knowing anything.

11:35 Isn't this not-knowing in the same place where you experience being existentially silent? Not knowing provides a powerful contrast to the rest of life, which is devoted to knowing, and remember, it only exists as "not" knowing because our whole experience is focused on knowing. So even the not-knowing seems to relate silently to knowing. But it is simply the blank slate in the matter, the open origins of the possibility of knowing, the starting point for existence.

11:36 When we die the knowing dies. But not-knowing or silence, like absolute existence, doesn't die. Perhaps we can see that in our experience not-knowing is as close to the absolute as we can get—shy of direct consciousness.

11:37 **Guided Meditation: Not-Knowing**

Focus on your experience of not-knowing right now—the place where you are completely blank, where there is only silence and stillness.

Does this seem like it is close to the very core of you? How does not-knowing relate to your basic experience of this silent-stillness? Don't assume they are different or in different places. Don't assume they are located anywhere. Just concentrate on this silent not-knowing.

As you reside in this experience of not-knowing, what tends to come next? Do you feel pressed to know again, even a little bit? Is there an impulse to think something? In contrast to not-knowing or the silent-stillness at the heart of your experience, what do you see is the purpose for your knowing—what is it doing?

Once again focus on this sense of not-knowing, on the silent-stillness at the core of your experience. Here, in this silent not-knowing, is death an issue?

Among the great things which are
to be found among us,
the Being of Nothingness is the greatest.
Leonardo da Vinci

Transcending Survival

11:38 Direct consciousness of who and what you are is possible, but as long as the assumed individual self-object remains the central and dominant distinction in your experience, the operating principle will be the survival of this self. Although we identify with being an internal and separate uninspected self-object residing within the body, this is only convention. Therefore, it is possible to "re-identify" what self is, or at least commit whatever self seems to be to something other than the cultural norm. Of course, such a shift is unlikely, but it points to an interesting possibility of freedom, so give it a try. It doesn't really matter what you attempt to be, just choose something that is clearly not your self-experience now, even at its root, and try to make that your experience of self.

> *Before we can become who we really are,*
> *we must become conscious of*
> *the fact that the person*
> *who we think we are is at best an imposter.*
> Thomas Merton

11:39 Although a shift into a new kind of self-experience may seem transcendent and beyond survival, it's not, because the foundation is still the self no matter what you come up with. It might be beyond the survival of what you conventionally are—an exclusive inner-self-object—but getting beyond survival altogether is another story. Contemplate what that would be; see if you can find an "experience" that has no survival context or content at all.

11:40 The principle of self-survival is not wrong. It is not right. It just *is.* At the same time, our experience within the context of self-survival is so dominated by right and wrong, and focused on ourselves, we're unable to recognize this principle for-itself and as-itself. Although the self-principle is necessary for a self to survive, when we consider that self is whatever is interpreted *as* self, then we also see that self can be almost anything. Self is a *distinction* within consciousness.

11:41 When the distinction of self is applied to particular aspects within the field of perception or experience, those aspects are then identified as the self and the impulse to maintain them arises. If "self" is wrapped around a specified number of cells, then that will be what must persist. If self is wrapped around a set of ideas or characteristic behavior patterns, then those are what need to survive. Within the context of the self-principle, a distinction is made that categorizes everything as either me or not-me, and then goes to work to make sure "me" survives. But this distinction doesn't need to persist and clearly won't at death.

11:42 Independent of any self-awareness, a consciousness exists that is in no way bound to perception, mind, or survival. This is the stuff known only through direct realization. Realizing that the true nature of one's self *is this very Consciousness* reveals that the self is already non-existent and unnecessary.

No matter how massive, detailed, complex,
and real your "house" of self seems,
it is not and never will be YOU.
You can walk out of this house at any moment.
And you know what? You won't miss it at all.
Ralston

11:43 The truth may be that your nature is not a distinction and will not die, but as long as you are identified with and experience yourself as an inner and isolated self-awareness, you need to tell the truth about that. Whatever you experience as self is what will persist in life and die in the end, therefore you need to transcend self and survival. Yet, it is fruitless to fight self-survival because such a struggle will still be founded on the assumption of you as a self, and so can't transcend self's existence. Instead, get that it is already unreal and unnecessary to begin with, and be free of it. Commensurate with that effort, consider that your entire perceptive-experience of reality is a superimposition upon what is ultimately true.

For-Me, For-Itself, As-Itself

11:44 To better tackle this difficult material it might be useful to understand three distinctions I make regarding reality and our experience of it. These distinctions are: for-me, for-itself, and as-itself.

11:45 Normally, our experience is dominated wall to wall with a "for-me" perception, which we've seen is a function of self-survival. This means the brain automatically relates everything encountered to the distinction it makes of the self. By so doing, huge amounts of overlays are added to the mere perception of anything that are appropriate and valuable only to that particular self. Such additions include meaning, value, good and bad, emotional charge, function, use, label, history, associations, and so on. This is useful for the survival of the self, but it isn't an experience of what's there for-itself.

11:46 The "for-itself" distinction means we perceive the subject without any of what is added by the for-me perception. Once we subtract out all the self-referencing interpretations—which we can do with some attention and practice—we perceive the subject in its most basic form, for itself. This means it has no label, meaning, value, good or bad, charge, function, etc. This also means the thing is no longer useful for survival and so becomes uninteresting to us. As soon as we stop deliberately attempting this shift, it will fade away and be replaced once again with a for-me interpretation.

11:47 "As-itself," on the other hand, is the real nature of the thing. This is not a perception or an experience and not something we can grasp simply through attention and effort. It is only gotten through direct consciousness. As-itself is the true nature of the subject, not how it relates to us or how it is perceived by us, and so is not anything we normally access at all.

11:48 Why do I bring up these distinctions? Because we see that attention on death is immediately related to the self and so becomes a for-me experience. This is then seen as negative and unacceptable, and so is resisted. It also leaves us with no way to relate to this subject except by making stuff up—as in adopting beliefs, imagination, or religions—and therefore, basically burying the matter.

11:49 If we take death out of a for-me experience and try to get it for-itself, again this is difficult because the only place we can put our attention is on no-me—not a popular subject—and if we succeed to some degree we lose interest and return again to our for-me world of experience. Yet within the for-itself possibility we might be able to find a way to actually become complete in our experience of life. When we get life for-itself we are not reacting to it or engaging in the drama of life, we are soberly viewing the subject without meaning or charge, history or belief, or any other self-referencing addition. This at least frees us from relating it to ourselves and provides a more real and non-reactive assessment of what's there.

11:50 Yet, for-itself is only useful to create some freedom while alive because this ability ceases at death, as it is based on perception. In death clearly all for-me aspects will die, but so will for-itself. Still, our for-itself ability is useful for tackling the subject of death. Here, we can see both life and death in a new light. Gone are the self and social concerns regarding attainment, worth, value, and so on, and for-itself also eliminates our automatic aversion and rejection of death. When we experience either life or death without ourselves—and so our survival—getting in the way, we can see them far more clearly and with detachment. In this way, we can more readily access an ability to create being complete as a person and being complete with life and death. (We'll address being complete in the next chapter.)

11:51 But it is the as-itself consciousness that provides the essence that is beyond life and death. For transcending life and death, grasping what exists as-itself is essential. That is a job for deep contemplation.

Consciousness Beyond Death and Perception

11:52 Getting back to our contemplation on life and death, let's keep pushing into the matter. Once again, dwell on the fact that as does life, death "comes with the package" at birth. Death is inherent in being alive.

Beyond Death

11:53 As we've seen, the only places where we find any possibility of "life after death" are in beliefs or religions. These, however, are strictly conceptual stories and don't change our condition or alter the facts in any way. Because we are so attached to life and self, death is seen as bad. Beyond avoiding it, we've seen our overwhelming tendency is to ignore death as a real and present possibility.

11:54 Instinct obviously plays a role by programming each biological creature to avoid death at all costs, but this imperative extends into the mind as a struggle against any possibility of death, and penetrates the intellect, pushing attention away from even considering the reality of death. How does the intellect grasp or survive death? It can't. Since self-survival is the principle of our perceived world, death is dismissed and ignored because the fact of death undermines the "destiny illusion" of survival. Neither resistance nor ignorance, however, is a viable option when trying to grasp the truth.

11:55 As a child of six, I entered a spontaneous contemplation regarding time, which led me to an experiential realization that my death was occurring in the very same moment that I called now. This made death into a presence rather than merely an idea. Perhaps it was one of the events that turned me toward studying the nature of existence as deeply as I have. It certainly made apparent that being alive as an eternal activity is an illusion. Yet our main mental relationship to this inevitable outcome is to ignore it, pretty much completely.

11:56 If death were an immediate and known presence in your experience, perhaps it would motivate you to seriously pursue the real nature of life and death. I don't believe Buddha's exposure to death was inconsequential in initiating his total commitment to understand the true nature of life. As a result, he went from a pampered and wealthy prince to tossing off all of life's distractions and enticements, and committing himself to becoming free of life and death. Although an uncommon relationship to life, it turned out to be a fruitful one.

11:57 If death appears to you as a categorically negative subject, you may think we've already spent way too much time on it. Yet consider again what some of the past legends of freedom or enlightenment were up to. As mentioned, Gautama, Ramana, and Jesus had death as a central theme. Or consider the courage demonstrated by Sir Thomas Moore and many other exceptional people who chose to honor something greater than life. Each of them came by their courage through personal efforts, since moving toward death is the definition of counter-intuitive. To become conscious of what life and death really are, however, we need to get past our automatic rejection of death so that we can look into the truth of absolute existence.

Remember the story of the warlord?

In ancient China a terrible and ferocious warlord
was ransacking the countryside.
Coming upon a Zen monastery,
his army began killing and pillaging.
When the warlord entered the inner courtyard
he found the abbot of the monastery
sitting in a chair.
The abbot said firmly:
"Get out of my monastery."
The powerful warlord walked up to the abbot,
sword in hand, and said:
"You don't understand, I could kill you
without blinking an eye."
The abbot replied:
"No, you don't understand. I could
die without blinking an eye."
After this, the warlord became
a devotee of the abbot.

11:58 It certainly sounds like the abbot was complete with life and free of death, doesn't it? Can you match that disposition? Your instinct to avoid loss or death becomes a gigantic obstacle to your conscious progress. This instinct may be biologically rooted, but it permeates every aspect of your experience and intellect. When death is approached honestly in contemplation, you've seen that your mind will tend to quickly slip off any sense of death as a real presence. Once more, let's try to contemplate and stay with it for a longer period of time than most people can.

11:59 **Guided Meditation: Death Focus**

Again, keep your attention on your own inevitable death, not merely the thought but the presence of the reality that you will end completely—no you.

> Let go of all fantasies or consoling thoughts. Focus on the upcoming reality of no you. See how long you can stay there.
>
> As you do, contemplate what will exist—if anything—after death when there is no perceptive-experience, self-awareness, or life. In all likelihood you will find nothing, that is appropriate and normal. Thoroughly eliminate the notion that anything will survive death.
>
> Now go back to focusing on contemplating the upcoming reality of no you, setting out to grasp the presence of death. Stay with it as a present reality for as long as you can.

11:60 Contemplating what you are can be challenging, but contemplating no-you as a present reality is almost impossible to maintain long-term and with intensity. As seen, penetrating the true nature of death is difficult since it seems you don't have actual death to focus on. You can only focus on the created "presence" of the "absence" of you. Yet you do have another viable window into the real nature of death: absolute consciousness—starting with becoming deeply conscious of what you really are.

11:61 Becoming conscious of the true nature of all entities, as well as objective existence, shows this nature to be absolute and so free of both life and death—not because this absolute is eternal but because it has no element or relative existence at all. In this consciousness, death isn't an issue, and neither is life.

11:62 But such realizations tend to demand a great deal of commitment and dedication to discover. Believing in such an assertion does nothing, your beliefs will die completely when you do! A consciousness of your nature is not what you think, and anything related to the activity of self and life even after such consciousness will also die. So only deep and direct consciousness will do, not hearsay or belief. What's worse is the fact that if you pursue the truth to get something from it, you are pursuing the wrong thing. The truth must be pursued for its own sake, even if you end up doomed to realizing something you may not want.

Beyond Perception

11:63 What anchors us to an experience of being a located inner-self are our perceptions. We assume and conclude that we must be located behind our perceptions, and that perception reflects an objective world that is fixed and we are simply a part of it. This is a natural conclusion. One thing to keep in mind, however, is we aren't just perceiving, we are assuming and interpreting. Another thing to consider is that what is perceived is indirect, it is not the "thing-itself" and so real reality is unknown.

Reality is merely an illusion, albeit
a very persistent one.
Albert Einstein

11:64 **Contemplation: You Without Perception or Life**

Let's do a guided meditation to try to work our way past perception as the defining factor of who we really are.

Right now, as best you can, work to imagine you exist without any perceptions. Without sight, hearing, sensation, or any other perception, what are you?

You might conclude that you are your mental activities. And yet thought, emotion, memory, and all mental activities are perceived just like anything else. Are they you? Who's perceiving or experiencing them?

Imagine that you also have no perception of thought, feeling, or any other mental activity. What is left?

If you are what's perceived or experienced, then of course at death you will be gone. If you're not any of these perceptive-experiences, nor are you found within them, then what are you? Notice you can't grasp this by trying to perceive it! What is existence without any perceptive or mental activities at all? What is the nature of awareness without perception?

Try to honestly grasp that you do not directly experience existence through the activity of perception, and so what you perceive is irrelevant to your nature. It is indirect phenomena that are very limited relative activities arising to serve a purpose, and so are not reflective of absolute existence or reality as-itself.

If there is no experience or perception whatsoever, is there anything left? When you die, are you conscious of anything—beyond perception, awareness, or experience of any kind—that cannot die? Don't make anything up, look into the matter.

When you are without perception, mind, or experience of any kind, what are you? Focus on whatever is left as consciousness.

Concept Dominates Your Self-Experience

11:65 Before we go on to experience being complete in the next chapter, I want to re-focus our attention on where so much of our experience lives. I want to back up a bit, and address something that is often overlooked and not fully grasped.

11:66 We've seen that our experience of self is bound to an existentially alone and separate inner self-awareness. One thing we tend to miss in this, however, is that this very seemingly solid experience is actually founded on concept. This is not to say it is whimsical or intellectual. Concept goes far deeper than we think, and actually constructs our experience of our selves and lives.

11:67 Yet, notice that this entire experience of being separate and isolated is conceptually produced. It depends on conclusions and assumptions—such as overlooking the fact that you have never found this inner self-object, you just assume it. Stop assuming such things and you won't experience being separate. That might sound like a high bar to hurdle, but grasp that it's possible. Beyond this one rather central assumption, I invite you to start to get how much of your entire experience is based on concepts and stories.

11:68 We think reality and life are solid physical events that we simply observe. But this isn't true at all. We barely experience the objective world as it is without adding a great deal of conceptual overlay to it, and beyond handling physical tasks most of our energy and attention live within stories.

11:69 Watch your mind and see how much of it occurs as and in concepts and stories. Clearly, every conceptual "experience," such as fantasies, imagination, internal dialogue, daydreaming, your life-story and memories, anything regarding the future or past, and so on, are all conceptual activities, mostly in the form of stories. These create an imaginary reality you live as if real. Can you see that? Do you get that your internal world is filled with stories and these stories dominate what you live as "life"?

11:70 Consider what stories you tell yourself. What is the plot and purpose of these stories? Notice that no matter how seriously you take them or how much they seem to relate to objective reality (or not), they are all completely conceptual. A story is any scenario you act out in your mind, even if it is only a fragment or is nonsensical. If it is not a perception of an object in present time, it is a story. Can you see the domain I'm talking about?

11:71 Notice all such "life" activities are based completely on concept and are simply imagined. How much of your life energies are given to imagined and made-up realities? Try to grasp how much of your entire experience lives in the stories you tell yourself, be they minor or major. Observe and study this for a while.

11:72 To go further, beyond the imagined "movie" aspect, notice you can't tell a story without the existence of language, and as we've seen, language is totally a social function, and so is not possible without sentient self and other. We understand language is an invention, but it has become the central aspect of our experience in many ways—labeling, internal dialogue, thinking, reasoning, even emotional or psychological reactions are explained by us and understood through language.

11:73 Yet, we should ask what are the consequences of living inside imagination and language? We don't usually entertain such notions. We live within the experience that we have and assume it is simply reality. Consider it's not, that reality exists independent of and beyond every invention within it. Whatever we assume and whatever context we live within will always have consequences. In other words, depending on the context we live within, some possibilities will be unavailable because of it, and others will dominate and limit us because of it. So one of our jobs is to become conscious beyond concept, language, imagination, and stories.

11:74 **Guided Meditation: Beyond Language and Story**

Right now, remove all imagination, stories, and even the existence of language, and work to merely observe life in present time. Once you've done that, you will notice a difference in your experience, but may miss the fact that you are still very likely engaging in stories.

For example, you will likely still have a background story of your life and the story of what life is, you'll have judgments and assessments that are created by story scenarios, you'll have projections and interpretations applied to what's perceived, and these are conceptual and could be called forms of story.

There are also stories applied to what you observe, telling you what it means, where it's going, and how it relates to you and how you should relate to it. Try to notice all the conceptual activities occurring within your experience—making sense of what's perceived and fabricating a reality—and get that, in the end, they are really just stories.

Once you are sensitive to this level of story, eliminate that whole domain, including language at its root. What do you have left?

Notice even now you likely still have very present and basic stories influencing your experience of the objective present moment. You might have a story of time passing, or what seems to be simply observations such as 'that is my cup,' 'I am sitting here in a room,' 'I am contemplating,' or what-have-you. Eliminate even these notions and ideas. Now what have you?

What do you experience when you don't have even a fragment of a story or concept about the present? Without comment or explanation, without interpretation or assumption, what do you experience? Without internal dialogue, language, story, or concept at all, what exists?

11:75 You can see that once again you will close in on a state of not-knowing, or a blank slate of experience, because eliminating all stories and conceptual activities pushes you toward an unknown. Still, you do seem to perceive, but if you can't say what anything is or means, if you can't even "know" or make distinctions within perceptive phenomena, whatever is experienced as existence in this moment is open-ended and unknown. Seek a consciousness prior to or independent of language, concept, and stories.

11:76 Given our experience is primarily based upon concept and stories, we should acknowledge that we suffer the consequences of these stories. Our entire sense of being incomplete—feeling like something is missing, or wrong with us—is solely generated through the concepts we have and the stories we tell ourselves. These might be "deeper" stories than most, and it may not be obvious to us that they are stories. But they truly only exist through assumption—and this is a conceptual fiction. Although they may seem as if they are real observations, they are not. Realizing how they are created changes our experience of them.

Chapter Twelve
BEING COMPLETE

12:1 We've jumped back and forth from addressing existential matters—about the nature of existence—to looking into your experience of self and mind. One of the subjects we have worked on is moving toward an experience of being complete. Yet, why should we be complete? Like I've suggested, once we can free ourselves from the endless drama and personal suffering that dominate so much of our attention, we not only have space to engage deeply with seemingly more abstract matters, we will have learned to control our minds to a much greater degree, and in this way will have experientially realized how much of our experience is self-created. This puts us on a new footing, enabling us to better tackle deeper levels of consciousness.

Why Aren't You Complete Already?

12:2 As seen earlier, your experience of life is fundamentally based on a fabricated social world. Although death eliminates any social context and perceptive-experience, while alive you will continue to attend to the demands of life using both social elements and perceptive faculties. But if you are pursuing a life agenda based on trying to remedy what ails you, your experience will always be burdened by feeling incomplete.

12:3 Why is that? Remember in the earlier section on "Being Incomplete" (Chapter Six), we postulated that chasing fulfillment, pursuing ideals, needing meaning, and mistaking not-knowing as a malady to resolve all contribute to a sense that something is not right or missing within your very existence. As it stands, at the root-bottom you likely experience yourself as separate, alone, and fundamentally ignorant, and this condition in itself is seen as a malady. People long to be connected, whole, knowledgeable, and at one with life and the universe. But their experience inevitably tells a different story.

12:4 Although these so-called maladies seem inherent or existential, all of them are produced conceptually. Being incomplete is solely conceptually created and therefore can be eliminated. All the drives and impulses in our lives that are attempting to remedy dissatisfaction or lack are based on what are actually false concepts. Even though they don't seem frivolous but as essential aspects of life, when we eliminate such concepts, those maladies and drives disappear.

12:5 What if the pain of feeling incomplete—like something is missing that needs to be found or added, or that something is wrong within yourself that needs to be fixed—is not only unnecessary but unreal? Instead, consider it is a myth, generated on purpose as a sort of red herring to push the self to survive within a social context—this is akin to the analogy of our mouse running on a wheel after unattainable cheese.

12:6 The social domain creates a self-experience, and this self is required to fit into a social world. But how is this done? Since the whole social domain is an invention made up collectively, no individual inherently knows exactly how to fit in, and for most of us fitting in is not a small matter. But why is trying to remedy being incomplete a common drive serving self-survival?

12:7 Since our self-experience stands upon many existential assumptions—as we're beginning to see—we think our very existence is dependent on maintaining and managing these assumptions in order to get through life. Because of existential assumptions that are viewed as negative—such as: our very person is isolated, alone, and ignorant, is missing something essential, and is perhaps broken, wrong, worthless, or what have you—we think we are incomplete and this sense of being incomplete drives us to try to attain goals to make us whole and happy and remedy our distress. This dynamic produces a life agenda we think will do just that—never mind that it hasn't worked so far, and never will.

12:8 This dynamic is quite circular because assessments of our value or wholeness, or our sense of separation and isolation, etc., are solely a function of our collectively invented social world. Without this social context we wouldn't have any assumptions about worth, missing something, or even the possibility of connectedness. We wouldn't compare our self-assessment to some other way of being, or have the notion or need to attain some ideal or standard that we lack. These only exist as imagined possibilities, and they only exist as a result of social values. Therefore, our attempts to remedy what's wrong with us are not only created by our social world, they are how we try to fit in and achieve the self, experience, and life we think we're "supposed" to have.

12:9 We imagine if this goal is accomplished, it will allow us to finally fully feel happy within our own skins. All of this keeps us working consciously and unconsciously to attain some solution that resolves our existential lack. But this dynamic perpetuates the assumptions upon which it's based. Although such explanations probably seem overly intellectual, this matter usually doesn't show up in our intellect, it shows up in our heart as a form of pain or suffering that we simply live with, unconsciously driving attempts to make it go away. Even though our efforts fail to complete us, they contribute to our character and how we are known as a person—and this is how we fit in and survive in a social world. So, our specific way of being "incomplete" and our strategies for resolving that are a large contributor to the characteristics that make us a unique individual.

12:10 I know this can be hard to follow and work out, so let's look at it again in a different way. Your self-experience is generated through making the distinction of self and other, thus creating a social context. But there are far, far more others than you, and so this reality is heavily weighted on the side of others. Even though no one is the sole source of creating the agreements, values, and assumptions that make up this world, collectively whatever view is shared by everyone will have the power of being lived as a reality or at least a convention.

12:11 This is the reality in which you have to fit in. Whatever ways you attempt to live up to shared standards and ideals, or rebel against them, characterize you as a social person. Noticing that inherently you are not all-knowing, or perfect, and don't live up to accepted ideals, you assess you are wrong and broken and try to fix yourself in some way so you can be what you are supposed to be. Yet, try as you might, your self-experience still seems unfinished. And because you live in a private inner world, you think you're the only one with this problem—even though the truth is everyone suffers these same challenges.

12:12 For example, given you live as a self-object you will always seem to be separate and isolated—that is the nature of being a self-object because in order to exist you must be distinct from not-you, and that separates the experience of yourself from everything else. Although you share the assumption that this is true, you also see it as a malady because of social values and ideals and assume you have to correct it, not realizing the malady itself is socially created and shared. For all you know, you may be the only one feeling this way. Even if others share with you that they also have this going on, you still see it as something that needs a solution, and conclude it's your fault as an individual, when in fact it is a shared social dynamic based on shared human assumptions. Yet, even within this separate self-experience it is possible to be complete.

12:13 The truth is that if you stop comparing yourself to imagined possibilities not present, you are already complete as you are. That doesn't mean you attain any ideal, or experience being something you're not, just that what you experience as your "being" is a done deal. It is complete as it is and needs nothing else in order to exist.

12:14 Remember, this is the you that will die. Yet, this entire experience of being separate and isolated depends on conclusions and assumptions you make—such as being an inner self-object. But you really don't know this to be true because it's not true. You just overlook the fact that you have never found this self-object, you just assume it.

12:15 This whole social self is conceptually constructed and so can be eliminated from your sense of being because it is existentially unnecessary—except as needed for participating within the social world. Although this very conceptually created self is going to die, why would you care? In the end, it's just a bunch of concepts. Ultimately, it is not you, and not true.

12:16 Can you entertain the possibility of being complete and fulfilled, even if you experience your existence as an isolated event? If you can, does such an imagined experience conflict with your current experience? Regardless of what you assume or don't assume, experience or don't experience, are you complete and happy with your core experience of self and life now? Probably not. So, how can you become complete?

What Is Being Complete?

12:17 Clearly, our concern with being complete is to experience being fulfilled and self-contained—so that there is nothing missing, nothing needs to be resolved, and nothing about our nature is broken or flawed, there is nothing to achieve or attain at all. In this way, we are complete. This may sound too good to be true, but it is actually far easier to attain than people think.

12:18 To get a better handle on what we're talking about with being complete, let's look at some definitions from the dictionary:

Complete:

As an adjective:

1. having all the necessary or appropriate parts; entire; full
2. to the greatest extent or degree

As a verb:

1. finish making or doing
2. make whole or perfect

Origin:

From old French: 'fill up, finish, fulfill', from *com* = expressing intensive force + *plere* = 'to fill'.

12:19 In this work "being complete" means you are exactly as you are, and this is experienced as complete and whole, and not in need of anything to make it so. You are at peace and content with your existence as-is. If that is deeply the case for you, great. If not, why not? Let's look at some possibilities.

12:20 Among other contributions, because we are not all-knowing—but we believe we should be—we develop a sense that we are incomplete and somehow flawed. Most people have some sense of being broken or missing something essential. From this buried existential sense of malady, the mind will develop two background activities that dominate much of one's life. These are the creation of ideals—images we think will fix or complete us once attained—and an agenda that generates a life strategy to attain these ideals or in other ways try to manage or resolve our sense of being incomplete. As we've seen, this shows up as characteristic perspectives and behaviors.

12:21 Contrasting being complete to your normal state probably shows that you are not complete. Why? Because you live as if there is something out there to attain in order to be completely satisfied and happy. Because of this, you live with a constant experience of feeling incomplete—even if it is often in the background. This leads you to look to the outside, trying to make your experience be as it should be, or to somehow fix or improve yourself so that you have the experience and life you think you should have. You imagine that by achieving these things, you will finally become whole and happy. As long as this continues, you never experience being complete.

12:22 Becoming complete is obviously a tall order if it means we must transcend the very strong impulses and beliefs that our entire world and self-view are based upon. Yet there are reasons that such assumptions and beliefs, no matter how entrenched, are not ever going to accomplish what we think they should. That is why we continually fail to realize our "perfect" self and life.

12:23 In life, within our central and powerful goal—survival—being complete is already seen as a main goal, unconsciously or consciously, and this is why we are drawn to pursue it even if unsuccessfully. It takes the form of trying to feel fulfilled and happy with ourselves and our lives. Although sometimes we seem to be getting closer to our goal, in the end we always fail to get there. This is because we mistakenly assume that being fulfilled and happy is based on circumstance—achieving something we don't have—and not on being complete where we are and as we are right now. So our struggle to be fulfilled can't ever be achieved—as we saw in the myth of the "promise of out there."

12:24 Because of this condition, over the years we may begin to think we will never get there, or we might simply feel beaten down by our attempts and failures, or perhaps we just blindly hang onto a vision that our achievements will finally pay off and produce the result of endless happiness. If I'm right, though, this cycle of struggle and achievement never ends, and so never allows us to finally become complete.

12:25 Adopting a blind belief in a fantasy of achieving a positive world and future is perhaps the easiest way to create an upbeat experience; of course opium works pretty well, too. There are plenty of people offering such beliefs—religious, spiritual, or even outrageous other-worldly or mystical fantasies—and when the mind accepts them, they offer a blissful image of reality and so a beautiful experience. How can we pass up such tempting possibilities?

12:26 The fact that they are not real could be contested. After all, who knows? Of course, a direct consciousness of this reality shows that all those magical fantasies are no more real than all the accepted humdrum or bleak views of a negative world. They are all conceptual inventions, and so not existentially real. In fact, no form of sound and fury is real, although some are very positive and some very negative.

Chasing after a dream only keeps you asleep.

12:27 We have seen that finding something outside ourselves in the "out there" is a myth and won't work to resolve our distress, because nothing adopted actually changes our fundamental condition. Even trying to fix ourselves within—although this may produce more fruit—still won't make us complete, because there is nothing wrong with us. All these so-called problems and their solutions are produced solely through concept and imagination.

12:28 But real life occurs in objective reality, not concept, and death eliminates both the objective and subjective, and it is certainly not a concept or image. Being complete with life and death has to be based on what's true, not what's imagined. And it has to exist in the same place as your self-awareness.

12:29 The distinction of being complete—which is different from chasing after ideals and resolutions—is a rather new one for most people. Yet, if our goal is to be complete in life we need to have access to such a possibility. Faux solutions can fool us until we die, and in this way we will never get to the end of the matter.

12:30 But being complete with life and death demands we get to the end, that we realize there is no more that needs to be done, we are whole as-is. As a being, we are what we are, and there is nothing missing or that can be improved because it is already as it should be. This is a hard reality for us to confront in life, because normally we experience quite the opposite, and we would have to change the whole foundation of how we experience self and life to get there.

12:31 You may still think that being complete means getting everything you want, or having an ideal experience. It doesn't. In that way, you are looking for some experience to make you happy or to feel fulfilled. Being complete really has nothing to do with all of your various experiences, or needs, or desires—all that is just sound and fury.

12:32 An experience of being complete means you are stripped of social drama and comparisons to any other possible experience. Instead, you grasp and experience you are an entity exactly as it is, that you simply exist, however you exist. If you think you are a body then you are that and there is nothing missing; if you think you are an awareness or conscious entity then you are just that. This is not compared to anything else, or any other possible experience you could have. It is your experience of existence in this moment and there is nothing else needed or missing.

12:33 A rock is completely and only a rock as it is, that is its existence, there is nothing missing or needed for it to be a rock. Get it? It is the same with you. You exist just because you exist. There can be nothing missing because it is your experience of existing, no matter what that is.

12:34 As an entity you are always that entity and you are completely and only that. The only way you could not be complete is to have concepts that you should be some other way or that you should attain something not true of you now. Without comparison and imagination, being incomplete can't occur. So eliminate all those concepts—ideals, judgments, comparisons, assumptions, and so on—and you are completely you in this moment. "Is" just is. It needs no justification or attainment, it already is. You already are, and you are complete—unless you say you're not.

12:35 It seems that most people don't really get what is being said, and that it is true! Their brains override what's being said. Even as they intellectually understand it, they still neglect the reality of it. Sometimes a reaction to such statements as "you are complete unless you compare yourself to something not present" or "unless you think you are incomplete" is to hear these statements as some pseudo-psychological notion or positive thinking attempt. They really aren't. They are true existential statements. Control your mind and stop generating being incomplete, and you will experience being complete—whole and happy just being.

12:36 Another form of resistance to doing what's needed to be complete is the idea that if you did you'd have no motivation to get things done, or to achieve your ideals without discontent spurring you on. This is another red herring. Has the feeling of being incomplete worked to push you to accomplish great things? Of course not, because that's not its job. All these "incomplete" dynamics are false. You can accomplish whatever you want without being incomplete. As a matter of fact, being complete is a more powerful experience from which to pursue anything, especially because it clears up the many false agendas and ideals that just keep you spinning your wheels fruitlessly. In this way, you can actually create, accomplish, and do whatever, all while experiencing being complete.

12:37 Eventually you should see the benefits of being complete to your experience of both self and life. But how does being complete apply to death? Death seems out of bounds for such discussion because it ends both self and experience. Yet, experience is an aspect of life until death, and so your relationship to death is central to your experience of life and being complete within it. You become complete with death when you can grasp that you are already non-existent and are completely happy with that. Then, during life you are complete now, and the fact you will end at some point doesn't diminish you because you aren't looking to the future to be fully alive.

Being Happy As-Is

12:38 You can't be complete with your existential existence by engaging in distractions or achieving social ideals—which are the most common attempts at a remedy to imagined maladies. You can't be complete through the accumulation of thoughts, beliefs, or conclusions. You can't do it through any distractions, fantasies, or attainments.

12:39 You can only be complete when you let go of all social concerns and the hope of attaining something outside yourself or something not present within yourself that you think will make you whole. You'll be complete when you let go of finding a solution by following desires or attempting to attain some ideal. You can only do that when you stop comparing yourself or your life to others or to other imagined circumstances, and so stop desiring anything not present that you think will fix you.

Freedom is not achieved by satisfying desire, but by eliminating it.
Epictetus

12:40 To be complete with life, just be in this moment without worldly concerns or comparing your life to something you imagine would be better. I'm not saying you need to live a monastic life or be an ascetic. Simply begin by existing without flaw—not because you are perfect in a social context, but because you are complete as-is—and don't compare yourself or your life to anything outside or not present. In this way you want for nothing, you are happy as you are.

I am happy because I want nothing from anyone.
I do not care about money. Decorations, titles or distinctions mean nothing to me.
I do not crave praise. I claim credit for nothing.
A happy man is too satisfied with the present to dwell too much on the future.
Albert Einstein

12:41 Knowing how to make this shift of mind allows you to experience being complete with yourself and within your life. You may think this is hard or impossible to achieve, but it isn't. Consider the popular notion of the solitary monk or enlightened being sitting peacefully without want or distress. This gives you the sense that it's possible. Yet, you may think their peace is because of some "attainment" that you don't have and probably can't achieve. This is a false view. No achievement accomplished this peaceful state—grasping the truth did. Through recognizing those unnecessary mental activities that keep one incomplete, the monk simply stopped engaging them. Just so, control your own mind. Stop generating the concepts—even if they live in the background and aren't obvious—that create this world of suffering, desperation, and dissatisfaction. That's all it takes to be complete in life. But how do we get complete with death?

12:42 On your deathbed, even if you have loved ones all around, you must say goodbye. Why? Because you die alone, no others can follow you, revealing that the end of your existence is independent from any experience involving others. Since your experience of self exists only in relation to not-self, to be complete with death you must also be willing to let go of the distinction of self and not-self.

12:43 You might jump to the conclusion that this means you have to struggle to eliminate the self. But this is not what I'm suggesting. In trying to eliminate the self, you would still be the main feature in experience, as "you" struggle to eliminate "you." See the rub? Therefore you would not become free, you would just be creating more struggles of which you are the center and the source. Instead, you have to transcend this whole notion of being separate. By eliminating the distinction of you and not-you, you eliminate the experience of separation. This may seem a difficult possibility to entertain until you grasp that the self already doesn't exist.

12:44 Along these lines, consider letting go of mind and perception altogether, and so letting go of all concepts and experience that are generated from the reality created by the distinction of you and not-you. I'm not suggesting you try to push them away or fight with them, but to allow your consciousness to exist independent of them by either being directly conscious of your nature or abiding in not-knowing or the silent-stillness at the core of your awareness. Within this not-knowing silence, how can you insist you and others are separate and don't exist in the very same place? Without the distinction of self and not-self you are not separate, and thus you have already let go of self.

12:45 **Guided Meditation: Completion**

Right now, grasp that for mere existence, or non-existence, a social world is unnecessary. Eliminate any social concerns right now and allow yourself to experience being complete. As you experience being complete, get that your existence is a done deal, there is nothing missing or needed, you are that and it is complete—given you don't add unnecessary forms of "thinking" to the mix!

This includes the very core experience of you—alone, if you assume you are a separate self, and as you are, no matter what you assume. As either a separate self or as a not-separate consciousness, by being complete you are freed of social struggles and drama.

Once you are complete, you exist without the need for anything else. Simply experience the raw existential existence of you as-is. Be OK and happy with your existence in this moment. Work on this until it's true for you—not attempting positive thinking, or overriding or suppressing your experience, but actually changing your experience and being complete. Consider this pushes you toward who you really are.

After you accomplish being complete with your self-experience and life, dwell on an experience of you dying alone, without others able to join you in any way. Experience a sense of being complete with no self and no others or perceptive-experience. In other words, be complete with your non-existence.

Sound and Fury Revisited

12:46 Since your mind might be freaking out about now, resisting this apparent death-loving cult or dismal focus, thus rejecting it and clinging to the glories of life, again contemplate this quote by William Shakespeare:

> Tomorrow, and tomorrow, and tomorrow,
> creeps in this petty pace from day to day,
> to the last syllable of recorded time;
> and all our yesterdays have lighted fools

the way to dusty death. Out, out, brief candle!
Life's but a walking shadow; a poor player,
that struts and frets his hour upon the stage,
and then is heard no more; it is a tale
told by an idiot, full of sound and fury,
signifying nothing.

12:47 What I hear in this quote is a comment on life as we live but ignore it. Each day the activities of life creep on and on into the future without resolution, and the past simply reveals our way to death, until all too soon, death occurs. We hold life as a serious affair when it comes to ourselves, but it is really just motions gone through that, outside of a social context, have no meaning and end without fanfare.

12:48 Yet this is exactly the life that is being objectively lived, there is nothing else and no need for anything else—not to mention there is no other way it can go down but the way it goes down. Being totally OK with the simple and present life unfolding as it does from moment to moment, no matter what is experienced, is to be complete.

12:49 When you take *you* out of the picture it becomes obvious. What captures your attention and passes for "life" is all story. It is a tale told by an idiot—the self—full of sound and fury—drama and struggle—but ultimately it goes nowhere, it has no meaning. A harsh-sounding view perhaps, but a true one nevertheless. It is only because you are focused obsessively on yourself, and caught up in the self's drama and story, that it sounds harsh.

12:50 Since the whole domain and experience of life and all life activities are founded on the self and self-survival, how you experience yourself determines your experience of life. Given you live as a self-object you will always experience being separate and isolated. That appears to be the nature of being a self-object.

12:51 What's also true, however, is being distinct from not-you doesn't actually mean you are separate from not-you. "Separation" is a distinction, as is "object." When we apply the distinction of separation to our experience of self, we will not only be distinct but also separate.

12:52 Ordinarily, our experience lives as if separate and isolated, because we assume we are an inner self that is an uninspected self-object. As an object we must be separate from other objects, because that is the nature of objects. Assuming we are this inner self-object makes our self-experience separate and isolated. This is because, in this way, we have placed ourselves "within" as opposed to "without," creating an impenetrable barrier between the two, thus isolating ourselves from all other conscious-entities and objects. But this isn't ultimately true, and needn't remain as if it is.

12:53 Unless we think we are a body, we are not an object. If we can grasp that self is not an object at all, then we can be distinct from not-you, but not necessarily separate from not-you. That would be a different experience, wouldn't it?

12:54 If you aren't getting the difference between a distinction and separation (which is a distinction itself), consider the rock. We make a distinction of the color, shape, and weight of the rock, but that doesn't mean these distinctions are separate from the rock or from each other. Just so, as a self we are distinct from not-self, but that doesn't mean we are separate from not-self. Consider your experience in this light. Imagine being, but not being separate or isolated, except as a function of your own mind and assumptions.

12:55 **Guided Meditation: Freeing Self from Assumptions**

Experience being whole and fulfilled without any impulse to resolve something missing in yourself because you are already complete. You exist because you exist, and you exist exactly as you are and there is nothing missing or needed. Right now, be complete as a conscious entity.

Remember, this is not a psychological exercise, trying to convince your brain or engage positive thinking. It is about realizing what is true and being conscious of the facts, then simply shifting your experience to match the truth.

Now, put your attention on your sense of being separate and isolated, on being existentially alone. Challenge this notion. Realize you are not a self-object somewhere unfound within. If you can't realize this, then again, admit you have never directly found the ethereal object that you are, and so it is just an assumption that your self is objective in nature.

Consider that, although to be a self you must be distinct from not-you, you are not separate from not-you. Realize or at least imagine that you are not separate from anything, even though this doesn't make sense within your perceptive-experience. Bask in such a possibility until you can make it seem real. What changes in your experience when you do that?

From an experience or at least a possibility that you are not an inner object and aren't separate from not-you, how does that influence your experience of the end of this distinction, *ergo* your death? If you aren't alone and separate, what changes about your idea of dying? With this freedom in mind, meditate on the end of you as a reality.

If your self-experience is simply a distinction and activity that is not objectively real, how does that change your experience of life and of death? Does this help you be complete with the inevitability of your death?

12:56 There are more steps for us to take, but the realizations asserted so far are the stepping-off point, without which we can't take the last steps. Let's briefly review some of these.

12:57 Again, dwell on the sense of being an isolated self and see how it is held as a malady—feeling incomplete because you have the idea it should be otherwise. See that this belief is just a convention, a mistake, a social assumption—assuming that you are in need of something missing. This is founded on the assumption you are a self-object within, and that this object needs to persist. It also makes it seem that you can be created and be destroyed, that you start and stop. As a self this is obviously so, but what if you aren't this self?

12:58 Conventionally, having not-knowing as the base of your experience makes it seem as if you are broken, incomplete, and just haven't accomplished the final resolution that will make you whole and happy. But this isn't true, it is a mistake. This not-knowing is a doorway to your nature, not the cause of your maladies. On the other hand, when you can get yourself as nothing, or at least as a silence without any objectification, perhaps you can be complete in life and with death. If freedom remains your fundamental existential principle, and not the bells and whistles of any experience, you can be complete with both life and death.

12:59 A quick reminder: you should be contemplating this whole time, not waiting to get to an answer. If you think an answer is the solution, look at the end of the book and see what good that does you! You should contemplate each subject as we go, making breakthroughs, having insights, and becoming more conscious. If not, this book is worthless to you. I know it is easy for all this chatter to slip into intellect, or just be confusing. Remember, your job is to look into your experience and find how these assertions apply, then go beyond your experience and become conscious of things you never knew existed. This a "work" book, not a novel. Now, onwards and upwards.

Chapter Thirteen

THE MYTH OF SELF

Transcending the Myth of Self

13:1 You identify as a self that is related to or exists as some kind of awareness, or a source entity that perceives and produces thinking and feeling, right? Where do you think this awareness and mental activity come from? How is it generated? Do you think it spontaneously pops up from the universe all by itself? It kind of seems that way, doesn't it? At one point you didn't exist and then you did—like magic. But let's look at this more closely.

13:2 We accept that our perceptions come from and relate to the brain and nervous system—giving feedback about our bodily existence and environment. Without these elements—brain, nervous system, and perceptive organs—how could we find an experience to identify with? On what would our awareness or attention fall? We imagine we could simply exist as if in empty space because we assume we are existentially real in and of ourselves. But is this true?

13:3 We tend to overlook the fact that this sense of entity, and the conceptual activity it enjoys, is produced by the brain. This suggests that the existence of an immaterial entity independent from the body is a myth. Regardless of what's true about the nature of consciousness, consider that "you" or your "self" is not independent of brain activity, it is produced by it.

13:4 If it's true that the self is a result of conceptual activity produced by the brain—no matter how complex or convoluted, and in spite of the idea that concept or awareness can exist independently from the brain—then when this brain-activity stops, so do you. Besides such anatomical observations, you have only abstract notions that aren't grounded in the reality of your experience. If you don't identify with physical elements, you will undoubtedly identify yourself as being the source of concept and awareness.

13:5 Humans generally assume they are located at the source of perceptions, and linked to the awareness of what's perceived. Beyond such passive assumptions, however, you have an active component as well. In this case, you seem to be something like an impulse-creator having and using a will to create movement or thought. You can command an arm to move, or a thought to occur. You can deliberately take a breath or hold your pee. These kinds of actions firmly suggest you are behind them and doing them.

13:6 Clearly there is a function of the body that directs the body's gross actions regarding the environment. So an impulse-creator role is a necessary aspect of any advanced multi-celled creature. Is there some unfound conscious entity sourcing impulses and thoughts, or is the brain doing it? In either case, you don't know. It is possible that the problem-solving ability of the brain not only creates the thinking that produces the idea of a self, it also generates impulses that appear to be willful because you assume that you, as a conscious-entity, are commanding the brain to do them.

13:7 **Guided Meditation: Breathing**

Watch what you can do willfully. Start with breathing. Right now command your body to take a deep breath, and let it out.

It probably feels nice to do that, doesn't it? But how did it happen? It seems you read my instruction and understood the request, then did something to comply.

> This demands a complex series of activities. Right now, try to experientially trace the origins of all these activities—reading, understanding, and producing an impulse to take action. Use your breathing right now to study and look into these activities.
>
> Although "you" seem to be behind these things, what is this *you* that is hearing, understanding, and breathing? Although you probably attribute such actions to the idea of a conscious-entity, consider that all that activity is simply a sophisticated function of the brain. Contemplate this possibility.

Brain or You?

13:8 It seems you can breathe upon command, but breathing also goes on without and independent of your will, or even your attention or knowledge. With or without your command, breathing continues non-stop. Just so, you seem to be able to purposely have a thought. Yet thinking also continues non-stop—at least while you're awake—whether willfully done or not. Take a look. So, being capable of initiating some impulse or action doesn't mean that activity can't arise on its own, and when it does we certainly attribute that to automatic brain activity.

13:9 Still, how is a willful breath or concept created? You don't really know how it comes about, just that somehow you can "will" it to occur. But as you see, it continues even when "you" aren't purposefully doing it. Notice you don't have any control over or knowledge of the vast amount of physiological activities occurring within the body—the heart beating, the immune system working, the Krebs cycle in the mitochondria producing energy, active transport, oxygen and carbon-dioxide exchanges, liver and kidney function, or trillions of other activities both micro and macro. Being able to take over breathing and thinking is a rather minor ability compared to the massive amount of physiological activity taking place in every moment and in every cell and system of the body of which you know virtually nothing, and over which you really have no direct control.

13:10 What's also true is you don't even have the control you think you have. In other words, if you wanted to move your arm but it didn't move, you could do nothing about it. The ability to do any willful act can be taken away from you and you have no ability to bring it back. Just as when you die, you cannot change this outcome. You can't recreate life because you have no idea or consciousness of how you or life came to exist in the first place. This bursts the bubble of your self-important sense of being directly responsible for even those few things of which you seem to have control.

13:11 Again, the brain is clearly seen as responsible for physical actions taken, but the notion that thought and awareness are independent of the body has taken hold. Let's challenge that notion. As an analogy, consider the possibility that the brain is like an old-time vinyl record in which the activity of rolling a needle in grooves produces music. There are tiny bumps within these grooves that vibrate the needle, creating sound. This sound is directly related to and comes from the record. But these sounds, as beautiful as they may be, are not actually the record even though they don't exist without it. The music isn't of that same nature as the record, yet they are totally interdependent. In this analogy, the brain is like the record and concept is like the music produced.

13:12 In the case of this analogy, music is actually objective because the needle, connected to speakers, vibrates air molecules that vibrate the eardrum. Just so, concepts are also produced objectively through brain activity, even though, like the music, they are not themselves an object but the product of an activity. It is probable that neurosynaptic activity produces the apparent non-physical or conceptual domain where you seem to reside, as well as the idea that "you" are the source of the content of this domain. Thinking you are an independent conscious entity that is the source of concepts is like thinking there is some hidden entity within the record that produces music.

13:13 Within the cells and flesh of the body, you can't find this "conscious entity" that seems central to your self-existence. If all this mental and physical activity is done by the brain, then you are really just produced by the body. This busts up the fantasy that self is some ethereal and detached entity existing on a higher plane.

You are your body, the rest is bullshit.

The Rock and Survival

13:14 The thing is, if you are a body—of which you know very little—you're kind of like a rock. You attribute no sentience or awareness to the rock since it seems to have none. This is exactly the same for your body. Does a leg or an arm have sentience or is it aware? Obviously not. So it's easy to conclude that as an independent awareness you aren't anything physical. Still, beyond imagination, you can find no self outside the body or what the body produces. Although the possibility may still exist that your nature is not limited to the brain, it is far trickier and stuck in paradox than you think.

13:15 Why is it so difficult to stop identifying with stuff that can easily be seen as not real? To answer this, it is useful to revisit the survival principle. Remember, survival dominates everything we experience and do, and clearly we think that whatever we identify with must survive. As we've seen, this whole idea is false. We are created through the distinction of self, and whatever we identify among experience as this self—much of which is social and based on shared human assumptions—is what we're driven to maintain. None of this is necessary, but getting free of any of it is difficult because of our blind commitment to survival.

13:16 Therefore, de-identifying with anything you identify with—or believe in, or want, and so on—is a challenge, most often only attempted as an intellectual exercise or an act of will, not a conscious freedom from anything. This is like saying you're not your breathing and to prove this claim you begin holding your breath. Yet, soon you will resume breathing because it is a constant for self-survival. That still doesn't make any of it ultimately true.

13:17 By accepting the observation that your self and awareness are a product of the body, you can eliminate the idea that self is an independent entity separate from physical reality. In this case, self is nothing but a by-product of the body. Notice you can't find this mysterious conscious entity or soul or whatever immaterial self you think you are. Without the thinking, and without the conclusion of being at the source of perception, you find no such self. If you throw away the taken-for-granted notions humanity has generally accepted over the centuries, can you experience what's really true without resorting to such historical assumptions?

Beyond Humanity

13:18 Over millennia humanity has held self and life in various ways. Yet, we seem to have moved in the direction—mostly through religious ideas, fantasies, philosophical and spiritual theories, and other desperate attempts to avoid the idea and finality of death—of adopting and accepting the notion that the self is separate from the body, and is perhaps endowed with special qualities that might survive death. It isn't too hard to see how we could fall prey to such beliefs. They give us the hope of "life after death"—which, if you think about it, is a really stupid notion, since if there's life after death it isn't death, is it? This whole imagined world is most likely born of ignorance without any real or direct consciousness being involved.

13:19 Consider, why do people disdain the body or at least hold that the body is less than the conscious entity that seems to reside within it? Why has this relationship to the only object that produces both life and self taken hold? We see a long human history of detaching self from body, choosing the mind or the soul as our existential domain, and viewing the body as merely a dumb physical object. Yet, it is highly probable that "you" are a product of the body. What's more, the body itself is far more complex and brilliantly designed than any of the conceptual opinions and beliefs you hold in high regard.

13:20 Entertain the possibility that you are simply a mythical by-product of the problem-solving brain. If this is the case, your real existence lies in being a body. But you know nothing about the body directly. You have no "consciousness" of each cell or organ. These so-called living objects are not really any different than a rock. If the rock has no self-awareness or perceptive capacity, neither does the body itself.

13:21 When you do your best to discern the experience of a rock, what do you come up with? If you were a rock, what would you experience? Nothing! A rock has no experience. Your entire existence would be unknown and your perceptive-experience would be non-existent, wouldn't it? Can you get that? If you are the body, then like the rock, without awareness, imagination, or concept, there is no "conscious-entity," no perceptive-experience. Soak in that reality for a moment. A very unconventional possibility, eh? You are stuck with a conundrum hard to square. Clearly there is awareness but objects don't seem to be aware. 'Tis a puzzlement.

The Activity that Is Self

13:22 So a body without conceptual by-products has no independent awareness. The brain may be producing activity, just like the intestines produce gas, or the skin sweats, but these by-products aren't independent of the body, they are produced by it. What's also true is an object isn't aware and can't perceive or think, so this must be true of you as a body as well—awareness and thinking are just activities of complex living objects.

13:23 Don't fall into the trap, however, of thinking that if you don't exist then there can be no perception. To be clear, I'm not saying there is no perceptive activity going on within experience. I am saying there is no self. If there is a distinction made between a body and all that is not that body, this could be called a specific animal, and because it is living it will create abilities and actions that promote the body's life and welfare. But this is not a "self that resides within."

13:24 If there is a function that is performed by or attributed to what is identified as the self, this function can still occur without the myth of being an inner self-object or conscious-entity separate from everything else. No one thinks music is independent of the record, or hearing is separate from the ear, or a stomach ache has nothing to do with the stomach. Why assume the self is independent or separate from whatever creates it?

13:25 If we grasp that self is a myth, it becomes obvious that it has no objective reality. It is rather more like a vapor emanating from the body. Although this perspective may vex us, it kicks serious ass when it comes to the self we've been assuming we are. It frees us of the self concept, but not from the body. So, at this point, we have to ask the question: What is the body? Freed of this conceptual nonsense and the myth of self, we still don't know what the body really is any more than we know what any object is. So, there is more to resolve.

13:26 It seems that if you are an independent awareness then you aren't the body. If you are the body then you aren't really an independent awareness. We may prefer to nail all this down, and choose one or the other, but that might just be a cop-out. Trying to become conscious of what is really true in this case is like balancing in a kayak. If you tilt to one side you flip over, if you tilt to the other side you also flip over. Choosing the body as self flips you, choosing the mind as self also flips you. Can you look beyond these options?

13:27 **Contemplation: Beyond the Myth of Self**

Using all these unusual and disruptive considerations, contemplate what is true about your nature, as well as your self, without all of humanity's past accepted conclusions and assumptions getting in the way. What is actually true about your experience of "being" when you eliminate all the conceptual inventions you and everyone else has taken for granted?

13:28 Consider that you are not what you think you are. You are an activity, a distinction, and a function of the brain evolving a problem-solving ability that becomes abstract. From this conceptual activity the observation is made that concept can't be found in the physical domain, and so the idea forms and a conclusion is drawn that a self is at the source of conceptual activity and is independent from the physical.

13:29 This is accompanied by the conclusion that this same self is located behind perceptive organs, and so is located within the body as an immaterial self-object, the nature of which is of the same substance as concept or awareness. But I want you to consider that all this is false. Instead, consider that your self is a by-product of the body and produced from the activity of the brain, nothing more.

13:30 You can see that I am using rather unprecedented arguments to lay out totally reasonable but unconventional observations. Of course, these can't produce the consciousness necessary to grasp what's really true, especially since what's really true is mentally incomprehensible. But they can push you to the brink and perhaps give you a shove over the edge. They certainly put a fly in the ointment of any spiritual fantasies or beliefs you may have. But remember it is the irritant in the oyster that produces a pearl. ☺

Beyond Location, Beyond Knowing

13:31 Again, what is the nature of your existence, is it body or soul, or something else? That's a matter for direct consciousness to resolve, but as I repeatedly suggest, your real nature is not the self you experience, but it isn't elsewhere either. Consider that what is being referred to is not this self but is still inclusive of the self, that it involves a paradox hard to square. Yet you will still likely hear this as if it applies exclusively to you—see the rub? To proceed, let's see if we can create a doorway to possibilities beyond the norm, by looking into the nature of something we experience but overlook. Then, perhaps we can consider this matter in a different light.

13:32 **Guided Meditation: No Location**

First, find the silence within your experience, where there is no activity, no thought or images, no known experience, just silent-stillness.

Outside of this silence, see your entire experience, no matter what it is, as sound and fury. Instead, focus on that aspect within your experience that is silent and always has been. It may not have gotten any attention before now, but make it the star of your attention now. Silent-stillness. Find it.

Now, abiding in this silence, notice you likely think of it as within you. Yet this is just another assumption. Drop that assumption, and grasp that you have no idea where this silent place is. If you don't relate it to you as being the source located behind perceptive-experience, notice you can't really say where it is. Consider that it actually has no location at all.

This might seem difficult to consider because your awareness is stuck in and dependent upon perceptive-experience, which tends to locate you. But get that if you are not "behind" your perceptions then location is also an assumed conclusion. Notice that without perception, you really can't say where you are or where this silence is. When you can allow the silent and still aspect of you to be without location, embrace the possibility its nature is really nowhere and is without element.

13:33 Consider the possibility that this so-called "silence," whatever it is, may remain once you die. I hesitate to use the word "remain" because that suggests persistence, but it doesn't persist because it never "existed." This not-knowing-silence is experienced by you, but it is what it is. Whatever that is, it isn't hard to see that you don't know. Your knowing and perception cease to apply within the sphere that you encounter as this silent place. Therefore, it exists in the same domain as not-knowing. In your experience, you only encounter the edges of silent-stillness of which you know nothing. Because you are bound to the constraints of knowing and perception, you can't see beyond these limited activities.

13:34 Consider it may also be a doorway to grasping where real consciousness exists; that it is simply a manifestation or indication of this nature accessible within your limited domain of experience—even though you don't know what it really is. Imagine it is not related to time or location. When you look into it, you can't really tell where it begins or ends or even where it is, can you?

13:35 This exercise could be a doorway that might offer possible insights. Yet it can't produce a direct consciousness of whatever is true, only consciousness itself can do that. You'll need to contemplate this until you directly grasp what is true.

Let's do another exercise to keep pushing the edge of the envelope.

13:36 **Guided Meditation: Not Knowing as Universal**

In your conventional experience it seems you are separate from others. In the world of "knowing" and perceptive-experience you appear as an individual and a separate self-object. Because you are unique and different from others, you experience being isolated and separate.

But when you look into this place of not-knowing or silence, you can see that it cannot be different from any other not-knowing or silence. They are identical because there is no element there to be different. Notice that since it must be the same for everyone and everything, it also could be the very same one, and in the same place, so to speak.

Put your attention on this core sense of not-knowing, the place of silent-stillness. Now try to grasp the real nature of not-knowing, without relating it to knowing in any way. What is it as itself?

What is silence without being related to sound, and stillness without being related to activity? What are they as themselves? Consider the possibility that they are all the same experience.

Grasp that here there is no difference or separation from anything. In this place, if you also stop assuming you are located, you are not separate from anything or located anywhere.

What's to say that this very silent not-knowing place isn't universal or connected to everyone and everything? Get that it is certainly possible because you don't see the limits or boundaries of this "condition" of not-knowing, or nothingness. So it might be that existence here is not separate or alive—and so can't die.

Will the Real Reality Please Stand Up?

13:37 Where does a thing that is only perceived or thought actually exist? In vision, for example, what is perceived is light stimulating the eye and the nerve synapses of the brain to form an image. This is all objective activity. And yet where is the image in all this? While looking at a flower, you're not seeing the light as light, or perceiving your eye or the synapses firing, you are perceiving a flower. Yet notice that there is no flower in any of the perceptive activities taking place—light, organ, or synapses.

13:38 Just so, a computer may be programmed to generate the image of a flower, but the computer doesn't see it, only you do. The computer never perceives the results of its own processes. In other words, the computer doesn't observe the flower or anything else; it only moves through mechanical processes just as you do with the eye and synapses. Whenever this synaptic activity stops, the "knowing" of the flower stops. Nowhere in this is the actual presence of whatever the flower is, only various independent activities and the knowing of the results of these activities.

13:39 The thought of the flower follows the same basic dynamics. The only activities going on are what is fabricated from the brain, none of which look remotely like a flower. In all these indirect and relative processes, where is the perception or the thought?

13:40 In some unknown way, "you"—whatever that is—"know" or experience a thought or perception of a flower. Notice that, within this process, there is no actual thought or perception that is being known as itself. This whole dynamic makes everything that is perceived or thought into an activity that is generated to serve a purpose other than the existence of the activity itself. In this way, perceptive-experience is always indirect and not ever the thing-itself.

13:41 Therefore, we could say that both thought and perception are illusions—something like a dream if the dream is held as objectively occurring. We're not directly grasping any true nature. Within all these indirect activities, perhaps the "substance" that doesn't come or go, regardless of any changes in thought or perception, would be "consciousness," yet we don't know what that is.

13:42 Mind, thought, and perception don't have any substance to them. These activities produce a result that isn't actually "there" when the activity occurs and obviously doesn't exist when the activity stops. There are infinite possibilities for thought, perception, feeling, etc., but no matter what is experienced it is only a form of mental activity. We've already seen that the essence of whatever actually exists is, at best, unknown, and perhaps even non-existent.

13:43 Since nothing is really added to or subtracted from reality, we see that the "essential substance" that remains without coming or going is its true nature. Consciousness in the form of "mind" provides the activity of thought and the "knowing" of perception. Perhaps consciousness without form is the "substance" that remains with or without any activity—and yet there is really no substance whatsoever that is this consciousness. Perhaps you can glean this consciousness directly when it is not being filled with mind or perceptive-experience.

13:44 **Guided Meditation: Object Beyond Mind**

Pick an object to look at and use as the subject for this contemplation. Looking at the object, notice how much of your experience of even this object is subjective mind activity. Now, focus on the presence of the object and see it for-itself.

As you shift to seeing it for-itself, put your attention on that quality of objective reality that is constant and unmoving. As you focus on the unmoving and steady aspect of objects, watch how your mind *is* moving. Now, bypass this mind activity and continue to focus on what is outside your control and is unmoved by your mind.

Consider, is this object what you think it is? Get that it is not your interpretation of it. Could it be just a perceptive phenomenon, an activity showing up as a "that" in your mind? Could it be energy—whatever that is—forming a particular activity that appears constant and defined? Could it be something other than your experience suggests?

Now that you have questioned it, look again, and again focus on that element that seems constant and unmoving—and is outside your mind and even your perception. Once you are focused on this aspect, stay there for a time. What happens?

Can you stay there? Take a look at the fact that most of your experience is a completely subjective mind activity, seeming to occur within your internal state. Is it possible to experience a truly objective reality without any influence or domination from your mind? Take a look and see. What comes up?

Genius is the ability to independently arrive at and understand concepts that would normally have to be taught by another person.

Immanuel Kant

Getting Who You Are

13:45 Perhaps you see life as an opportunity to connect to others—without life, that isn't possible. But consider further. The only reason you desire to connect is because you experience being separate. If you aren't separate you don't need connection—or to say it another way, you are already connected.

13:46 Yet, in a culture and society that have been built on this sense of being an isolated individual, getting free of both a social context and the desperate need to resolve the sense of isolation is hard to do. Consider the possibility that you don't have to, that it's only powerful assumptions—that seem self-evident—keeping you in this experience and struggle.

13:47 **Guided Meditation: Being Nowhere**

Again, put your attention on yourself and dwell on your sense of being existentially alone and separate. Now dig deep into this experience. How is it that you can claim you are really isolated? What do you experience that suggests you are separate and alone?

Consider that this experience is actually generated by an assumption. Do you know what the real nature of self and other is? Consider again that the domain where there is only silence might be the very same place that both you and other exist. It could be that you really aren't located like you think, that this aspect of your nature does not reside as separate or alone.

It only seems you are isolated because you can't experience any other "conscious entity" within your private inner world. But notice you don't experience *anything* in this not-knowing silent place. Why conclude that it is of the same nature as that which you *do* experience?

Keep your attention on the core place of your experience that is silent, and is the foundation for all the "noise" that you experience within yourself. Notice you can't do anything with it. You can't think it, feel it, identify it in any way. It is silent and still, and without attribute.

Let go of whatever ideas you have about yourself and consider that in this silent "place" you may not be separate from others and also you may not be your self-mind. Consider, your self-mind might be just noisy activity you do—including the assumption that you are separate—but not who you are.

Abide in this silent "place" of your nature and notice you know nothing about it, except that it is a core and authentic aspect of your experience. Drop all assumptions, even what seems totally obvious, and don't conclude anything. What is there without any thought or activity, belief or assumption? Does that tell you something about who you really are?

13:48 In the end, if you can be complete with your experience as it is, and grasp the true nature upon which it is built, and if you can allow the nothing or silence at your core to be your base, you can be happy no matter what experience comes or goes, and no matter what you do or don't do. Further, if you can grasp that your real nature, what you really are, is not found within any of the activities of life, and is without location or element, you are complete with life and complete with your inevitable death because you realize you aren't going anywhere. You are already there.

Silence without location, stillness within activity.
The Nothing that is infinite is already
the true nature of existence.

13:49 People often miss the fact that Buddha was NOT advocating for life, he advocated for the end of life. We cling to ideas of life in any form, but even though we may like the idea of Buddha and complete enlightenment, we still miss the simple fact that he was pursuing having no more self or life forever. Why is that? It flies in the face of everything we want out of life and every idea of attaining a better experience someday.

13:50 Could it be that, among other things, he got that life is not just full of sound and fury, but always a source of suffering? Is it possible that the experience of struggling to survive as a self is itself suffering? Not just suffering the struggle of trying to turn the unpleasant into the pleasant, but that the nature of being a self is itself a form of suffering.

13:51 **Guided Meditation: Inherent Suffering**

Right now put your attention on your self and life experience. Don't specifically engage in any of it, just notice it taking place. What does this feel like? What do you experience as a self living a life?

Now, imagine being totally free of both self and life, and completely open in your experience, without any attachments or worries, without any concerns or demands put on you to survive in any way, even subtly. Feel completely free of having to be any way in particular or to do anything at all. Be without limit or constriction, without definition or form.

Imagine being completely free and open and without restriction or limitation. Imagine an experience of no self, no isolation, no separateness. Work to let go of struggle and self. Instead, allow consciousness to be nowhere and open, free and unlimited, and without your self existing at all. Soak in this possibility—total freedom without form or limitation.

Now, shift back into an experience of being a self. Watch how contracting your experience into a self is a form of suffering. Notice that being a self is not free or open.

Consider that consciousness being reduced and squeezed into a self is a form of suffering. Contemplate the reality of that experience.

13:52 As a mere idea this does little good. To pursue this consciousness, start by getting who you really are. This is having a conscious experience of your unadorned and essential being, absent of any social context, history, identity, or any other conflation.

13:53 Look into your experience right now. Consider that what you experience could be called the self-mind or a self-awareness, which is composed of an elaborate conceptual social-self. The fact that this experience is actually conceptual is overlooked. This self-experience will disappear at death. But if it is really conceptual in nature—although it seems solid and real—it is only a figment of mind, and so at death you are simply letting go of what amounts to a domain of thought.

13:54 **Contemplation: Who You Are**

Experience yourself just being now without any social context or mind, without history or identity. Experience just *being*—unadorned and without location or attachments. Contemplate who you really are.

13:55 Once you're conscious of your non-social presence and can experience just being now—without comparison or a social context—you can be complete in life because here there is nothing missing and nothing to seek. Yet, getting free of the social drama that entangles you, even if only temporarily, might seem very difficult. The reason it seems so difficult to let it go is this is where you live and exist. You find your "self" in this drama and story.

13:56 Without your particular story and all the ceaseless mental activity that keeps it alive, your self would be unrecognizable as it is, and without any story at all a self-identity couldn't exist. So it is challenging to let go of this story because your mind is committed to self-survival and you identify with your story. It creates the context for your social-conceptual self-awareness.

13:57 Since it is unlikely you will let go of your story altogether, you can still move toward gaining some freedom from it. You can also at least craft it to be more honest and open, more effective and empowering. If it is not, why are you telling and living that story and sticking to it? To help get some detachment from your story, if you hold it like you would a game, you get that the game is just serving a purpose and is unreal in itself. The key, of course, is to remember it is a game while you play it, and know it as such—experiencing it as unreal and unnecessary. You are then able to stop playing it or step outside of it whenever necessary or useful.

13:58 Although transcending your self-story alone is a herculean task, there is still quite a bit more to be done. You can, at least temporarily, let go of all stories and just be present without the domain of thought or a complex story or social context dominating your experience, and this sets the stage for the "more" of which I spoke. But it should be acknowledged that this unadorned self-experience will also become a story, even though it will be a very simple story that depends on whatever "cosmology" you adhere to.

13:59 Remember, "cosmology" is a word I use to refer to how you see yourself in the universal scheme of things. This is the fundamental reality you think exists, the background belief about how the world is basically constructed. It can be practical or strongly influenced by a belief system, but it is actually not true. It too is an invention.

13:60 To give you an idea of the general ballpark I'm referring to, let me offer some simplistic examples of partial cosmological subject matter:

- I am an inner self-object living in a body surrounded by a world of physical objects.
- I am an embodied spirit suffering the mortal world, eventually to return to the bliss of universal love.
- I'm an animal surviving in an unfeeling world of dog eat dog.
- I'm a fragment spinning off the evolution started by the big bang.
- I'm a soul tempted by the weaknesses of the flesh trying to get into heaven to be eternally saved by god.
- I exist as an awareness perceiving objects from moment to moment.
- I am my mind, so concept is all there is, and the world is an illusion.
- The physical world is all there is, I am just a biological creature living within it.
- I am a special being realizing my destiny.
- There is only one self of which we are all aspects.

13:61 This is just a sampling of fragments of possible perspectives to give you an idea of possible cosmologies. Look into your own case and consider what sort of "cosmology" you hold to be true about reality and your role in it. After getting a sense of the cosmology that founds your self-experience, let it go and experience who you are without it.

13:62 If you still have trouble getting who you are, free of all that mind stuff, perhaps another way to approach this is through realizing that the real nature of your social self is conceptual. No matter how real it seems or how important it is to you, it is just a story. You can grasp that no story really needs to exist. Stop telling it and it doesn't exist. Then you have already let go of the story that is you and your life. Once this is done, perhaps you are left with who you are in its most basic form.

Language Assumes Self and Not-Self

13:63 Communicating beyond the restriction of you as a conscious-entity is quite challenging because it is virtually impossible to convey a consciousness outside of you and not-you. This is because language, our only tool to use for communication, is founded on the distinction of self and other. We've seen that the creation of a sentient-self and a sentient-other is necessary to be able to create language. Without this distinction language couldn't exist because there would be no possibility to communicate. In other words, it wouldn't be possible to share the experience of one person without the existence of another person, therefore selves are taken for granted within the language itself. Can you see that?

13:64 We overlook the fact that language is completely structured around the self and not-self distinction. Therefore, everything said inherently includes this distinction and assumes a self and other. There is always a subject and object. We are always referring to an assumed world of self and not-self, and so it is very difficult and almost impossible to talk about anything outside of this world—whereof one cannot speak. Yet to tackle this unprecedented subject we have to find a way.

13:65 The first thing I must do, of course, is point out the above impediment so we are alert to this fact and its challenges. Then I need to assert that self and not-self don't really exist. But it probably still seems that that just goes too far, doesn't it? It seems so obvious that you are a self, and that there's lots of stuff that is not you.

13:66 Yet, in order to have this "obviousness" in your experience, the distinction of you and not-you must be made or it can't be experienced. You may acknowledge this but continue to wonder how this distinction is made unless you make it, and if you make it then you must exist to make it, so isn't it made already? When you say "you" make this distinction, this inherently assumes the distinction of you and not-you since you are the one making it. See how the language assumes self?

13:67 But it is not too far-fetched to consider that something existed prior to this distinction dividing up all perceived experience into either you or not-you. This suggests that consciousness, and even consciousness in the form of perceptive-experience, exists prior to and independent of this distinction. However the distinction is made or comes to pass, it is still a distinction and so it can be unmade or transcended.

13:68 It could be said that "consciousness" is making the distinction, and that's how you get to exist to "make the distinction." By eliminating this distinction, you experience that "you" are just a fabrication. Yet, if you are a fabrication how can you be the center of all this experiencing and the making of distinctions? With such a conundrum, it would seem there has to be room for experience to occur without it coming from and being based on you. Therefore, to understand all this, you might have a challenge on your hands.

13:69 The point is that language, the very means we use to communicate about this, is inherently structured around the distinction of self and other. So when talking about eliminating you and not-you, it will still come out as if you are doing the eliminating. Everything said to or about you will be centered on the idea of you, it's in the language. This is something we just have to live with, remembering there is no way to speak about this subject without the you/not-you distinction being assumed by the language. Simply see past this structural challenge to grasp what is really being referred to without getting overly caught up in semantics.

Chapter Fourteen

TRANSCENDING LIFE AND DEATH

Challenging Perception

14:1 After the fundamental non-social experience of who you are is attained, you will still have perceptive-experience going on. This tends to produce the conception that there is a reality in which you live and are located. So, at this point, you must transcend perceptive-experience as well. You might think this is impossible, that perception and objects are just facts of life. But neither is going to survive death so you can't continue to cling to them.

14:2 Begin by letting perceptive-experience be just a phenomenon, as if a dream or an illusion if you like. This may seem hard to do, but start by noticing that you perceive a world around you filled with whatever objects are present. The nature of what's there is not perceived because perception is an indirect sensory and conceptual activity, as if a radar pulse from which distinctions are made. Therefore, this very experience itself can be seen as unreal and irrelevant.

Concerning matter, we have been all wrong.
What we have called matter is energy, whose
vibration has been so lowered as to be perceptible
to the senses. Matter is energy reduced to
the point of visibility. There is no matter.

Albert Einstein

14:3 Whether objects are real or not isn't really an issue when considering death. Your inner self is not an object, and in the end all objects will vanish at death. So your indirect perception of them is irrelevant except that it pushes you to experience yourself as an object and as located while alive—this will also die.

14:4 Your entire relation to objects exists solely through perception. Consider, perception itself is just a phenomenon that has no substance or reality, like a dream world has no real substance when you realize you are dreaming. In truth it is all indirect and subjective.

14:5 If you can lock onto the infinite nature of reality, you should be able to transcend perceptive-experience. This frees you from identifying with a perceiving-self-awareness and so opens up the possibility of not being bound to life and death. It is important to be able to grasp a consciousness freed of self and perceptive-experience of any kind; otherwise you are likely to be stuck in being located and objective.

Immanuel Kant said something like:

> *Mind so influences our perceptions that our perception of reality can't be trusted as true.*

Beyond Perception

14:6 Since perceptive-experience is your sole connection to an objective reality and your main proof of existence, it's useful to press into it more deeply. There seems to be an impenetrable division between the experience of you and all that is not you. Focusing on objective reality, you find a lack of depth in your intimate knowledge or direct encounter. In other words, it exists outside your self-awareness and your direct consciousness. You are only conscious of reality through indirect perceptions. To get a better handle on this do the following exercise.

14:7 **Exercise: Object Known**

We are going to investigate what we actually or directly know about something, what we actually or directly encounter. Look at some object that you can easily see. We will use that as the object of our investigation.

What do you know about it? You and I say there is something there. But what is actually there? Your first task is to get it for-itself. Therefore, you see that it is not the name you give it, it is not the function or value it has for you, it is not your memory or associations, it is not the concepts you have about it. It is without meaning. It is just itself. So first pull off all the stuff you normally automatically slap onto any perception. Can you do that? Get it for-itself.

Even without all that stuff, it still seems like something is there, doesn't it? What is that? What have you got left? What do you get as there using just perception without interpretation or any other conceptual add-ons?

Right now you are looking at it. Looking at it is a function of light bouncing off it. If we eliminated all light and it was pitch black, you wouldn't know it existed. You'd get nothing. Can you see that what you are experiencing is the light, not it? Without the light you get nothing. You are not indeed encountering the object, you are encountering the light—and only the light it rejects not the light it accepts, and you get only what light itself can carry as a medium and what you can see and discern.

This means you aren't really getting what's there, just some phenomenon of light that is not the thing itself but an independent activity. With sight you only perceive light bouncing off the outside of an object, you get nothing of the inside or the real substance, and certainly not the nature of what's there.

You might think that if you touch it then that would prove something, but what does it prove? You have a feeling, that's all.

Is it your feeling? If we snipped the nerves that relay such sensations to your brain you wouldn't perceive anything, get it? So without light and without sensation, what do you get? Nothing.

I want you to experience that all perception is indirect. It goes through a medium and you can only receive what you can from that method of perception. For example, with sight you don't get the weight, or temperature, or sound of something. It is the same with sensation or smell or sound and any other perceptive-experience. None are the thing itself, and all are restricted to the mechanics of that organ and the medium used. Perceptions are just limited aspects of an infinite reality made distinct to serve a purpose.

Our next task is to get it as-itself. If you take away perception because it is not direct—in other words, it is not actually the thing-itself—what do you have as an experience? What do you have without perception? Nothing! I want you to get that you have no direct experience of anything. You don't know what anything actually is.

14:8 An object may be perceived, but not its nature or the source of the act of perceiving. When we consider this source—the origin of which seems to be "us"—we have to confess that it is also unknown since it is not found within our perceptive field. So, when it comes to our self-perceptions, we suffer the same condition and limitation as we do with our perception of objects.

14:9 Given this source is unknown, without identifying with a separate self-object, we can't say that non-self and self are separate or in two different places. We identify with being located at the source of our perceptions, and though we can't locate this source we assume we are somehow "behind" our perceiving. Like when we look through a telescope we experience we are behind the scope. But consider, why assume you are located behind the organ of perception? All you need is to somehow be conscious of what's perceived.

14:10 You perceive a thought, but although you might unthinkingly imagine you are a self-object floating around inside your skull somewhere—assuming this is where the thought is—you can't locate yourself in relation to the thought because you don't know where the thought is or how it is you perceive it. So why assume you are located behind any perceptive organ?

14:11 After all, what is actually there behind the eyes or between the ears? Physically, behind any perceptive organ we find only nerves and brain tissue. Does any of that look like what you hold as you? Not even close, is it? So either you are somehow floating around inside of or located within this tissue, or we've got it all wrong about being located behind perception.

14:12 When we take consciousness out of a dependence upon or confusion with perception, we find no location except as an assumption. When we transcend location, again we may discern no difference between self and not-self. There is no reason to locate yourself behind perceptive organs or even at the source of them. This information comes into your consciousness somehow, but you don't have to be located at all for that to happen.

14:13 **Guided Meditation: Transcending Perceptive Phenomena**

Right now put your attention on your perceptions, and notice if you locate yourself because of them.

Now let perceptions be, but don't locate yourself anywhere. You could be anywhere or nowhere. A phenomenon of perception is taking place, but don't assume you are located because of it. If it helps, hold that what you are perceiving is unreal like a dream—simply a phenomenon.

Sit and experience consciousness as independent from perception. Work to transcend perceptive-experience.

14:14 Sorry we are continuing to push into what must seem abstract and difficult material. I imagine your brain must be about to burst. Hang in there. Try not to hear this stuff as abstract metaphysics, but as real conscious possibilities you can experience. Ground it as best you can, but don't believe it if you can't find the reality behind the assertions. You have accomplished a lot so far. If you can't jump these last difficult hurdles you will still have much to work with.

The Self-Perception Myth

14:15 We are stuck within the myth of perception. As said, deep unknown existential assumptions influence and bias our perceptive-experience. So, let's continue to work to free our consciousness from both assumptions and perceptions.

14:16 Even if you hold that you are not wed to perceptive-experience, it is still difficult to grasp that there is no "non-objective self-object" behind the scenes. Since you find yourself in a perceived world of objects, you are drawn to assume that either you are what's identified within your perceptive-experience—primarily the body, which is the only object identified as you—or that you are some source-object that's being expressed in and as conceptual activities experienced within the body.

14:17 If you toss off the notion that you are an undefined self-object within, still, the mere presence of thinking, feeling, and perceiving seems to suggest that you must exist, especially since these are further held to be expressions of you. This does appear to almost "prove," even if indirectly, that you exist as something behind the scenes that is simply not perceived.

14:18 But you don't have to be so roundabout, you always have the body to identify with. Outside the distinction of being an internal self-object, the reason it seems like you're a body is because the body is all you have that indicates a you; even the perceptive organs—behind which you tend to locate yourself—are a function of the body. Still, existing as a by-product of a body and its brain doesn't provide a consciousness of your real nature or even the nature of the body.

14:19 Yet, the body is perceived like anything else and then identified as oneself or as one's body. This suggests a distinction between the awareness that is doing the perceiving and identifying, and what is being perceived, and so this awareness seems separate from the body and perhaps residing within it. But remember that being a body is not an experience of being inside the body or being a part of the body, which is usually how we experience self as it relates to a body.

14:20 As we've seen, being a body is a very different matter than we think. It is like being a tree. Can you imagine the "mind" of a tree? It's beyond quiet, without thought or reflection, only silence. It is being the tree itself, not a thought about itself, or a perception of itself. There is no mind, and no reflective activity—try to experience this possibility.

14:21 **Guided Meditation: Being the Body**

Experience being a body like a tree experiences being a tree. This kind of awareness is not found in observing the body, or having a thought about the body, or even feeling the body. As already seen, in this case, your perceptive focus will be outside of and other than the body.

Again, if you are just the body, then—other than bodily sensations—you perceive from the body out. So, do that now. Move your perceptive-experience outside the body. When you do that, notice your mental activities dissipate, and the inner self-awareness disappears. Soak in that, and take a break from your internal-state activities.

Now go further, and experience being the body as an object only, without perception at all—again, like what we might imagine is so for a tree or a rock. No concept, no perception, no self, no awareness, just "is." Contemplate that.

14:22 Now, having an experience, even if temporarily, of being free of the inner-self, you can see that the central mistake made about not being a body is that you then tend to experience yourself as "a one inside" (or elsewhere), and this becomes the immaterial object that implies you're something other than a body. Here is where the belief arises that the self is a "little man within," or a soul, or an entity, or some other form of being a self-object.

14:23 Because it is inconceivable to you that your self is not an object or substance of any kind, you invent a distinction of an immaterial self-object. Maybe you see yourself as "pure awareness," or "the witness," or some other notion of a "real" or "source" self. It may seem like this is an advance, but you would actually be closer to the truth if you were to say, "I am nothing but a body" because in this way at least you wouldn't be divided or conceptual. Your identification with objects may be necessary for living life, but this insistence that you exist in some form within, no matter how ethereal it may be, is an obstacle to becoming conscious of the nature of existence.

14:24 Even those who've directly experienced their true nature often don't get this point, because the mind will insist on formulating something to be "known" and this will inevitably become some "thing" even though it is the "nothing thing." Getting beyond this takes a much deeper consciousness of the real nature of reality and existence.

14:25 The first few beginning enlightenment breakthroughs don't stop the mind from going down roads of assumptions that bind us to life and perception. Yet to transcend death we need to get beyond both life and perception. So, let's do another exercise to see if we can make a little more headway by creating a new possibility of being conscious without perceptive-experience.

14:26 **Guided Meditation: You Without Perception**

You have no consciousness of creating or choosing to be a human body, so you might just as well have experienced being an infinite number of creatures or forms. Get that you could be anything at all—it makes no difference as far as being a "you" is concerned.

Say you were born as a worm. Imagine you are a worm with no eyes or ears, *ergo* no visual or audio perception, nor any idea of such things. What would that be like?

What would it be like if you were a single-celled organism with no perceptive organs at all? Work to create such an experience.

Without perceptions, or any memory of perception, and without language, are you able to think? Try it. What happens?

When you close your eyes, what do you have in your experience? Mostly darkness for vision, maybe hearing some sounds, breathing in some smells, feeling sensations. Now, remove all these perceptions, even sensations. Remember, this is possible and could actually happen to you—you could lose all your perceptive faculties, and eventually you will.

So imagine that is the case now. You are blinded, you can't see a thing. Your eardrums are broken, you can't hear, total silence. Your body goes numb and you can't feel anything, or perceive in any way. What do you have left? Notice what you experience now.

Now imagine that your brain malfunctions and you can't think, imagine, remember, or sense anything. What is there now? You still are, but you have no perceptions or mental activity at all. Don't assume anything, be completely open.

Now, also eliminate the idea or memory of space, so there is no experience of space, or objects, or location—which are all dependent upon perceptive and mental faculties. What are you now? You will lose all these at death. What are you then?

14:27 Clearly, self and self-reflection, mind and self-awareness, aren't needed for life to exist—as we see in many other forms of life. Beyond this observation, although we perceive and relate to life as if there is something there, actually there is no such thing as biological life outside the distinction of biology. There is a distinction that we call "life" and a more specific one that we call "entity," and neither actually exists as something. To say it another way, they can't be found because there is really nothing objectively there—like you, they are activities not objects.

14:28 Although life clearly exists as a distinction, if it has no substance, not even an ethereal one, then it seems that it also doesn't inherently exist. No one can seem to locate the essence that we assume is life. Consider the possibility that there is no substance to life, and that its existence is perceivable only as an assumed distinction we make in relation to what we experience.

14:29 Just so, the distinction of self is also an activity, and whatever is included within that distinction is what will be experienced. For example, if I make the distinction that an image is the sight of a real and solid table, then that is what I perceive as there. If, on the other hand, I see it as a hologram of a table, then those aspects of it being objectively solid disappear and my distinction is of an image only. So it is with the distinction of self. If self is seen as separate and isolated, then that is what's experienced as there, but if self is seen as distinct but not separate, then that becomes the experience of self.

14:30 I know most people will not be able to experientially realize much of what I have been saying, as with what I just said. One reason this is so is that they don't understand what I mean by "distinction" and how central it is to our experience. One huge domain of distinctions is concept, and we can see that this whole domain can be made or not made. So, the experienced reality that is created from these distinctions is not inherently real, and we can eliminate or change any or all of those distinctions.

14:31 When we make "object"-ive distinctions we consider them outside our own mind—but even then we determine what constitutes those distinctions, as seen in the table example above. Still, there is something we consider non-conceptual and so outside our own mind and interpretation. This is quite an important distinction—as we'll see in the next chapter.

14:32 But beyond objective existence, every conceptual distinction is something that comes and goes. Conceptualizing is an activity, and so concepts can be easily changed or eliminated. Therefore if you look carefully at the assumption that you are separate and objective and discover this is in fact conceptual, that means you can stop conceiving this assumption, and in so doing, stop assuming those distinctions. Consider this is true of all distinctions, especially conceptual ones, but we will find it is true of objective distinctions as well.

14:33 Although we seem to perceive an objectively occurring body and environment, our "self" lies within the distinction we make that is experienced as our self-awareness. This is where life and self exist for us. We have seen that without the assumption of being an inner-self, and so on, our existence and non-existence is not really an issue. Therefore, freeing ourselves of assumptions, distinctions, and perceptive-experiences, we might find a way to be free of life and death.

Transcending the Life Illusion

14:34 Now, let's return to your experience of life as a subjective and perceived process that is biased. Consider that every possible view within "life" and "reality" is, necessarily and by design, insular and limited. Viewed from the history of humanity or the entire cosmos, or from the Absolute that contains it all, it is easy to see that your entire experience of life and reality is only a temporary blip in the scheme of things, and that a limited and myopic view sets the stage for how you perceive reality.

14:35 To get some freedom from the assumed importance and necessity of self and life, remember William's quote:

Life's but a walking shadow,
a poor player, that struts and frets
his hour upon the stage,
and then is heard no more.

Sound like something to desperately hang on to?

14:36 In the context of time, "having a life" is viewed as a conceptual experience where each moment is seen in relation to every other moment of remembered experience that comprises the past, as well as an extrapolation of the future persistence of this same life—and, by definition, this is all conceptual and therefore not existential or necessary, and certainly not absolute. We are distracted from the real moment by our ambition to actualize some story plot, be it minor or major. This is a departure from what's true in favor of what's "planned." Now is the only place existence shows up, so you must acknowledge that your context for experience of both life and self only exists in this moment as a concept. The only place where your life and personal history seem significant and enduring is within your own self-mind.

14:37 In this way, grasp that your life experience is a story, making it conceptually generated and therefore not intrinsically real. Notice that the story of your current life-experience hinges mostly on the months or year preceding it, and if that year was preceded by similar years then it all represents your current life being lived, and if not, then it represents life as it seems to be occurring 'round about now. And this recent unfolding story relates to an upcoming future story of whatever your plans are and however far they extend in the story of the life you are living.

14:38 This past and future story is the focus of and considered to be your life being lived. Take a look—doesn't that more or less constitute your life as it is currently experienced? Get that all this is conceptually created. Dwell on this for a moment and see if you can get a hit on what's being said here. What is life without any story linking moments? What is awareness without any story whatsoever?

14:39 The only place where your life and personal history seem significant and enduring is within your mind. Imagine that all the perceived activity and drama of your life and world, no matter how intricate or momentous, still amounts to nothing but a speck of a dream within a cosmological dream—none of which is Absolute. Whether we're talking about your life or the entire universe, it is all relative and conceptually generated—it goes nowhere and means nothing, except for what you make up.

14:40 When you are inside it, it seems real and important and all that you have in life. But if you step back from the immediate distractions and activities you engage, you see that it is all founded on your story and that you view it in relation to both immediate and long-term imagined goals. But all this is conceptually generated, it is not existentially real or necessary.

14:41 Can you grasp what existed before the Big Bang, before any relativity arose, and will remain long after everything is gone—after the "Big Whimper"? Make no mistake, however, the Absolute is not really *before* or *after* anything because it isn't relative. The above is just a way of speaking.

14:42 **Guided Meditation: You as a Blip**

From the vantage point of infinite existence, you can see that everything you know and perceive is as if in a small bubble of perceptive-experience created by and for you, looking at itself from within. What would occur if this bubble popped?

While such imagery is inaccurate at best, it may help rein in your fixation on what you experience and know as life and world. Contemplate this possibility.

Try to get that everything you experience, perceive, and know is a temporary and relative activity, and that every bit of it will dissolve. Can you grasp that?

Now you can consider existence more broadly and without limit or specificity. Is there anything that is not based upon you or life or perception?

Acknowledging the limits of your experience, set out to grasp what's not limited, grasp what doesn't come or go, start or stop. Grasp the nature that has no element yet is the source of all elements. Get that consciousness-existence is of this nature.

14:43 Outside of self-survival and a social context you are free and independent of life and death because you have no element, no location, and can't come or go, because "you" don't exist. But for this to be realized you have to be conscious of a nature that is free of those activities. "Is" doesn't come or go, absolute Now doesn't start or stop.

Your Objective Existence

14:44 Although the self doesn't exist, that function or activity has the job of helping to keep the human-animal alive as it interacts with the environment. Whether or not there is self-activity taking place, the body is what exists as the creature that we experience being. Since the self-activity is based on the objective world—in other words, on the body without which we wouldn't exist—let's make some distinctions and experience some possibilities about this object.

14:45 **Guided Meditation: Your Objective Existence**

Start with being a body. In a previous exercise, you made a shift in your experience to being a body, so do that again now. Simply experience being the body and so perceiving from the body out. Have the body be the self-object so there is no inner self.

Now go further. Eliminate identifying with abstract brain activity and have no thought, no inner or conceptual world at all. Just be the object of the body.

Although you don't have the perceptive capacity to experience this, as a body you are completely made up of cells. Stand on this knowledge and experience yourself as a conglomerate of trillions of cells acting in concert to form an organism. Notice that these cells—making up the reality of you—themselves have no concepts, intellect, or awareness. Be nothing but cells. Soak in this as a reality.

Now, let's go deeper. All these cells are physical matter and so are made up of atoms and molecules. These may seem infinite in number but experience being the molecules and atoms that comprise this object. Keep your mind focused on that reality.

From here go beyond the cells and particles that make up the body and do something completely different: de-identify with such particles. This shouldn't be difficult since you have never experienced yourself as these unseen atomic particles and they don't seem remotely related to an experience of being human, even though admittedly they are fundamentally what you are made of.

Dwell on the fact that matter is unfathomably small particles whizzing around. What is the space between these particles? Is that you too?

What if these particles stopped moving—what would exist then?

Entertain the possibility of a reality that is of a nature beyond, but inclusive of, matter and activity, even if such an experience seems out of reach. If this matter and activity stopped moving, what would exist then? What is as if "beyond" such stuff?

It is said that Buddha said something like: the smallest particles of matter exist and don't exist a trillion times in the blink of an eye. More recently such notions were scientifically confirmed. In addition to such a discovery, the nature of this particular matter was said to have no mass and no dimension. Sound familiar?

Regardless of all this hearsay, and beyond your capacity to think or perceive such things, consider the truth is that in essence matter doesn't actually exist at its root. If this is true then even as a body ultimately you don't exist. Soak in that possibility. Then ask what are you?

Getting What You Are

14:46 Imagine a consciousness that is independent of the distinction of self and not-self. A consciousness that does not reside in three dimensions or have a location, and is not related to perception. What could that be? It seems it would probably be a consciousness that is absolute in nature, wouldn't it? In this consciousness, both life and death would be irrelevant, because here nothing can change, this nature can't come or go.

14:47 Remember not to confuse cognition or awareness, thought or perception for consciousness. They are limited forms of consciousness but not consciousness itself. The nature of consciousness is beyond the distinction of both self and not-self. Ultimately life and survival are unreal and unnecessary.

14:48 In life a phenomenon of perceptive-experience exists, but the nature of existence itself is not limited to that and so is free of it. With death, you must realize you already have no element and so nothing comes or goes. Obtaining such consciousness begins the last steps of this work. Since there is no element here, when perceptive-experience disappears in death, it doesn't change a thing.

14:49 This is cold consolation, however, unless you realize and identify with what's absolutely true. Yet, even shy of this depth of consciousness, there is much that can be done to change your mind and experience in such a significant way that it places you on the threshold of making this leap in consciousness. That's one of the most significant steps for this life and death business, so let's do more work to move in this direction.

14:50 **Guided Meditation: Consciousness Beyond Perception and Awareness**

Perceive whatever you perceive, inside and out, but let go of any notion that you are located behind these perceptions or related to perceptive-experience at all. Keep working on this until it's real for you. What do you experience when you do that?

Now, concentrate on awareness without any location at all. Simply pure awareness without any other activity taking place. Here there is no form or substance, and so there is nothing to be aware of.

When you have your attention on this unformed awareness, work to detach from the awareness to seek a consciousness that is prior to awareness. Find it.

Notice this consciousness is without any element whatsoever, it has no location or substance, it is not thinkable or imaginable, it doesn't span time, it is Now, and it is Nothing.

When you find it, keep your attention on this consciousness. Don't look elsewhere. If you get it, it's obvious that it *is* reality, and that you are *it*—if not, you didn't get it, there is no doubt or guessing or conclusion necessary. What did you become conscious of?

14:51 I would like to ground this all a lot more for you, but unfortunately "ground" is a function of mind and life, and we have to move past those. Still, I've done what I can to make all this as accessible as possible, even though through a normal human lens it is all clearly absurd and impossible. Yet, this next section can help you bring it together in a way that can push you beyond your comfort zone and create the possibility of letting go of life and death, so pay attention and work hard to make it real.

Getting Free of Life and Death

14:52 What would it be like to experience being free in life and of death, and so unburdened by taking self and survival seriously? Sounds like that would be a fantastic experience, doesn't it? Of course, beyond the fantasy, to access this experience you'd have to get past the domination of self-survival, which creates good and bad experiences; therefore, this new experience couldn't be good or bad.

14:53 Even so, the freedom involved in transcending life and death does come off as a rather positive experience. Certainly, a sense of ease and lack of struggle—the opposite of which are the hallmarks of life in survival—would accompany such an experience. Yet, if we focus on such an outcome—rather than holding it as a side-effect that may or may not occur—we are focusing on the wrong thing. Our focus needs to be on what produces that outcome, which can occur only if we get free of the sound and fury and, instead, abide in the consciousness of the real nature of existence.

14:54 Much of what's been said up to this point might be hard to follow and may seem way too abstract or out of reach. I don't want it to be inaccessible, so let me go over some of the main points briefly to see if I can ground them a bit. Attempt to experience each of these points as we go over them.

- First, grasp who you really are—this unadorned and unattached experience is free of any social context, story, or identity; and it also reveals that you are not an inner self-object.
- Then, grasp what you are, your true nature, and realize you are without element or location, and that your nature is a consciousness that transcends your "self."
- Realize that perceptive-experience is just an indirect phenomenon, and free yourself of being separate from objective reality—grasp the nature that is the same for absolute Now and absolute Consciousness (we take a more in-depth look into this in Part III). If you haven't done that, at least abide in a not-knowing silent-stillness until you do.
- Grasp a consciousness that is prior to and free of the distinction of you and not-you.
- Realize that since consciousness has no element, no quality whatsoever, the nature of existence cannot die because it never lived, and that you (and everything else) are of that nature.

If you can be directly conscious of all these elements, you can transcend life and death. A tall order for most perhaps, but doable, and now you have a roadmap to help you work on doing just that.

14:55 Although you might trust me and imagine I know what I'm talking about with all the assertions I've made throughout this book, if you don't prove this stuff for yourself by becoming conscious of whatever is true, the danger is then making it into a belief system, like a religion, and this is unacceptable. So take care if that is the case. Of course, you may simply have no idea what I'm talking about or think I'm nuts—a totally reasonable conclusion—then that obstacle won't be a problem. But I still invite you to consider these possibilities and contemplate to see where it goes.

Be complete in life, and absolute in death.

14:56 On the other hand, if you do realize what's said, or at least parts of it, the likelihood is that these will occur as insights and breakthroughs that confirm the truth of the assertions. But the drama of life is where you live, and so it will probably overwhelm your insights once life's drama takes hold again. No worries, that's natural.

14:57 You live where life occurs for you, and that is primarily within a social world. It is very unlikely that you're going to give that up. Perhaps it would be useful to have some way to remind yourself of, and keep you connected to, the truth when life takes over. Whether you do or not, know the truth is unchanged no matter how distracted by life you become. In addition to getting over yourself, a possible placeholder or reminder that could be used to ground you in at least lightening up about life and death is to simply remember a short version of William's quote:

Life is full of sound and fury signifying nothing.

14:58 Also, a paragraph from my book *Ending Unnecessary Suffering* might offer a useful perspective for this reminder effort:

> It is very useful to get that your mind is not always your best friend. Although it may be difficult to grasp and admit, it is powerful to acknowledge that in so many ways you're "fucked in the head." This simply means that your mind has been programmed to automatically generate an endless stream of suffering-causing activities. It is also very useful to create some humor around your suffering. Admitting you're fucked in the head should be a comedic act. If not, it's likely to just create more drama and cause suffering. Once you admit that your mind often goes down unfruitful roads, and you can laugh at your own folly, it gives you a lot more space to let go of this ridiculous behavior.

14:59 In life a sense of freedom from the binding qualities of survival, along with freedom from a resistance to death, is a completely different experience than almost any human attains. Once attained, however, we have transcended both life and death.

14:60 But already too many ideas have been proffered and words spoken—rather ironic for a book titled *Whereof One Cannot Speak*. Just grasp the real nature of consciousness—prior to but inclusive of you and not-you. If that doesn't happen, grasp the place that is silent, that has no thought or mental activity, and is completely and authentically itself—and contemplate a lot. In this way, you get closer to the truth without having to know or think anything. After all, all this life turmoil and drama is just sound and fury. The silence is constant, whether noticed or not.

14:61 **Guided Contemplation: Completing Life and Death**

Do you still harbor desires and hopes for some attainment "out there" that will make you whole? Can you get that there is nothing "out there" that will resolve the malady of your sense of being incomplete?

Can you allow yourself to exist here and now, without any concepts about having something missing or being incomplete? Get that without a social context you are already complete, because you just *are*.

Experience being complete right now.

Put your attention on your present perceptive-experience. Notice that it is created and dominated by self-survival, and lives within "for-me" perceptions. Work to transcend this domination of your experience, and experience existence for-itself.

Since sentient self and other are created together, the very experience of your existence and self-awareness exists within a social context. Notice the role that your internal dialogue and mind plays in maintaining a sense of self in relationship.

Now, imagine a world in which there are only objects—without the existence or possibility of others, now or ever. Notice that here no internal dialogue can exist, since there is no one to talk to. Use this to shift your experience outside of the social.

Eliminate a social context.

Look into this notion that you are a separate inner self-object. Can you find it? If not, consider that's because you are not an inner-object of any kind, material or immaterial. Make the body the only object of self. Take a moment to experience *being* your body and so perceiving from the body out. Notice that this eliminates the inner-self idea.

Without this inner-self, who are you? Can you be directly conscious of Who you are independent of a conceptual social context?

Get who you really are.

Eliminate the distinction of self and other (selves). What is left as experience when you do that?

Put your attention on absolute Now, grasp that it doesn't span time at all. Notice that this Now is the same as existence, and therefore the existence of you and consciousness. Use absolute Now to grasp that your nature also cannot span time, and that therefore you have no element, no location, and no substance. Can you get that this nature can't come or go, that it never began and can't end?

Grasp what you actually are, the real nature of existence.

Notice that the mere activity of perceptive-experience tends to suggest you are located behind perceptions. Can you see perception as an indirect meaningless phenomenon? Notice that perceptive-experience does not and cannot exist in absolute Now, and so can't be ultimately true, because perception demands process and is a form of knowing and so spans time. Grasp the nature that is prior to the activity of perception, which is absolute Now and absolute Consciousness.

Eliminate the distinction of you and not-you.

Grasp and abide in a consciousness that is free of both you and not-you, so that not-you is you, and you are not-you—there is no distinction. It is all of a nature, a consciousness-existence, that is not restricted to you but includes both you and not-you. Find this consciousness.

When all this is real for you, realize Consciousness-Existence is of a nature that has no location and exists in absolute Now; therefore, in this way, you are already free in life and of death. Is this real for you?

After you have worked through Part III you might want to come back and revisit this long guided contemplation. Your work in Part III should make a difference in contemplating these matters in more depth.

Part III

INFINITE EXISTENCE IS ABSOLUTE CONSCIOUSNESS

Becoming free of life and death eliminates you, but strangely this is still about you, isn't it? Going beyond the self, we can grasp a consciousness independent of both self and not-self and realize the absolute nature of existence. This section is devoted to that effort. Such deep consciousness will also serve you to let go of life and death in case you didn't quite manage it so far. This section is quite advanced, requiring even deeper consciousness than life and death—if you can believe it.

I'm sorry it took me so long to get down to brass tacks, but as you will see, these "brass tacks" are beyond easy comprehension. As we enter the beginning of the end of this presentation and begin to focus on the real truth of the matter, we get to the point of revelation: Colonel Mustard in the Parlor with a Candlestick. But even these revelatory clues are not easily deciphered, therefore the game continues, demanding further investigation. So gird your loins and get ready to contemplate even deeper!

Chapter Fifteen

CONSCIOUSNESS: KICKING ASS AND TAKING NAMES

The Power of the Not-You Reality

15:1 Sometimes people argue that everything that exists only exists in their experience, and then conclude that therefore they are the source and creator of all existence. A valid observation perhaps, but an erroneous conclusion. With this deduction the nature of not-you is overlooked. When the distinction of self and not-self is made, although self indeed creates your entire perceptive-experience, not-self has a significant say in the reality that you share with it. This is why there exists in your perceptions aspects over which you don't seem to have control, like objects and others.

15:2 Not-you has an incontestable say in what you experience as reality. When the distinction of self and not-self is made, not-self is as much a part of that reality as is the self, and clearly, the not-self is not controlled by the self. This creates a reality that is outside the self. This not-self is experienced by you in all sorts of ways, it is loved, feared, despised, ignored, and so on. But it is not controlled by you—although it is interpreted and related to by you.

15:3 This seems to be the reality in which we live, but what if no such distinction were made? We would then see not-self the same as self. But how would we experience or even imagine such a thing? It seems nearly impossible because our entire experience and perceptions are created through the distinction of self and not-self.

15:4 How can we approach such a shift in experience? First, we have to be willing to entertain the possibility of a consciousness beyond the experience of ourselves. Perhaps we could envision that although not-self is not what we experience as ourselves, it is still an aspect of existence and perhaps consciousness, and therefore, a consciousness of this existence can't be limited to the experiences of a self. So, within this quintessential existential-consciousness, not-self would be perceived to be the same as whatever was previously perceived as self, and self would be the same as not-self. We may still have a hard time imagining whatever that would be, and might think we would be one-with-everything or some such. But if "I am one with the universe" this still assumes the distinction of "I," and that makes it tricky, so let's look further.

15:5 I have mentioned that my take on the Lucifer myth is that it represents the self—ruling in a limited and isolated world rather than "serving" absolute reality. But in this consciousness the self would be eliminated or bypassed, and the absolute would be the only reality, and this absolute would be inclusive of all that is relative. To continue considering this matter, again embrace the possibility that a rock and you are the same thing. Still hard to accept or even imagine, isn't it? Yet, within this context, that would be the case.

15:6 I don't see how any of this can be heard as anything other than bullshit or as spiritual dribble. I don't support it being heard either way. So ask the question: Why assume a consciousness that is existence is the same as or only resides within your mind or is limited to yourself? When you think about it, such a limitation is kind of a ridiculous notion, isn't it? There is no reason consciousness has to be limited to you or to any self.

15:7 Normally we hold that self is the source of consciousness, that consciousness arises because of the self. But we are confusing cognition and perception with consciousness. Instead of the self generating consciousness, consider that consciousness creates the self. This is not only easily possible, it turns our consideration on its head.

15:8 You have no problem thinking consciousness resides within your awareness and experience, yet why stop there? Imagine that an object is also a form of consciousness. What form of consciousness could it be? Exactly that—exactly what it is and even how it is perceived. You attribute no awareness to an object and so assume it is not conscious—but again, you're confusing perceptive-awareness with consciousness.

15:9 An object may not have perception or awareness, but that doesn't mean it is not *of* consciousness, or is a form of consciousness. It is the unimaginably silent and selfless aspect of consciousness-existence. It is consciousness that is not self-serving, that is not self-referencing. It is the foundation for reality. In a way, once we get past our own arrogance and get over our obsession with ourselves, we might see objects as the best form of consciousness manifesting in the relative domain.

Objective reality is the unimaginably silent and selfless aspect of consciousness-existence.

15:10 I know this is an impossible possibility for people to consider. Experience seems to contradict such an assertion in a big way. But I invite you to consider it anyway. Consciousness is and always has been far beyond limitation and self-orientation. Again, be clear, the consciousness to which I am referring is the same thing as existence, including the infinite or absolute nature of existence. You can easily see that the limits of a self-mind can't embrace the "consciousness" of absolute existence, and existence must be outside of and not limited to a self's mental cognition or perceptive capacity. That is why I sometimes use the phrase "consciousness-existence." Keep remembering that here the nature of existence and consciousness are the same subject.

15:11 If we entertain the notion that consciousness is everything, however, what is this *everything* that we imagine? We are stuck thinking in relative terms, so when we imagine "everything" we might imagine lots of objects and space. Yet we hear that space, *ergo* objective reality, is infinite. Even intellectually considering the matter, we see that space has to be infinite, because no matter how far we go or how much we include, if it were finite it would have to stop somewhere, and then we must ask what is on the other side of where it stops? Our inability to grasp infinity makes our "everything" suspect, doesn't it?

15:12 The thing about infinity is it's absolute. That puts it out of bounds concerning our conception of relative "everything." Although it is inconceivable, consider the possibility that Infinity is the same as Nothing—that is how it works to contain everything and be infinite. Yet we also can't conceive of this absolute Nothing because it has no dimension, no space, no time, no objects, no distinctions, or anything else—and, paradoxically, isn't separate from anything. Therefore, Nothing is the only name I can come up with that refers to the absolute nature of existence itself.

15:13 Hard to understand, I know. This absolute Nothing, or absolute Consciousness, is beyond and inclusive of the distinction of you and not-you. In this way you are the same as not-you, and so you neither exist nor not exist. Instead, you are of a consciousness that includes you and not-you. Don't turn this consciousness into a notion like God, or some pie in the sky fantasy. Ground it in this reality occurring right now. OK, now that the stupid things have been said, let's get on with it.

15:14 Again, notice there is an aspect of not-you that is not controlled by your mind, as I said earlier: you have no choice but to succumb to the fact that a tree is not a car and a car is not water. You interpret them and can judge them, you can give value to or ignore them, but you can't change the fact they are not you or your mind.

15:15 But what if in some overlooked way what you experience as not-you is actually you? Strange-sounding possibility for sure, isn't it? Yet, consider if you didn't make the distinction of you and not-you, there would be no separation between the two, and so no two.

15:16 Of course you will still have a hard time imagining what would be the case without self and not-self because, as seen, all your perceived reality is based on this distinction and is determined through the lens of self. What's more, as asserted earlier, your entire language is based on this distinction and so everything said and thought via internal dialogue will inherently have the distinction within it. To entertain the possibility that consciousness is prior to and inclusive of you and not-you, you can't identify with or be limited to a perceptive-experience that is based on self and not-self.

15:17 In a normally perceived world you see objects as separate, and as a body you are separate from all other objects. Yet, remember, objects, including your body, are limited forms of this same ultimate existence. If existence is everything, why would we restrict existence to a self? As a body you are an aspect of existence, so you must share the same nature as existence—whatever that is. If you separate yourself by identifying with an immaterial self-object, it is still part of existence. But why imagine you are of another domain separate from objects and independent of physical existence? If you remove the idea that you are a unique and transcendent entity within existence, then you clearly are just one aspect of existence and so are of the same nature as everything.

15:18 How can you approach experiencing such a possibility? By becoming conscious that the Absolute—the foundation of all existence—is not separated in any way from anything. Here, there is no difference between self and other, you and not-you. They exist in the same place, so to speak, and only show up as separate when a distinction is made within experience. The nature of existence is clearly prior to and not limited to perceptive-experience of any kind, and therefore, here, there is no distinction of you and not-you, and so no separation.

15:19 From all this talk you might well imagine a different sort of world of perceptions emerging, or perhaps a transcendent consciousness floating around without perceptions. But consider, all that I'm saying is true now, within the very reality that you experience exactly as it is. Nothing needs to change, this nature and consciousness is already the case, you are just very likely ignorant of it. Trying to make everything disappear or some such is not only unnecessary, it is not a fruitful endeavor. Instead, grasp a consciousness that is already true and already beyond you and perception.

Self Is an Activity

15:20 As we set the stage for more, let's revisit the myth of self. We can see there are many activities a self does, but there is something even more existential that is overlooked. You likely still think of yourself as an entity and as real, existing in the universe on its own. I want you to entertain the notion that you actually don't exist as something at all. Instead, you exist as an activity.

15:21 Imagine that the very sense and experience that you have of "you" right now is actually an activity. It is something you are doing. Or more accurately, it is an activity that consciousness is doing. It's like squeezing your hand into a fist: if you are the sensation produced by this act, you can see that your existence as this sensation resides solely in the activity of the squeezing. No squeezing, no you.

15:22 It is as if consciousness is being squeezed into a limited form of self and mind, contracting into the sensation and distinction of a self. You *are* this squeezing. Perhaps we could say that you are *doing* the squeezing, and in this doing you are *being* that activity. Start by seeing if you can feel or sense that this is happening.

15:23 You exist as an activity. A strong and persistent activity perhaps, but an activity nevertheless. Since you identify with a self, you are committed to the persistence of that self. If this is an activity, as I assert, then you are committed to continuing that activity. If this activity stops, so do you.

15:24 It's clear you are committed to survival, and you maintain life by engaging the physical activities to do that, such as breathing, eating, avoiding danger, and interacting with others and the environment. But, for the most part, these are activities you willfully direct your body to do. Even though you might adhere to the popular notion that self is a soul or independent entity, you still do these things because you reside within the body and so need it to stay alive in order for you to persist, but you may still feel detached from being the body itself.

15:25 Just so, you also maintain lots of mental activities. No matter what they are, they are rather constant because their presence is necessary to maintain the sense of an inner-self or self-mind, which you identify as you, and within which you seem to exist.

15:26 Although you don't know you are responsible for activities such as perception and interpretation, they are also created by you through automatically relating everything to yourself. Even if you acknowledge that such activities are a result of the existence of self and self-survival, you still aren't in touch with doing them, since being conscious of what's going on with all these activities is not your job, doing them is.

15:27 Just so, you aren't in touch with doing the self either. To be clear, when I say self is an activity, I mean the very experience of being a self—no matter what that is—not what self does. The simple experience of self is an activity being done, not an existential fact observed.

15:28 Dwell on the sensation and notion of being a self, and grasp that this is an *activity* not an object, nor is it inherently real. It arises to serve a purpose. No activity, no you. How does this assertion change your experience of yourself? If it is something being done, it can also not be done. Consider it.

A Joy That Is Hard to Come By

15:29 I have been trying to share something incredible that could easily be missed, as it's buried in a lot of material. I really don't want it to be missed, it is the most important aspect of this whole book. But there is no way to share this consciousness directly, and yet the joy, humor, and happiness that are available with this depth of consciousness are too good not to give it a try. As you've seen so far, it's possible to make headway with most of this material, even if in the end it is up to you to make the final leap into a consciousness that is generally unavailable to people and is literally inconceivable to the human mind.

15:30 My commitment is to what's true, not to what a mind can conceive. Therefore, you must create, or at least entertain, the possibility that consciousness and becoming conscious are not limited to mental conception. Still, I want to continue attempting to convey the very nature of existence. Not just the existence of you, which usually gets all the attention, but the existence of anything and everything. There is a huge paradox in all this, yet if we chip away at the edges of this paradox perhaps we can lessen the leap needed to square this contradiction and enigma.

15:31 The following sub-sections are really an exercise, a guided contemplation of stuff, most of which has already been asserted in various forms. But since there is so much to say in this whole "guided contemplation," I will put it into the form of prose instead of an exercise. Although much of what's to follow has been said already, hear what's to come as an opportunity to contemplate and really experience it—find the consciousness of which I speak. Without trying to tempt you with fantastic claims, I do want to repeat that once freed of the normal human restrictions in experience, an unbelievable joy lights up the heart. This may only relate to the relative and to the self, but hey, such joy is hard to come by. It is beyond anything I've ever experienced so far—and I've experienced some really great stuff. In order to approach this consciousness, your first job is to get rid of yourself.

Beyond the Self

15:32 Once we can lighten up on our obsessive focus and worship of our selves, we have room to look at this in a more objective way. If we are open to considering reality outside or beyond ourselves and our experience, we might be able to see that our experience is limited and based on overlooked assumptions. Most of this sub-section is a review and deepening of assertions already made. Study it and contemplate to deepen your genuine experience of what's said. For example, we have already seen that most life-forms have no "self," therefore life doesn't automatically produce a self, and self is not necessary for life to exist.

15:33 Despite the fact we spend all our time on and devote all our attention to ourselves in one way or another, we actually know precious little about the reality or nature of this self. We've seen that we refer to self as that inner activity only we are privy to. This leads to the assumption that we are located inside our heads. Yet, we observe that we don't actually directly perceive this, we just assume and conclude it is the case. But I have asserted that's not true. Although this may be sinking in by now, it might still be hard to get past.

15:34 So, let's re-think this matter. When you run is running an object? No. Your body is an object but the running is an activity. When you have a thought, a concept, is the concept an object? No. It's brain activity, and just like the running, it's neither an object nor necessary. So, for the umpteenth time, where is this unfound self-object?

15:35 It doesn't exist. Self is a product of brain activity, it is not an object, nor is it existentially real. Consider, the brain engages a sophisticated array of activities that produce many concepts, and this function has evolved to create many abstract and imaginary concepts as well. From this activity the idea of a source that is separate from the body is created, and a self is born. Without the activity that produces the distinction of self, and therefore an experience of self, the self doesn't exist. The self is a distinction. Without making this distinction no self exists. This is a huge shift in our accepted reality, isn't it? But what if it's true?

15:36 We've seen that we thought consciousness was a function of mind, yet consciousness existed before any creature ever drew breath. We misunderstand the real nature of consciousness and limit it to mental functions. But if we expand our notion to consider that consciousness transcends all limitation, we can view this matter differently. In this case, we see that self is not the source of consciousness; instead, consciousness is the source of self!

15:37 If this is so, it alters the context in which we hold both consciousness and self, and it becomes possible to eliminate the self without ending consciousness or even perceptive awareness. Such a realization radically changes our notion of consciousness. Yet in order to get that consciousness is creating self, we have to create a new possibility about the nature of consciousness. We must open up to the notion that consciousness is the source of all existence. This is a radical change in how we hold consciousness.

15:38 Normally, you keep an obsessive and automatic focus on your self that dominates every moment of experience. You are always the central aspect of reality and relate everything to and through this self. Yet, consciousness transcends this very self. When you finally get beyond yourself, so that this self distinction is not the dominant operating principle for experience, a new consciousness can emerge.

15:39 Remember, the apparently unassailable experience and seemingly existential reality of self only exists within the distinction that divides all perception into you and not-you. This distinction is not necessary. Eliminating the distinction of self and not-self is possible and recommended.

15:40 To be sure, as you attempt such a shift, notice that very likely it is "you" that is attempting it, and so it will still be based on "you" trying to be conscious beyond the self. Which won't work since you are still the central aspect of all experience. Consider this consciousness is independent of you and is not restricted to your mind or your perceptive-experience. The distinction of you and not-you needs to be dropped—or, if you prefer, "transcended." To be clear, nothing needs to change, the true nature of existence is already true, even when you and not-you exist. Simply drop the notion that this distinction is set in stone or is an observation of reality. It's not.

15:41 You should be able to at least imagine that the ultimate nature of consciousness, or existence, can't be restricted to the experience or mind of a self. Clearly, true and direct consciousness must be independent of the limitations of a self. As mentioned several times, conventionally, it seems the self is the only source for consciousness, that what arises into the mind and perceptions generates consciousness, without which it can't exist. But, as I've asserted, it is the other way around: consciousness is that in which the distinction of self and not-self can even be made.

15:42 Further, consider that this consciousness-existence is the source of the biological activity that allows a self to arise, as well as the source of the objective reality that allows space and objects to exist. Yet, you don't need to grasp the nature of biological life or of objects to get past the distinction of sentient self and other, and to abide in a consciousness independent of an obsessive focus on the self-experience and one that is not limited to a self-orientation. This provides a freedom unthinkable from the self-viewpoint.

15:43 But if you go further and eliminate the distinction of self and not-self (objective reality), you find a consciousness free of self-referencing, and a "oneness" with even objects and their inherent and silent wisdom. For this to sink in, entertain the possibility that everything you experience—as self, mind, perception, others, and objects—are all limited forms of consciousness sharing the same nature as absolute existence. Although the self doesn't exist as anything but an activity, you are still a form of consciousness. But before you pat yourself on the back too hard, remember, a rock is a form of consciousness as well—that should assist in modifying your view of you and consciousness.

15:44 As I keep asserting, not only are sentient-self and sentient-other limited forms of consciousness, even objects are a form of consciousness. I know this seems like a bridge too far, but you're not asked to stop perceiving or experiencing anything—since it is all consciousness already, just in limited forms—simply grasp what the nature of it all is.

15:45 Remember, we're talking about the nature of existence, therefore, this consciousness is the same as existence, nothing is left out. Perhaps objects are not a form of consciousness that manifests as awareness, but they are the selfless and silent form of consciousness that allows for the universe—the relative world—to exist. Standing on this possibility, or realization, get that you are a very limited aspect of this consciousness, and then let go of the myth of your "self."

15:46 Of course, given that life and especially social life continues to remain the context for experience, a self will remain an available and probably constant activity and distinction in order to relate to an invented social life. But you don't have to believe it is real—it is just a tool. You can see it for what it is and not identify with it. Remember the tale of Nasruddin making this point?

How are you?
Perfect, thank you. I'm traveling incognito.
Oh? As what are you disguised?
I am disguised as myself.
Don't be silly. That's no disguise. That's what you are.
On the contrary, it must be a very good disguise,
for I see it has fooled you completely.
Sufi Mullah Nasruddin

15:47 Perhaps the realization of a consciousness outside the distinction of self and not-self will be temporary and infrequently visited, but it should be real and contribute a new perspective from which to think and view. It provides a freedom that influences the continued use of self as a tool in order to participate in life. In this way, if such consciousness is repeatedly visited, or at least remembered, it assists in getting beyond identifying with the self. Therefore, the self clearly becomes something you are doing, rather than something you are being. (Also, it allows for a huge increase in humor. I tend to laugh a lot whenever I engage this reality.) Consider that you and not-you are invited to this depth of consciousness.

Get Over Yourself!

15:48 One catchy phrase I like, that works on many levels, is "get over yourself." This can be heard in various ways, but the power of it is easily overlooked. In a conventional social setting it is usually used as a put-down said to someone who seems to be arrogant and full of themselves. But what I'm pointing at here goes much deeper than a mere put-down.

15:49 As seen, we keep constant attention on ourselves no matter what is experienced. No matter what disposition we adopt, the self is always the centerpiece. So, to create some space outside this oppressive focus, we can use such a statement to help wrench away our obsessive focus on ourselves, at least temporarily.

15:50 Take a look. Isn't your attention always on yourself one way or another? Aren't you always there, always a part of your experience, even if only as the one doing the experiencing? Everything perceived or experienced in any way is related to you. Everything in every moment is really about you. "Getting over yourself" is about transcending the entire dynamic of this self-focus, as well as going further to actually eliminate the distinction of being a self.

15:51 This is clearly a novel idea. No one thinks they can do it because *they* are the essential ingredient in all experience, and life is really all about them. You probably think it is impossible to stop being a self, that it just can't be done. Try as you might you find no way to undo your self-focus because you are the one trying not to focus on yourself. But you are looking at it in the wrong way. No worries, everyone does. No one knows they aren't a self or that self is a distinction being made by consciousness.

15:52 Even when someone has an enlightenment experience, they will still say, *"I" know what I am* or *"I" know what life is,* or some such. Even this direct consciousness—which is actually independent of the self-activity—will still be related to the self when the mind gets hold of it. Experience always seems to orient around "I" no matter what it's about.

15:53 Ultimately, to get over yourself is to eliminate the distinction of you and not-you. Then what remains is a consciousness without you and without a separation between you and not-you, or between you and the objective world. Sound impossible? It's not. But you have to start by getting over yourself.

15:54 People are solidly stuck within this self and not-self world. It may seem impossible to drop, but it's best not to start by fighting with yourself, struggling to make self and not-self disappear. First, just let them be, and grasp a consciousness that is prior to or exists independent of this division.

15:55 Perhaps as an analogy, it's like reading these words right now. You know that language is a human invention and without it you not only can't read these words, they cannot be seen as words. But because you have created and so thoroughly adopted language it seems impossible to see these markings as anything but words. Even if you work hard to jumble them and make them nonsensical, in the background you likely still hold there's language happening here.

15:56 So, to get free of language, instead of trying to eliminate it from your experience, simply grasp that it is an invention and not existentially real or necessary. Be conscious of the fact that you are creating it, and how you are creating it, and so become conscious of a reality that is prior to language completely. Not just as an idea but as a consciousness that influences your experience in such a way that even as you acknowledge the miracle that language is, you also transcend it in that same moment.

15:57 Remember there was a time in your life when you didn't have language, and words did not exist. There was also a time when self didn't exist, but this reality tends to be overlooked. It isn't difficult to imagine that even after birth something existed before you ever became aware of a you. In the domain of life and "being," clearly some form of consciousness was occurring before you came to experience being a self. Just so, if you can create a self, you can also eliminate it. Consciousness is not limited to the self. So when you "get over yourself" you move toward eliminating both self and not-self.

Your Better Half

15:58 If you identify with consciousness taking the form of perception and experience—formerly attributed to being an exclusive function of the self—as well as consciousness that is objective reality, consider that you might say objects are the best part of you because they balance out that aspect of consciousness that takes the form of entity or self, and so free consciousness from a self-centered focus. Since the entire world has revolved completely around self and self-survival, this "surrender" to *being* objective existence, as well as awareness, is a dramatic shift in experience and identity.

15:59 Still, prior to such unconditional consciousness taking place, it's hard to imagine what would be experienced without self and not-self. We might think that some new experience should arise where our selves disappear or are inaccessible, but let's play this out in a different way. As I say:

Consciousness doesn't make you stupid.

15:60 What I mean by that is an increase in consciousness doesn't make anything that you can do or know now disappear or become inaccessible. If you can make a distinction now, you can make that distinction after grasping a consciousness far removed from it, even if you recognize that the distinction is unreal and unnecessary. Perhaps some distinctions or activities, like certain attitudes, perspectives, mental states, assumptions, and whatnot, might cease to be something you generate because you see them as untrue, ineffective, or not useful. But that doesn't mean you are unable to do them, you just don't want to.

15:61 Of course, in this new consciousness, if the self-distinction is eliminated or placed on the back burner, self would not be the source of or center for perceptive-experience. Perception can still occur, and everything experienced now can still be experienced then; nothing has to change except the depth of consciousness about the nature of it all. Once done, however, your overall experience does change because now there is a new context in which things are held—seeing you and objects as sharing the same nature certainly changes how you experience both—but the perceived content doesn't have to change or disappear.

15:62 Consider my assertion that consciousness occurs in many forms—as an entity and as an object, as mind and as perception—that these are all forms of consciousness. Therefore nothing need change, except for eliminating the obsessive focus on the self and constant self-referencing. The activity that produced the assumption of self can still exist, all the while knowing self isn't real or necessary. That's an increase in consciousness, not a change in conditions.

15:63 The consciousness that arises as awareness and perception still occurs, as do creatures and objects. But all these forms of consciousness are seen as the same consciousness. Distinctions may be being made within it, but there is no separation. Everything is the same consciousness no matter what it is. To be clear, I'm not saying your mind is conscious of everything that exists or is possible, I'm saying that the very existence of objects, space, mind, awareness, and so on *is* consciousness, that their very nature and existence is that. It is all the same substance and reality.

15:64 So, identifying exclusively as a self-activity may be gone or set aside, but whatever that function served is still one aspect of this consciousness. Another aspect of this same consciousness is the objective consciousness formally known as objects. This consciousness doesn't need objective distinctions, and whether they occur or not is irrelevant.

15:65 Yet whatever an object is perceived to be, its essence is simply that non-sentient, silent, completely selfless, and immovable aspect of consciousness that arises as objective existence. This consciousness contains the limited form of consciousness that used to be called objects, as much as it does what used to be called you. Falling into being all of existence, including "yourself that is not a self," is a huge shift in experience as well as consciousness.

Friend, our closeness is this:
anywhere you put your foot, feel me
in the firmness under you.
Rumi

15:66 So you can see that the "get over yourself" principle goes very deep. It can be applied to foster various experiences and insights. Getting over yourself ranges from the simple act of not focusing obsessively on yourself to not being limited to a self/not-self reality and becoming conscious of the true nature of existence.

You Have to Go

15:67 Obviously, the path being suggested demands that you challenge the very existence and reality of yourself. This is not to say that you generate the notion of a higher self or true self that you can jump to, replacing your current self experience. Instead, it is getting rid of you altogether. Strange as it might sound, you are in the way and need to go. Yet, no one wants to entertain not being anymore—that's death—but this is what needs to happen. Therefore, you need to let go of yourself while alive.

15:68 Again, I'm not inviting you to war with yourself or try to make yourself disappear. Such activities would still be based on "you," and so such efforts would fail, because in this way you would remain the main focus and central orienting principle. Instead, I invite you to realize you are already not real, that you already don't exist. Or to say it another way, you are not an object, nor are you existentially or inherently real. You're an activity and a distinction, and this activity and distinction do not have to occur. Any activity can stop and any distinction can not be made, or at least be recognized as more like a thought than a reality. This is so for you.

15:69 Consider it. Dwell on your experience of being you, and try to grasp that it is just an activity generating a sense that you exist. Now eliminate the distinction of you and not-you. Again, I'm not asking you to try to eliminate perceptive-experience either, but to imagine perception is simply happening as a function of the body, not as a function of you—it's more like you are a function of it. Instead, eliminate the idea and sense that you exist as a self that is separate from everything not it. What happens in your experience when you do that?

15:70 Even now, most people will still think this impossible. Without the distinction of you and not-you, *you* don't get to exist—or at least are put on the back burner as an unnecessary activity. Your reactions to this are still likely to be in the domain of confusion, disbelief, and impossibility. It's not even something you want, and more than that, it's not seen as something you can do, and again, why would you want to? This is a natural reaction because your whole life and entire experience have been lived and based upon you and devoted to your survival. Where in this is any room for even the notion of getting rid of yourself? There is none.

15:71 If such a notion can gain no traction because your experience screams the opposite reality, how can you punch a hole in this perspective? First, you may want to take another look at some basic assumptions upon which such a stance is taken. For example, without thinking about it you probably still assume that the self is the source of consciousness, that without self there is no consciousness. Yet, in this case, what is being talked about as consciousness?

15:72 Again, we think consciousness is found in our thinking, cognition, awareness, perception, intellect, and so on. These activities fall into the category of "consciousness" for us, and they all seem to relate to the self, and perhaps arise because of the self. Yet, what if it's the other way around, and self is not the source but rather a product of consciousness through such vehicles?

15:73 It is just an assumption and conclusion that has us believe self is the source of mental activities and that these activities constitute consciousness. Consider instead that these activities are producing self, rather than self producing the activities. The self distinction occurs and is made real because of and by these conceptual activities. This can be hard to experience, so contemplate the matter.

15:74 If you can get this, then it's possible to eliminate this assumption and distinction, and so the self that's generated from it, isn't it? This makes eliminating your "self" accessible. Simply experience that you are already unreal and don't really exist, except as a distinction that divides up everything into you and not-you. You exist because of an activity. If you see that this activity is unnecessary, you also see that you don't need to exist. Without you getting in the way, consciousness can expand to include absolutely everything.

Chapter Sixteen
BEYOND TIME AND SPACE

The No-Self Reality

16:1 To continue pushing past the myth of self, again, get in touch with the fact that the inner-self lacks any objective substance and doesn't exist except as a thought or an activity. Then, acknowledge the power and reality of objects, and entertain the view that the objective world is held as the most real domain of existence—and is possibly the best manifestation of consciousness.

16:2 Again, this turns our normal view of life on its head, doesn't it? We usually adore the self and pooh-pooh mere objects as insignificant. Here I'm inviting you to consider the opposite. That would mean you are unimportant and perhaps non-existent, and objects are better than you, perhaps "sacred" like you used to be. Weird turn-around, isn't it? Does it ruffle your ego-feathers?

16:3 In any case, how could this be true? Obviously, objects are just dumb things, they have no sentience or awareness and can't do a damn thing but sit there. Whereas you have awareness and are active and complex, and you use objects, bending them to your will without a whimper from the objects. So aren't you superior? Seems that way, at least in your world, doesn't it?

16:4 Perhaps such a leap or huge change in perspective could use a bit more explanation. Let's back up and consider again the animal that we are. We seem superior to other animals that don't have our intellectual problem-solving ability. Of course, as seen in the book *Ending Unnecessary Suffering,*[3] this ability has led to a great deal of suffering that those "lesser" creatures don't have, so our superiority might not be as valid as we think or assume it to be. To access a consciousness beyond the norm—which means beyond the self—we need to stick a crowbar between our self-experience and the truth of existence, and pry self away from continuing to dominate our consideration.

16:5 Let me re-introduce the overarching assertion that all of existence is absolute consciousness, since such an assertion gives us a very different way to relate to both self and body. This huge leap in the argument leaves our taken-for-granted experience and reality in the dust. Why should we entertain such an outrageous assertion? It sounds really stupid and impossible, or it might just sound like a fantasy that we simply want to be true. But, again, we don't want to go down the road of desire and fantasy as we're wont to do.

16:6 The greatest danger with this new assertion is to jump to the same conclusion humanity has invented in many ways for a long time: the idea of an independent and divine self. First, it may still be challenging to grasp that there is nothing that is the self, that it is simply an activity of the body, and the body is "consciousness" being an animal, just a sack of cells really—one that in our case generates the idea of a self. *That* may be conceivable, but now I'm asserting that the body is of a nature that is inconceivable, that the body is somehow consciousness itself. This is not how we have come to think on this matter. We continue to struggle with the question: How can objective existence be consciousness?

16:7 We don't grasp that consciousness doesn't "exist," it *is* existence. Sounds like just weird word play, doesn't it? But it's only seen as weird word play

[3]Peter Ralston, *Ending Unnecessary Suffering* (Inner Traditons, 2025).

because within our cognition and awareness we can't conceive of such a thing. Still, how can there be a distinction between existing and existence? If something is existence itself, how can it not exist? Seems paradoxical, but this isn't our first encounter with paradox.

16:8 If consciousness is existence, and neither absolute consciousness nor infinite existence exists, what are we talking about?! Perhaps I should clarify my use of these words. Again, we confuse consciousness with cognition and experience. We limit consciousness to what we can think or perceive. But it's not too hard to realize that our experience and mind are limited and so not capable of easily grasping anything outside that domain. And clearly the nature of existence can't be restricted to our own limited self-mind and its conceptions.

16:9 If existence is consciousness, it too can't be limited to this self-domain. Existence "is" and *is* just is, it is infinite and absolute. Therefore it can't be anything at all, it can't be limited to the distinctions that we make and perceive. Get it?

16:10 Remember, "is" is the context for existence, not—as we assume—what's in it. As a way to think of it, imagine infinite empty space versus all the objects that reside within that space. We can see that space exists whether anything fills it or not. Something existing, like an object, doesn't in any way change the existence of space. This might give you an idea why I say consciousness doesn't exist, it is existence. Absolute consciousness and absolute existence are the same thing, and neither is limited, and so can't be anything at all.

16:11 Why do I say infinite and absolute existence can't be anything at all? That just sounds like another stupid thing I'm saying, doesn't it? Again, how can existence not exist? We have touched on this before, so perhaps it's good to remember the uncarved block and infinite space. I know these make sense to some degree, but we still can't conceive the reality that there must be nothing here, so it bears revisiting. If there is no limit, no boundary, no distinction, where is this existence? If it is absolute, how could it be something, because if it exists in any way it is relative. Perhaps understanding this is still a bridge too far; if so, keep it simmering on the back burner as we proceed.

16:12 The truth is, although everything we think, perceive, and experience in any way is a limited form of consciousness, these activities can't access within themselves the nature of the very consciousness they are a part of. The absolute nature of existence is ... well ... absolute. That means it isn't any one thing or all things. It is the nature of everything that exists in any way or doesn't exist in any way. Is your contemplation starting to get pointed in that direction?

16:13 What if self, body, and objects are all just forms of an existence or consciousness that is absolute? Here, existence and non-existence are the same thing. In a sense we might say that consciousness is "doing" existence, and existence is "doing" consciousness. Such a statement helps us relate this assertion to the world we know because here it is all doing or activity, inventions and distinctions—which, of course, are themselves forms of consciousness. But it's more accurate to say consciousness *is* existence and vice versa.

Existence without Movement

16:14 As we proceed, we'll continue to move through some unconventional but grounded possibilities about our reality that may help us get a better handle on this. To start this aspect of our ongoing contemplation, put your attention back on objects. What is the most basic aspect of objective existence?

16:15 Normally, our response to such a question would relate to what we perceive and how we interpret stuff based on our own self-survival. This all occurs solely through activities. Yet, we can imagine that whatever existence is, it begins as just what-is without any movement or activity. After all, for something to move it has to exist first, right? And movement isn't what's there, it is an activity or process occurring in what's there. So begin contemplating the nature of existence—unknown at this point—as completely still, unmoving, and existing only in this moment—a world of absolute unmoving "is" without activity.

16:16 It may be nearly impossible to imagine this, but when we consider an atom or molecule—holding them as rudimentary to objective existence—we see we are already dependent upon movement. Particles whizzing around with negative or positive charges make these building blocks for matter possible. But in our non-moving existence even these atoms can't happen. There can be no process or activity here and no span of time because time demands change and change demands movement. So what is the nature of this original existence?

16:17 We don't seem to be able to find what's prior to objective matter. But it seems it would have to be an absolute, doesn't it? In the relative world, because matter is composed of movement, we've no idea what the nature of "is" is absent of the activities necessary to create objective existence. We are all familiar with Einstein's assertion of $E=mc^2$, which is simply saying mass or objects are "energy," or are mass moving very fast. This punches a hole in our thinking about objects, and we are still unable to grasp what energy is any more than we can grasp what objects are. Yet, it seems this reality is based on activity and so time. Since time seems to be at the heart of this business of movement and change, perhaps we should look some into the nature of time.

The No-Time Enigma

16:18 Let's visit a crib-notes version of absolute now—which we will go into in detail soon—and grasp that real now doesn't span time. It can't span time since if it did it wouldn't be now, would it? Spanning time, no matter how short the interval, would exist as a bunch of "nows" stacked next to each other and so couldn't be actual now—there is only one now. Instead, it would be a process, and since all perception only occurs through process, we grasp that absolute Now can't be perceived.

16:19 What we experience as now is a process. It is simply the most immediate process we can manage in order to perceive occurring conditions, and this is what we call now. Therefore, now is seen as what is unfolding in perceptive-experience that seems to be whatever's occurring "in the present," and yet this is not actually now.

16:20 When we make a distinction between experience and concept, we understand that experience only occurs in present time. Since memory is a concept (past), and extrapolation and imagination are also concepts (future), they can't be experiences, and so whatever they are conceiving isn't actually what is. Future and past, which are necessary for the idea of time, are concepts, not objective realities. Neither the past nor future is occurring now, meaning they are not actually occurring—except in imagination—and aren't objectively real.

16:21 If we become increasingly rigorous we can tighten this "now" span of time into smaller and smaller segments, and this will seem to be more and more immediate. But no matter how small we make it, it still spans time. So, we need to make a distinction between relative-now and absolute-now.

16:22 Relative-now is what we experience as occurring in our immediate perception. It is a span of time but a small and immediate span of time relating to our experience as it is occurring within life "presently." It is the smallest amount of time we can manage to reduce the process of perception and recognition to what we call the present. Absolute now, on the other hand, is real now, actual existence. Absolute now doesn't span time and so is imperceptible to the senses, because perception demands process and process takes time—no matter how short the span. Do you understand the difference between relative-now and absolute-now?

16:23 We should also make a distinction between what's immediately experienced, what we call present time, and how we hold time as if it exists outside the present, and in which now is just one small moment in a string of moments on an infinite line. This latter distinction of time is actually not real. It is a context or a way of holding conceptually experienced reality.

16:24 When we notice that it is always now, and that we never leave now, we begin to see that we were wrong about time. Now is the only place experience and life exist, it is not just a small moment among many small moments, it is THE moment and always has been. This changes how we see now, doesn't it?

16:25 Instead of assuming time, as if existence comes in bite-size pieces lined up in a row, imagine there is no time. Again, it is always now—this is usually overlooked, but when pointed out you can see that it is true. Your experience never leaves now. The only reason you invent time is because the experience of now goes through changes. Circumstance and conditions change but never leave now. Because you perceive changes in conditions and can conceptually remember and imagine conditions that aren't what you are currently perceiving, you invent time.

16:26 Yet, existence is always now, there is no time. Think about it. Where does time exist? Concept—which occurs now—invents time. But time doesn't have to exist, any more than an inner self, language, or mind do. Time is an invention, perhaps a useful one for many reasons, but an invention nevertheless.

Time does not exist - we invented it. The distinction between the past, present, and future is only a stubbornly persistent illusion.

Albert Einstein

16:27 Since experience occurs as process, it is easy to see it as a function of time. Yet, this so-called experience of time is really just changes occurring now. Because change occurs, it seems that one thing leads to another and so we call these changes "time." Yet, it is simply now going through changes. Study it.

16:28 Do you get this? Now never goes away. What is called time is observing changes occurring in the most immediate perception of now, and remembering changes not occurring and imagining changes that haven't occurred and so creating a past and future.

16:29 You never actually experience anything outside of or leave now at all. Stuff just changes in your perceptive-experience. The real error is then conceptualizing the idea of a time that doesn't exist, or "nows" that don't exist. These are called past and future, but they are made up completely of concepts. We live inside this imagined world as if it's real and we are traveling along inside it.

16:30 As an analogy, consider it is like being in a room called Now, and in this room the experience of now keeps changing. You never get out of the room—it is existence and is always the case. Given you have conceptual ability, you can remember changes not occurring now, and these are called memories, creating a domain called the past, with the idea that there are rooms you passed through that exist on the other side of one of the walls of the room of now. You can't perceive these "past" rooms, but you can imagine them and recall them, and so you think they are still there somehow.

16:31 You also imagine changes to come, and this is called the future. It is usually easier to get that the future is just concept because it hasn't happened yet, you haven't entered those rooms that are on the opposite wall of the room of now. You are extrapolating from the "past" and imagining more changes will come, and thus you will leave the now-room and enter future rooms.

16:32 This may seem a reasonable analogy fitting our idea of time, but what's overlooked is all this is done now and will always be done now. It is only concept that makes it seem like there is anything outside the room of now. Continuing and expanding our "now-room" analogy, drop the concepts that generate the idea of time having a past and future, and see everything as simply changes occurring now. There are no other rooms—that is an illusion!

16:33 Watch some movement occurring—perhaps move your hand and watch that movement. You see it is still now and you remember perceiving something you aren't perceiving now (concept) and so imagine time. But notice it is all in the same room of now—the seeing and the concept—and what is occurring are just changes in what you perceive.

16:34 Grasp the reality that you are always inside the room of now, existence only exists now. Life never occurs in any other place but now, and although life depends on changes, all these changes occur in relative-now. Beyond the immediately perceived world that seems to be occurring, we still have the absolute to deal with.

16:35 Having grasped that the room of now is always what is, eliminate every wall of this room and allow Now to include infinity. Remember, infinity is an absolute and has no substance or end. Embracing this paradox might help you see how the apparent incompatibility between perceived changes in relative-now and the stillness of real-now can co-exist.

16:36 To go further, consider, if all conditions occurred at once (recall the uncarved block), then where would time be? If infinite conditions all existed in real now, there would be no time. We'd have to pull out a distinct condition from infinity in order to perceive it, and this would create a comparison to whatever it is not, and so we'd conceptually compare one distinct condition with anything not-it. From this we create time. But what if it were all infinite and now? Then time would clearly be seen as an invention to create process, and yet the whole context of time as a past, present, and future could easily be seen as an unnecessary conceptual invention.

16:37 This means the perception of one condition being different from another doesn't require the invention of time to separate them. Both are occurring within the same now because this now is infinite and absolute, and what we perceive and conceive as time is as if contained within this now, not vice versa. Can you see all perceptive-experience as occurring now, just appearing as changing distinctions, and this change builds the idea of time that really doesn't exist, except as a concept?

16:38 I know it can be very difficult to grasp this point, but it's not impossible. To help the mind find some experience related to letting go of time, consider being a rock. You imagine the rock doesn't seem to change, and any change that might occur is so slow as to be impossible to discern. So, as this rock, the only thing going on in your "experience" is existence, not time. Even if any change occurs, it is simply what is so now and nothing else; it is not compared to any other form or condition and so it is only existence now. This brings us back to our notion of existence without movement. In this case, without perceivable change.

16:39 With such a shift in perspective, we can do away with the abstract long-term context of time and instead grasp that our experience is only occurring now. One thing this does is alter our view of now from a small fleeting moment in time to the only place for anything to exist, and so now becomes an essential aspect for all experience, turning it from a small insignificant moment to an infinite and absolute that includes all reality and all time. Quite a shift, isn't it?

16:40 In any case, this shift can make a difference in how one lives and experiences life in relative-now. For example, there is a reason we use the phrase "sleeping like a baby." Imagine the baby has little or no time, they only have experience unfolding in the moment. Therefore, although they are growing and are working out many things, their brain is not troubled by the slew of stress-causing mental activities that are dependent on time, such as worry, fear, ambition, longing, desire, resentment, disappointment, and many more, since these can only be generated through the conceptual invention of time. The baby's lack of disturbance likely relates directly to having no concept of time.

16:41 How can this same shift apply to your experience of life? It is possible to experience life now, getting that changes are occurring now, and never leave now, rather than live within an imaginary conceptual construct of time as if it's real. Such a shift is still relative, but it works to get closer and closer to the immediacy of existence. If we make the jump from the relative to the absolute, we can grasp the real nature of Now. This nature *is* existence, and existence is Now. With such a leap we get a little closer to being able to realize the essential nature of consciousness or existence, and grasp that they are the same. Revisiting the analogy of the uncarved block might help us here.

Revisiting the Uncarved Block

16:42 For us, consciousness is stuck in our own mental and perceptive capacities, and these know nothing about the real nature of anything, including consciousness itself or objective existence. Being restricted to perceptive-experience, we can only access objective existence from the "outside," so to speak, and therefore as not-us. Yet, not-us only exists within our experience, even though we rightly imagine there is more to it than what we perceive. We've looked beyond self and time, and yet we are still stuck in self and time via perceptive-experience. So how can we relate to this limitation effectively?

16:43 If we revisit the uncarved block analogy, perhaps we can make some sense out of this. As we know, the uncarved block represents infinite existence in its original state. The carving of the block is making distinctions and so creating finite boundaries within the block, and therefore creating separate things and a relative world. I use this analogy to point out that the real nature of both the uncarved block and the carving is exactly the same.

16:44 We can see that once distinctions are made, we have created separate things, and so, when it comes to life, one thing can perceive another, but only from an outside encounter of the thing, not the nature of the thing. Even though what's true about the nature or substance of existence is like the uncarved block, the world of experienced-existence is only known through the form of perceptive-cognition.

16:45 Therefore, this world is something we are doing *and* something done to us! Grasping this directly is difficult because our whole perception and experience of reality and life start with us. By that I mean, it starts by creating the distinction of self and not-self. So when we see that everything we experience—which is everything—is a function of us and so something done by us, this is only one side of the coin.

16:46 We also experience a not-us, and this not-us eludes our control and is clearly independent of our will. Even though it only shows up in our experience, we have no choice but to conform to it as outside of mind and self as it directs our perceptions. We may be able to ignore, tweak, project, and bias our interpretation of what's perceived, but we can't stop it from pushing its own existence upon us. This is because in the world of self and not-self, the not-self is that aspect of consciousness that is NOT self.

16:47 Yet if we go beyond being limited to self and not-self, we might be able to see everything as the same consciousness, at least as the same existence. To do that, however, we must get free of this dominant self-orientation, and being stuck solely in the carving, *ergo* perceptions. If we shift what we identify with from a separation within the uncarved block to the substance of the block—which everything shares as its real nature—we would identify with all of it, wouldn't we? To grasp the real nature of this existence, though, we must become conscious of what is prior to time and space. This can be done by grasping absolute Now.

Using Absolute Now to Help Grasp Absolute Consciousness

16:48 To continue pounding away, attempting to pry open a consciousness of the nature of all this, we will now use absolute Now as our subject. Notice that absolute Now and absolute Consciousness or absolute Existence share the same nature. See if you can use contemplating Absolute Now as a way into Absolute Consciousness. We'll start off slowly with rather grounded steps toward our goal then proceed into absolute existence outside time. With all the preparation work we've done so far, you are in a good place to really get this.

16:49 **Guided Contemplation: The Koan of Now**

Whatever *is* is true right now, in this moment. The *when* of existence is now. *Is* and *now* have a lot in common—they share the same "place," so to speak. When we speak of now, however, we fall into the trap of thinking of it as a moment in time—as though now is just one bead among many on the string of time. In this work, we cannot afford to hang on to such an assumption.

We've seen that it's always now. We think we go through many nows as we travel through time but fail to notice that we never leave now at all. We might imagine that we'll "get into" the future, as though it's some other place, but when we get there, it turns out to still be now—and also not exactly what we imagined. The past is experience that we say was, but this experience is a concept called a memory, and the memory is occurring now. "Past" and "future" are always only occurring now.

In the context of time, now seems to be a moment in a series of moments, as if on an infinite line. Yet if you work hard to discern the moment, you can't actually find it in your experience. Try.

What you find is a process, one of recognizing distinctions being made—this is perhaps a very short process, but a process nevertheless. This isn't now, since, within this process, how many more nows could there be?

You could say that the real moment of now is infinitely small, but what are you saying with that? First of all, you can't conceive of infinity, so that makes it out of bounds of your discernment, and thus a cop-out in your contemplations. If I'm to be believed, infinity and absolute nothing share the same nature. That would suggest that now doesn't really exist at all the way we think it does.

But I'm not inviting you to believe anything I say. I'm inviting you to grasp for yourself what's true in this matter. At this point, perhaps you are mulling over some idea of an extremely short—perhaps quantumly small—span of time. Drop that idea and try to stay with my assertion that now cannot be a span of time; it cannot be more than it is, nor can it be mixed with what it is not.

So what is now? Where is now? When is now?

As an exercise, start by experiencing this moment for-itself, absent of any for-me applications—you know how to do this by now. This perception might include your immediate physical surroundings and internal state, but minus the usual additions of meaning, association, function, or charge. It feels quite present and here, yet also perhaps a bit "ill-defined." Be as present as you can and keep trying to deepen your experience of this moment for-itself.

Going beyond experiencing the present moment for-itself, your attempt to grasp true Now pushes your attention toward the very moment that is *not a span of time.* If now spanned any time at all, no matter how short the time frame, it isn't actually now; there could be an infinite number of nows in that time span. There is only one now, and it is the same as existence.

Because of this, you must realize you can have no thought about it, or interpretation, or even perception, since all those are processes and take time no matter how small the amount.

As we've seen, perception is indirect and a process, it is not the thing-itself. Since Now does not span time, it can have no process and must be the thing-itself. Since you can't "do" anything with Now, not even perceive it much less think about it, you might have a hard time finding Now.

Remember to confront all this experientially, having insights as you proceed. It makes a vast difference to experientially work it to the best of your ability rather than just hear about it and intellectually understand.

If you become more rigorous in your investigation and grasp the fact that true Now is only now and does not span time, you will notice that you fail to find anything in your experience that isn't process. In this way, you grasp that you don't perceive Now at all. And yet something seems to exist.

We need to come to grips with the fact that absolute Now cannot be experienced or conceptualized. That's hard to do when concept and experience are all we have access to. We're loath to give them up, or perhaps—since we have no other place to put our attention—we can't give them up. Yet, if we can only recognize and "experience" something by going through a process, then we can't actually experience Now. But we can become directly conscious of it because becoming directly conscious is not dependent on process or experience.

Humans assume that the only way they can be conscious of something is by undergoing indirect mind processes to recognize an experience or perception. I'm asserting that there's more to consciousness than recognizing "experience." But the question people often ask at this point is "Then how do I do it?" The problem with the question, although reasonable, is that the "how-to" is about process. Essentially you end up asking, "By what process do I become directly conscious?" There is no process to get you to this consciousness. You must simply get it.

Another way to talk about this is to get that you are already *being* Now. This is the "process," so to speak, for getting it. It's not impossible to become conscious of Now, but it takes a direct-consciousness—and by direct, remember, I mean there is NO separation, NO distance, NO process, NO difference between Now and You.

Guided Meditation: Absolute Now

Put your attention on now. Dwell on this very moment. Keep your attention on now, beyond experience and concept. Stay here and try to become conscious of absolute Now—which is without any span of time whatsoever.

Don't think of it as difficult but as available. Remember, Now is in the same place as "IS," so put your attention on *is*. Grasp that existence *is* Now. Notice that it isn't what you're perceiving or experiencing but it isn't elsewhere either, it *is* this existence right now. Give up trying to perceive it, simply be conscious of absolute Now.

Try to grasp that the nature of absolute Now is the same nature as absolute existence.

16:50 Within the context of time, now appears as a moment in a sequence of moments. But within the context of Now, time is an invention. Time actually exists in the context of Now, not vice versa—except as a convention.

16:51 Now is always the case. Now is actually an absolute. Absolutes don't lend themselves well to any kind of model or understanding. They also don't "play by the rules" of logic, experience, or objective conditions. As an absolute, Now is infinite, has no location, and isn't elsewhere. It is Now! Which means it *is* existence.

16:52 Since self needs to perceive a relative and solid pragmatic reality in order to manage life, our normal perspective has no place for absolutes. Absolutes are generally viewed as mere abstractions, and worthless except perhaps as a pleasant philosophical diversion, or as mystical silliness. At times, they can even evoke a sense of threat, because survival can't take place within absolutes alone. We need consistent and objectified perceptive-experiences to remain cohesive as a self-structure and to successfully stay alive.

16:53 But don't worry, absolutes, like absolute Now, are already the case, and you're doing just fine—whether you look into them or not. Absolute Now forms the base of the reality within which you already live. You are likely simply ignorant of this truth because it has no use or place within your relative survival interpretations. That doesn't make it any less true.

16:54 There is a relationship between Now and enlightenment. Enlightenment is about what's True and what's True is true Now. If you want to become conscious of what you are, for example, it is what you are, and that means Now. You're not attempting to imagine what you will be or were, but to be conscious of what you are. So the *are* of you is only *Now*. There is no other place to look for the Truth. It has to be what IS.

16:55 Absolute Now provides a window into the inconceivable nature that tends to elude us in all this. Through focusing on this matter in earnest, if your mind can make the leap to grasping the fact that now cannot span time, be perceived, and has no location, you are on top of this nature and should be able to become conscious of it. It is ultimately the same nature as you, consciousness, and existence. So use this in your contemplations to break through the final envelope and have a deeper enlightenment.

Transcending the Object Illusion

16:56 Difficult as it may be to consider, entertain the possibility that the world of objects is created through perceptive-distinctions carved out of absolute infinity. Consider the possibility that in some unimaginable way objects don't ultimately exist as separate or real, it just seems that they do. Where an object begins and ends is rather a perceptive choice serving a purpose. Although it seems objects are completely out of our hands, there is a reason for that.

16:57 An object is a distinction we perceive. The truth or real nature of the object is unknown, so without that distinction the object doesn't exist, meaning it isn't perceived, and that's where its existence resides for us, isn't it? This doesn't mean this is whimsical or within our control, just that ultimately objects are not permanent or existentially real, even though they rightly seem to be the most inherently solid aspect of existence. Getting this can be an extremely high consciousness bar to hurdle.

16:58 Remember, the whole domain of self—and therefore self-survival and the perceptions that arise within this context—is created through the distinction of self and not-self. You perceive the activities of life in relation to you and not-you, automatically relating everything to yourself. This includes the perceptions of an objective world. When you perceive something, how do you do it? You see it (which is only just reflected light), you feel it (which is just a sensation), and if you tasted or smelled it do you really think that would tell you much about what is actually there? Perception is not the thing-itself and does not provide any information about the nature of what is really there. It only provides enough information for you to manage life.

16:59 But don't forget, your experience of reality isn't done by self alone. The moment a self separates from not-self, not-self is as much a part of creating this reality as is the self. In order for you to exist as a separate "thing," it is essential that there is a world of things from which to be separate. Get it?

16:60 If we shift our perspective to the notion that consciousness-existence is creating both you and not-you, this perceived world, both subjective and objective, could actually all be called a collective illusion, given it's held as ultimately true when in fact it's an invented activity serving a purpose—self-existence. Again, although you may think otherwise, you find your existence through being a body, and so objects seem set in cement because as an object this distinction is essential for survival.

16:61 As a matter of fact, the context of objective reality creates the possibility of being a body, and this in turn can then generate the notion of being a self. But again, we see paradox ruling the day. It becomes a chicken and egg conundrum: Does objective reality create consciousness, or does consciousness create objective reality? As it stands, objects, perception, mind, etc., are limited forms of consciousness, a consciousness-existence able to create the miracle of physics and life, as well as creatures and intelligence—which are all forms of an infinite or absolute consciousness beyond comprehension.

16:62 If it helps you to hear this, substitute the word "existence" for that of "consciousness." So let's hear the assertion again with this substitution: objects, perception, mind, etc., are limited forms of existence, an existence able to create the miracle of physics and life, as well as creatures and intelligence—which are all forms of an infinite or absolute existence beyond comprehension. Hard to argue that one, since existence has to be whatever it is. It may be beyond comprehension but that doesn't mean it is beyond access, simply not through using the limited faculties of human conception or perception.

16:63 Again, one big error we make is to assume that cognition is the same as consciousness. Remember, the assertion is that cognition, awareness, intellect, mind, perception, and understanding are all limited forms of consciousness, occurring in only one domain. That means they aren't consciousness itself even though ultimately they share the same nature—recall the uncarved block. We might be comfortable seeing these activities as consciousness, but when I also assert that an object is a form of consciousness, that throws a monkey wrench into the works, doesn't it?

16:64 Just as we saw that self is an activity of the brain—and this assisted us in eliminating the view that self is an inherent and existential aspect of existence—we might be able to do something similar with objects. To help the mind grapple with this, let's play an imaginary game. Imagine that the entire physical world is composed of infinitely small particles, in infinitely endless space. Picture this condition is the same everywhere, that everything that objectively exists is made of exactly the same substance, sort of akin to the uncarved block. If this is true, then what is an object?

16:65 As an animal we are limited to perceptions using specific tools that access light waves, molecular vibrations, and so on. Can we see or in any way perceive this reality of particles and space? No, of course not. We have no capacity to perceive such things. Instead, we are reduced to making distinctions within the perceivable swirls of particles and activities that "catch our eye," so to speak.

16:66 This is all done within only one layer or spectrum of perceptibility. This layer, or level of vibrational frequency, is the place where we live and so is what concerns us as this creature. Although here we can only "perceive" what we might call certain "wavelengths," this doesn't mean there aren't many more, actually infinite, "wavelengths" we can't perceive or fathom. Imagine that what we call an object is simply limiting and categorizing particles perceived in this one wavelength into a group to serve a purpose.

16:67 Everything we perceive as reality only exists in finite forms that are perceived as real because it is what in the universe relates to you, and this is the domain in which you—as one of those activities—exist, and where you need to survive. So, do you see the function of perception and why it is perceiving just a limited spectrum of possibilities? Beyond the specifics of this dynamic, consider that when you push one palm into another, a sensation is generated. This sensation (or perception) doesn't exist on its own, it is only the action of one thing pressing against another. Just so, imagine the existence of a you is "pressing" against not-you, as not-you presses against you, and this is creating the reality you perceive.

16:68 The absolute truth is true with or without any limited form of consciousness arising, so nothing needs to disappear, just a breakthrough in consciousness needs to occur. An object is what it is, so grasp the real nature of the object. I'm just messing around with ways for the mind to look into the matter. Whether objects are real or not, your job is to grasp their actual nature beyond perception.

Time and space are not conditions in which we live, but modes by which we think. Physical concepts are free creations of the human mind, and are not, however it may seem, determined by the external world.

Albert Einstein

16:69 It's sort of like it's all as if a thought, and thoughts don't exist. Although the form of consciousness that is a thought is limited and abstract, it provides a possibility of seeing how consciousness as an object is also unreal given it shares the same nature as the thought. If object and thought are as if aspects of the same "dream," we can see how none of it is real even though it is the reality we perceive and live. To say all this another way, the real nature of existence is nothing and nowhere.

16:70 We see intellect can't handle such a possibility, but no worries, if everything is a form of consciousness, then so is intellect and so are you—you're likely just ignorant of this fact. Stop separating mind from body, object from awareness, and get that it is all of the same nature. In this way, objects and body, self and awareness—not to mention a hot dog and the speed of light—are simply consciousness, and none of it is ultimately existent. It is all limited or finite forms or activities of an infinite or absolute consciousness-existence. That would mean the nature of objective existence is very different than what we perceive as space with objects in it, doesn't it?

16:71 Becoming conscious of absolute Now should help resolve the paradox of the reality and unreality of objective existence by providing a freedom from the context of space and objects. But the mind will likely still struggle with this conundrum as an impossibility, especially as it falls back into the accepted, solidly perceived world of objects. This should not be resisted or denied but embraced and questioned to a greater extent. The feedback provided by not-you is invaluable in your contemplations on the nature of existence.

16:72 The way to transcend this object-illusion is to become conscious of what it really is. This needs to be deep enough that you realize the real nature of the illusion or invention and not just grasp the fact of it. It is not unusual for people who have had some genuine direct experience of their own nature to still remain trapped within the self and life illusions.

16:73 This is a lot to grasp, but the freedom available through such consciousness, even if it's only a glimpse, lays a foundation from which you can pursue understanding such paradox directly. This section contains way too much unnecessary explanation, when what really needs to happen is quite simple and direct. Yet, transcending the object-reality illusion is rare, and just attempting to illuminate this possibility is very difficult.

16:74 Consider that consciousness, *ergo* existence, has no element, no location, and can't come or go. I bet you're getting tired of hearing that, so just get it and the words will be irrelevant. For this to be realized, however, you have to be directly conscious of what is ultimately true, and that it is actually true. With the freedom that arises from this depth of consciousness you stop resisting the existence of anything since it all shares the same nature, including you.

Enlightenment is man's release from his self-incurred tutelage. Tutelage is man's inability to make use of his understanding without direction from another.

Immanuel Kant

The Nature of Existence

16:75 **Guided Meditation: The Nature of Existence**

Let's continue to push the envelope some more to help clear the way toward a consciousness that transcends mind and self.

Imagine that an ultimate Big Bang in reverse (a sort of anti-Big Bang) suddenly blows up all existence. Absolutely everything that could possibly be experienced is gone. Add to that: time and space have also been blown away and are non-existent. So there is really nothing left at all.

Has existence ceased to be? Has existence disappeared or been diminished in any way? No. Not at all. We confuse perceiving things with existence. We confuse experience with what-is. Notice that with nothing at all, existence still is. It just isn't anything or anywhere. Contrary to our senses and accepted knowledge, existence isn't bound to space or time and so is not limited to process or experience. It can't come or go, it only *is*.

Focus on *is* for a moment. The nature of *is* still "is" even if nothing exists. If everything is destroyed, *is* remains. How can *is* go anywhere? There is nowhere to go. Grasp the real nature of "is." If you identify with *is* then nothing can come or go. There is nothing that needs to be or not be.

16:76 Again, to help stretch your mind beyond its breaking point, let's hit an absolute truth that doesn't make any sense at all but is still true. See if you can grasp this beyond it making sense:

The nature of form has no form,
the nature of space has no space.
Absolute nothing isn't the absence of anything,
it is the nature of existence.
Everything is Nothing, Nothing is Everything.

16:77 The nature of existence is not an experience or something experienced. It is not a perception or something perceived. It is not an object or even a subject. It isn't what you may define or figure out. It is not an idea or conclusion. It isn't a state of mind of any kind, nor is it a really big and wonderful world of magical phenomena. All those things may be experienced, but none of them are your nature or the nature of existence, no matter how much you may want them to be.

16:78 The real nature of consciousness is independent from all experience, life, self, persistence, time, and so on. These are all relative distinctions so they cannot be absolute. A direct-consciousness of the absolute isn't a distinction. The moment we "know" something, however, the moment we become conscious of an absolute, we will make a distinction between that and everything else, but this distinction will be a function of the mind and not the consciousness itself.

16:79 Everything you know and experience, however, *is* a distinction. Bring to mind enlightenment or absolute consciousness, for example, and notice what comes up. Those are all thoughts or images or feelings about a conceptual distinction you make, either imagining what has been said if you haven't had an enlightenment, or remembering what your mind has created to represent a breakthrough you may have made. Both are distinctions. Can you get that?

16:80 **Guided Meditation: The Nature of Existence**

Set out to be directly conscious of the real nature of existence. Watch what comes up.

Notice everything that arises is a distinction you're making and not a direct-consciousness of this nature.

Don't try to force yourself to have no distinctions, simply let them be—everything you think, perceive, or experience in any way—and continue to set out to be directly conscious of the nature of existence.

16:81 I know these matters can be aggravatingly challenging to grasp. It all seems so abstract and impractical. It may be that, but consider that the real heart of the matter is not restricted to self's likes or dislikes, or to your experience at all. So addressing or considering assertions that seem quite outside your experience or beyond reason is a must, even if they have to remain a mystery for now, or seem just plain stupid.

16:82 Along those lines, to make it even more challenging, do you remember the introduction of the unusual possibility that the domain of objects might be a form of consciousness? My invitation then was to consider it a silent, non-self form of consciousness. Recall also the assertion that the silent-stillness of your own experience might be the same as it is for everyone. What if it is the same for all of existence, just as is absolute Now? That would suggest that in some way you are one with or the same as others and objects, *ergo* all of existence. Since this not-knowing silent-stillness might be a doorway to the nature of existence, it may need more attention and contemplation on your part.

The Thinking Rock

16:83 Imagine a rock being aware that it is a rock. We can't imagine such a thing because for us objects have no awareness—the insignificant bastards! But imagine it anyway, and do it without projecting some version of entity into the picture. How could this aware-rock exist?

16:84 What if the awareness or consciousness is within the thing itself? This is a very unusual idea, isn't it? We have no way to process that. But what if it were true anyway? That the consciousness is in the rock itself, or *is* the rock itself.

16:85 Along those lines, imagine that a thought and its understanding are produced by the brain, and this brain and activity are themselves forms of consciousness. Consider an unheard-of possibility that the cognition and awareness that arise from the brain are forms of consciousness but aren't separate from the brain itself—that the brain itself is also a limited form of consciousness producing another limited form of consciousness.

16:86 All this might sound akin to the old attempt to push the idea of "intelligent design" postulating that objective creation is not random but is designed on purpose, suggesting a divine source behind it. Of course, at the time, this proffered theory wasn't honest, even though it could have been. It was based on a belief system Christians were covertly trying to sell by making an argument for their religion. But if we take the disingenuous origins out of the questioning it might still have merit. Yet, our go-to notion is to consider this "intelligence" behind the design of the universe as something akin to our intelligence or the human mind. This is far too limited to consider valid.

16:87 So, instead of a divine source behind reality, how about consciousness IS the creation itself—it is inherent within it, not something separate from it. This so-called "intelligence" exists *as* reality, not behind it. This is because reality is consciousness showing up in limited or finite ways.

16:88 As we go down this road, akin to the myth of god, someone might wonder if consciousness is so brilliant and all-knowing, why does it produce stupidity and suffering and limitation? But such questions stem from self and social human values—which are all forms of consciousness, by the way—and what we are considering can't be limited, and certainly not limited to such inventions. In this consideration, the mere fact of the invention, or the existence of anything at all, *is* consciousness, not what comes out of it—recall the uncarved block.

16:89 We might say consciousness doesn't care what arises, it's simply the possibility for it to arise. Here, all things are equal. For us, due to ignorance, we are stuck within perceptive and conceptual limitations and so miss that all this is infinite consciousness-existence arising as possibilities. To be clear, what I am referring to as consciousness is the same thing as existence. If there were any difference between them, it wouldn't be absolute, would it? So there is no daylight between consciousness and existence, just as there is no daylight between the nature of both, which I call Nothing. Because neither word by itself is enough, I coined the phrase "consciousness-existence" to refer to what I'm talking about when I talk about either consciousness or existence—since here they are the same.

16:90 Focusing on objective existence, we see that we group matter into distinctions we can perceive, and so it is a rock, or a planet, or a galaxy, or a body. Yet, when we make these distinctions, we get lost in them, even though we can see that none of it really exists as anything but activities that create the distinction and so experience of objects and space. When we understand the real nature of this activity, we might find that neither space nor objects are real.

16:91 Our struggle with this matter is based on our knowledge and perceptions, which are based on millennia of human contributions about what is true about reality. But remember this is only a snapshot in human history. An ancient Greek formulated the idea of atoms long before it became scientifically verified, and an ancient Roman came up with micro-organisms and their link to diseases long before any such thing was discovered and proven. If such notions that later prove correct can be produced by great thinkers of the time, what are we seeing now that is myopic and what are we not seeing now that is overlooked? A good and perhaps fruitful exercise but no matter what we come up with, it is only a snapshot of human conception and a limited notion of what's true. Our job is to leap beyond such limitations and embrace what is true beyond time and conception.

16:92 But back to our thinking rock. In all this objective matter, we still can't find awareness or an entity. Given the nature of objects, brains, and perceptions, we have seen that a rock, concept, and self are all activities, not existential realities in themselves. What is the nature of the existence that creates the space for these activities? What is the substance that these activities are acting upon?

16:93 Since we don't know what the substance or nature of this existence is, we could call it anything or imagine whatever. Our task is to grasp what's true. Quite a task.

16:94 **Guided Contemplation: Thinking Rock**

Put your attention on objective existence.

After being assaulted with so many perspectives and considerations so far, use the openness these create to deeply question and contemplate: What is the real substance or nature of existence without any activity?

Chapter Seventeen

ULTIMATE EXISTENCE IS ABSOLUTE CONSCIOUSNESS

17:1 Sorry, one more chapter about impossible stuff. I have laid out a great deal of incredibly challenging material and seemingly impossible assertions about life and reality that almost no human grasps. Yet, I want to push some more in the direction of the consciousness that is existence. As you can see, an inconceivable leap is needed to consider the level of consciousness that includes all this stuff, as well as realizes it is not real, even though it is reality itself.

17:2 As must be clear by now, this consciousness can't be easily communicated. But since a huge foundation has been laid out, I want to bring it all home by revisiting some of the most central assertions and then pushing again toward the nature of existence that encompasses both the absolute and the relative. To attempt to tackle this, I will repeat many things already said (what's new, eh?). Try to go deeper. Again, as we proceed, see this as more of our immense contemplation or guided meditation we've been working on throughout this book. Work to really get it this time even if you've heard it before. One more time into the breach!

Physical and Biological Consciousness

17:3 It seems physics involves a lot of activity—movement of positive and negatively charged particles—and from this activity objects and the universe are formed. Biology adds another layer where the natural dissolution of things is resisted for a time. Yet, nothing lasts forever (including the earth and sky). All life dies and all things are eventually destroyed and return to a simple form of matter. Where is consciousness in all of this?

17:4 Is consciousness limited to the awareness and conceptualizing of a creature? Seems rather limited, don't you think? Perhaps we might think that through life, awareness will eventually and naturally realize itself into the absolute. Now that seems like it would be an infinitely long process, doesn't it? As Buddha said, becoming completely conscious using nature as the process would be akin to the amount of time it would take for a dove with a handkerchief in its mouth flying over the Himalayan mountains, brushing the top peak with the cloth once a year, to wear these mountains down to nothing. Sounds like a really long time to me. In any case, the very fact that life is a pursuit of survival and not the truth precludes this from happening. Seems a more direct method is recommended.

17:5 The assertion taking center stage at this point is that consciousness includes everything that exists. Consciousness is as if "doing" it all—or perhaps more accurately "is" it all—including the self and all the conclusions formed by concept. It doesn't ultimately matter what comes or goes, it is all consciousness. Your job is to ask: Is this true?

17:6 If everything that exists is an element of existence—hard to argue against that, since it's axiomatic—then you are the same as everything because you are an element of existence. It's something like if you were a chunk of ice, it appears that you are distinct from other chunks of ice. But when it all melts there is no distinction among what were formerly ice chunks. So even during the separation, the ice is just water and is the same as every other form of water.

17:7 **Exercise: Distinction**

Notice that you make a distinction between a chair and a table. But you can stop making that distinction. It may seem impossible to you because you think that you are only observing what's there, and clearly there is a chair and a table, and they aren't the same thing. So what do I mean by saying you can stop making a distinction?

Let's play it out by starting with some simple examples. For instance, you could see the chairs and table as a dining set. If you only made the distinction of dining set, there may be different objects comprising the set, but they are all grouped into that one distinction. Try that now.

Just so, you can see the back and seat of a chair, but observe that you probably didn't notice this distinction when you were considering the chair and the table or the dining set. You can eliminate the distinction of back and seat and just see the chair. Do that now.

Of course you are likely to think this is just a matter of semantics and ignoring what's there, but it's still there. It is there in your experience, when it is. If you didn't make those distinctions, none of it would be experienced as that or as there. Consider that an ant or armadillo never sees a chair or dining set at all. Why? Because they don't make those distinctions.

You might then think, "OK, sure, but something is still there." For now, it doesn't matter whether there is something there or not. What's important now—and what creates your experience and reality—is how you perceive what's there, and that depends on the distinctions you make.

Just like the dining set can eliminate chair and table, we see that cells make up a body. But we don't make the distinction of cells in our perceptions, even though we have to admit the cells are what is there. We only see the body. Likewise we might see bodies as creatures, or creatures as species—it just depends on what distinctions we make, and how we apply them to our perceptions.

In the world of martial arts, for example, I certainly make many distinctions you do not, even if you are a martial artist. These distinctions—on many levels—are recognized, felt, and responded to in milliseconds. This enables me to consistently beat opponents because they do not share in these distinctions. We hire a doctor because they make distinctions we do not. We have no problem acknowledging that a physicist relates to a world most of us are unable to, and so on. Most of us don't share in these worlds because we don't make the distinctions found in that world. But there are many assumptions and worlds we do share.

Now that we have warmed up by getting in touch with making simple distinctions, let's look into some that are more fundamental and overlooked. For example, throughout this book we have explored many overlooked distinctions that humanity generally shares and accepts. Much of what we've addressed I say is false or not existentially real. You've probably been able to eliminate all or many of those distinctions as we progressed, or at least grasped that they are not true but instead are inventions.

To better get this possibility of eliminating or changing distinctions, even ones that have been accepted by humanity for millennia, let's look at a few we have already experienced and challenged, and some that we've created in this book. See the distinction that was made and then perhaps eliminated, challenged, or added:

- Realizing the inner self-object is not real.
- Recognizing that our obsession with ourselves dominates our entire experience.
- Grasping that self is a myth.

- Getting that self is not an independent individual that exists on its own.
- Getting that self and not-self are created at the same time.
- Realizing that our perceptions are not direct or accurate reflections of existence.
- Seeing inventions as inventions, not as existentially true—such as language, culture, society, self, religions, mind, and many more.
- Experiencing the difference between being a body and being inside of or perceiving the body.
- Recognizing the possibility that the brain's problem-solving ability is what has produced an imaginary world of self.
- Getting that perspectives can't be the whole story or true.
- Seeing that over time humanity has increasingly separated the idea of self from the physical.
- Coming to grips with our shortfall in grasping infinity, and so coming closer to grasping infinity.
- Opening to the possibility of the uncarved block, and getting that the nature of everything relative must be the same as the absolute.
- Entertaining new distinctions of the nature of existence beyond what we assume—such as objective existence without movement, absolute now, and infinite space.
- Tackling the real possibility that the nature of existence isn't found in our perceptions or mind.
- Challenging the assumption of location.
- Grasping that time is not the distinction we make and have accepted as true.
- Opening to the real possibility that you can get over yourself.
- and more

17:8 Can you see that all these examples are about eliminating or creating distinctions? Do you get what a distinction is and that they can be made or eliminated? At this point I hope you have a good handle on distinctions and how to make or eliminate them, because to go forward you need this ability.

17:9 **Guided Meditation: Universal Consciousness**

I want you to focus on your experience and perception. Everything in your experience is either you or not-you, isn't it? Notice what is you and what is not-you.

You might say your awareness, mind, and body are you, but the table, air, and tree are not-you. Become clear on this distinction. Now, ask why do you say one is you and one is not?

Keep seeing what is you and what is not-you. As you do this, begin to see that this is a distinction being made. You might think you have no choice about it, but consider that you do. Get that you are distinguishing what in your experience is you, or of you, and what is not-you.

Notice that you could consider that your foot is not you, just an object you claim as yours because you can move it. If this is so for your foot, what about everything else, the rest of your body, a thought, a feeling, mind? You could hold that all these things are not-you. Try that out.

Now, take it to the extreme, where you can't find you at all. In such a case, you must be unknown or nothing. Soak in this possibility.

Now go to the opposite extreme and hold that everything is in your experience and so is you—that even what you think is not-you only exists in your experience and so could be called you, or of you, or within you. In this way, see it all as you.

Now, drop all that, and again notice that you live within an experience of dividing everything up into you and not-you. You make that distinction.

Now, stop making a distinction between you and not-you. Eliminate it. Allow the activity of perceptive-experience to occur without it being divided into you and not-you, so that everything that was you and not-you is now the same thing. What occurs in your experience and in your consciousness when you do that?

17:10 **Guided Meditation: Object Consciousness**

Note: When I use the word "immovable" in this next exercise, I'm referring to that quality in objects that is completely independent and unmoved by your will and mind—that constant and steady aspect of objective existence.

Now, as an exercise I want you to put your attention on an object easily visible to you. Focus on this object and begin to grasp the quality of the object that is silent and completely selfless. Keep focusing on the object. See if you can (as if) grasp the "mind" of the object.

Soak in the fact, or at least the possibility, that objective existence is the silent, non-sentient, completely selfless, and immovable aspect of consciousness. Keep opening up to this possibility.

OK, now get that the object is completely selfless. Notice it absolutely doesn't care if you break it or destroy it. It is selfless and serves whatever is asked of it without a whimper. Can you do that?

Again, put your attention on the object, concentrate on that objective quality that is silent, selfless, and immovable. Begin to be like that yourself. Be like the object. Shift into a state of being totally silent, non-sentient, selfless, and constant.

> Now, notice that as a body you are an object, and so share these same qualities. Be the body, which is as silent, non-sentient, selfless, constant, and immovable as all objects. Allow yourself to be the same as all objects. You may be afraid to go there because you don't want to give up self-survival, but imagine what it would be like anyway, at least temporarily. Soak in it for a bit. Be a selfless object.

17:11 Without knowing what an object really is, consider the possibility that it represents that aspect of existence that allows for you and life to occur. When it comes to being a self, objective existence has generally been overlooked as unimportant and just background noise. Consider instead that once you get past the distinction of you and not-you, it is the best part of you. It is that selfless, non-sentient, pure existence that serves without any concern for persistence and sacrifices itself without hesitation or a whimper. Can you say the same about you?

17:12 Hold that objective existence is that form of consciousness that produces you. If there is no you/not-you distinction, then everything experienced is consciousness-existence, and it is all the same consciousness. It is relative, but without that distinction it is all simply the carved-up uncarved block in different forms. Objects and space are one form of consciousness, and life, self, and awareness are other forms of this same consciousness—they are not different or separate.

17:13 Get that objects are a form of consciousness, just like you are a form of consciousness. Entertain the idea that objective existence is better than you because it is pure consciousness not stuck in the illusion of self or survival. That's an interesting perspective, isn't it?

The Paradox of Consciousness

17:14 I know all this can be very challenging for the mind to tackle. It's like an Escher drawing that bends the mind, or an insolvable riddle like what came first, the chicken or the egg? Or a paradox that just doesn't yield to common sense. Remember, we are stuck in language, as well as a huge number of assumptions about reality, but to entertain this "unspeakable" consciousness these can't be our stopping point.

17:15 Standing on an assertion I've already made many times, we have a way to proceed. This assertion is that consciousness is the nature of everything, including the self and not-self. Everything that exists or will ever exist is a limited form of consciousness. But in order to get this, we must grasp that what I'm calling consciousness is very different than what we normally know of as consciousness. Remember this consciousness is the same as existence.

Infinity

17:16 Even in our relative everything world of space and objects, we acknowledge that it must be infinite. Objects and distance are limited forms of infinite existence, but the fact of infinity, although a logical conclusion, is rarely a direct experience. Infinite existence is absolute yet only shows up in limited and relative distinctions such as objects and distance, so the infinite nature of existence is missed.

17:17 We can't conceive this infinity even though we still grasp it must be true. There is no end to things, space can go on forever, and must be able to go on forever, even though this is inconceivable to us. As we've seen, if it didn't, reality would have to stop somewhere, and if reality stopped somewhere we'd have the inevitable problem of what is on the other side of its stopping point. So, it becomes clear that space is infinite and infinity is an absolute, and so it can't be what we think or perceive.

17:18 Just as infinite existence is absolute, infinite consciousness is also absolute. But what is meant by infinite consciousness? It's hard to imagine because, just as with objective existence where we only perceive objects and space, with consciousness we are usually focused on stuff like thoughts and images. Yet, as with objective existence, there is no end to making new distinctions, and so this too is infinite. This infinity can't be discerned, because it is not thinkable or imaginable. So we have to be open to a new possibility.

17:19 **Guided Meditation: Infinity**

Dwell on the nature of infinity.

Start with infinite space. Get that space can't stop anywhere, and yet you can't conceive of the forever of it. Dwell on this infinite space and be conscious of what is true such that space must be infinite. And then directly grasp this infinity.

Now, consider infinite possibilities. Grasp that new distinctions and new possibilities never end, they can go on infinitely. What is the nature or context that allows that to be the case? How is the infinity of space the same as the infinity of possibilities?

Now, focus on infinitely small. How is it that you could go smaller and smaller without end? No matter how small you get, there is always something smaller—how can this be so? Just like space where you can go infinitely farther, you can also go infinitely smaller. What is the nature of infinity that must be true even though we are unable to conceive it?

We see that numbers themselves can be infinite, we just don't want to try to count that high and so leave it as lots and lots and ignore the fact that we stop somewhere, but it doesn't. With a wave of a hand we acknowledge that numbers must keep going forever, as if we could, but we certainly aren't going to go there. Instead of ignoring this reality, make the final leap to get what it is that creates the context for going beyond lots and lots. Don't make infinity just a math problem, but a reality. Try to wrench infinity out of numbers.

Get that infinity must be of a different nature than can be imagined within the limits of relative distinctions. What is beyond lots and lots, yet still includes lots and lots? What is that nature? What has to be the nature of reality for infinity to be foundational to all of it?

Recall absolute Now. Notice that if you try to relate to now as if it's an infinitely small space of time you can always go smaller or shorter, so you never get to real now. What leap did you make that allowed you to grasp that now can't be a span of time but at the same time is the context or reality in which time can be created? Does absolute Now share the same nature as infinity? Notice this challenges the convention of how now and the infinite have been held heretofore.

Contemplate the nature of infinity.

Self-Survival versus the Infinite

17:20 Absolute existence and absolute consciousness must share the same nature because the absolute doesn't discriminate. If the real nature of everything we perceive or know is absolute consciousness-existence, this would include both physics and biology, and therefore all of objective reality.

17:21 This is a new way to look at consciousness and a new possibility that is hard to accept. Our whole lives have been lived with a very different assumption and restriction, primarily due to the fact that we have separated self from not-self, and self-survival dominates our entire experience of reality.

17:22 By entertaining the possibility that viewing something shares the same nature as what's viewed, a new opportunity emerges. This is not to say that an object is the same distinction as the perception of it, but that the perceiving is a function of consciousness and the object is also a function of this same consciousness.

17:23 Remember, what's carved out of the uncarved block is of the same "substance" as the infinite block before any carving. Along these lines, what if being conscious of the perception of an object shares the same nature as the object itself? Mind-blowing possibility, isn't it? This suggests that consciousness may create both perception and object, mind and body.

17:24 We think in terms of this and that, limits and relationships, awareness and objects. These tend to exist in completely different domains for us, so how could they share the same nature? We may not be able to mentally conceive of it, but we can grasp that the one thing they all share is they exist. Existence is their nature. That can't be too hard to grasp since it's an axiomatic statement, saying everything that exists exists, and so must share whatever existence is as its nature. Yet, we need to directly realize that if consciousness is absolute and existence is absolute, they must also share this same nature because they both exist. There is no difference between the two because they are not two. Still, our central question remains: What is this nature?

17:25 One thing to keep in mind is that although our self-experience is a limited form of consciousness, it is still a form of consciousness—that means the self is not separate from this nature. Therefore, consciousness is also acting through and as the form of a self. This doesn't suggest any value or meaning, nor whether it's good or bad, just that it's so.

17:26 A word of caution, however: although this may be true, a self might grab onto such an idea as a justification for everything it does, thinking this assertion makes it right. That's stupid. The most ineffective, crazy, or moronic activities or thoughts are forms of consciousness, just as much as are the most brilliant, wise, and sane activities.

17:27 Right and wrong, good and bad, effective and ineffective are functions of self-survival, and this whole activity—as immense and all-encompassing as it is—is still quite limited and self-referential. Although as a self we may be ignorant of the fact, even self-survival is a form of consciousness. Consciousness doesn't take sides.

17:28 Perhaps when you hear "consciousness is everything" and try to understand how this can be so, you might think that because, for you, existence only occurs within your perceptive-experience or "consciousness," you could say existence only exists within your consciousness. If you don't make a distinction that there is anything outside your conscious experience, you could say existence is only found in your experience and so is a function of your consciousness. In this way, you could see every object and thought as something you are conscious of, and so they are living within your "consciousness" and therefore sharing this same nature.

17:29 Yet, that view is still arrogantly based on the self as the source of all experience and so the source of everything perceived. If you eliminate the false division between you and not-you, you might see that the existence of everything could be called absolute consciousness. Even if only intellectually, you must acknowledge that the nature of existence is absolute and infinite and therefore without restriction or limitation, and so it can't be limited to whatever is generated by your self-experience and mind.

17:30 Why do we still have a hard time relating to the possibility that self and not-self are the same? Once the distinction of self and not-self is made, we side with the self, since that is our identity, and our job is to manage and maintain this self. In so doing, because it's not us, we turn our backs on and separate ourselves from not-self—which is the objective world, and yet is a world we need in order to survive. But this disposition creates not only a dependency but a rather adversarial relationship to it. Further, we identify with awareness, perceptions, and mind, and since these are not objective, we conclude that self and consciousness reside in a non-physical domain of reality, and not in the physical.

17:31 Since "you" are created through the distinction of you and not-you, you must hold not-you as, well, not you! Therefore objects and others cannot be contained within your limited consciousness and so can't be seen as the same as you. Yet, when you get over being stuck in and on you and eliminate the distinction of self and not-self, it becomes clear that consciousness-existence is prior to and not limited to any self. It includes you, objects, and others—it includes everything that exists in any way.

17:32 Because of language challenges—and just plain mental challenges—it sounds like you are doing all this. But that can't be the case, since "all this" is prior to you. So we are talking about a paradox again, unless of course you identify with the true nature of consciousness-existence, but you don't. So, try to get past how it sounds. Consider it may be more like a rock splitting in two: we can't say one half did it, but we also can't say it didn't; it exists because of the split and is as much a part of the splitting as is the other half. But it is also true that neither half had any say in the matter, and the activity of the splitting, or "carving," creates both halves. This metaphor is just a way of thinking to help ground the paradox. Our goal is to become conscious of the nature of all this. Here, we are looking at something even more challenging than rock splitting, we are looking at the impossibility of absolute nothing creating everything. You're just caught up in the mix.

Everything Fitting into Nothing

17:33 You may still have trouble coming to grips with a nature that includes infinite everything. That's because, contrary to common sense, or any sense at all, the nature of everything is nothing. Yet, how can everything be contained within nothing?!

17:34 When I say something stupid, like the nature of existence is nothing—that it has no dimension or location—this sounds like nonsense. Besides, you'll rightly persist with the reasonable question: How can everything fit into nothing? How can nothing produce everything? This is an unimaginable enigma and paradox.

17:35 We must acknowledge that whatever this Nothing is, it's not whatever we imagine, so it isn't the nothing that we know. Nothing for us is relative, it is the absence of something or of everything, and this is not what I'm talking about. I've also asserted that this absolute "nothing-nature" includes everything and all relative existence. This presents us with a huge paradox, and as we search our minds, we can't find a way to resolve it.

17:36 The word "nothing" might lead us down the wrong path. It is better grasped without thinking, and as prior to perception and space. It may also be useful to acknowledge that just like you can't conceive of infinity, in the same way you can't conceive of this nothing-nature; and as has been pointed out, this infinity and nothing are in the same place, so to speak. This should tell you something about the nothing to which I'm referring.

17:37 As you try to use your conception and your experience to grasp this nature, know that you cannot do it there. Instead, set out to be directly conscious of it—beyond logic or history or assumption or any other limitation. Poetically speaking, look right into the center of existence (as if you can) and be prepared to realize that this center is nowhere and everywhere, without having one speck of existence itself.

17:38 Here, perhaps you can see that everything is of the same nature, and so you might say it is all one. This might sound like a kumbaya moment, but it still doesn't at all answer the question: How does everything fit into nothing? Although we might see this consciousness as being one with everything, the *one* and the *everything* make it relative. Since the whole world seems to be made up of separate things or distinctions, it is hard to grasp how they can all be the same. Yet, as we're beginning to see, in order to share the same nature, this nature has to be absolute and infinite, not relative and limited.

Dreams and Quantum Physics

17:39 Since mind can't handle paradox, let's play with a metaphor or two that may give us a way for the mind to grapple with some of this. Once again, if we consider that the mind really doesn't exist as anything but figments—as concepts without substance—we see that although a dream will consist of a whole world of objects, space, and activities, these all exist within the mind that dreams it.

17:40 In the dream we might be ignorant of the fact that the nature of all that stuff is really non-existent and is just a figment of mind. Yet once we become conscious of this reality, we get that everything dreamed shares the same nature, so all of the dreamed space and objects actually exist within this mind-nature that itself has no substance or space. This analogy might help us realize how our perceived world of space and objects might "fit" into an absolute nature that is both nothing and infinite.

17:41 Another possibility that might help us manage this paradox can be found in physics. We hear that quantum physics has some puzzling and paradoxical outcomes and possibilities. We don't challenge these conclusions even though we can't really understand them. The world at this level seems to work in ways totally impossible as conceived by the normal and logical world of time and space that we perceive.

17:42 Since we are open to the fact that we don't perceive the molecular or quantum activities of this reality, why assume that our perceptions and conclusions are the end-all to existence? If we can wrap our heads around quantum physics as a viable possibility, why not go further and consider that all of existence exists in ways totally inconceivable to us and yet it is still true? It is not out of line to consider that the nature of existence must be absolute and not restricted to any one thing or idea, or even to everything all together.

Infinite Nothing

17:43 Ever wonder why I keep relating Nothing and Infinity to each other? You can't conceive of infinity, we've already seen that. Yet you will still insist that it must be found within the perceived reality that you do experience. This can't be the case, however, since objective reality is defined and known as discrete elements that are limited to the boundaries or parameters of each element. Clearly, infinity, even as it relates to the universe of objective reality, can't be limited to those same boundaries because it has none.

17:44 What tends to be overlooked is that the reason infinity can go on forever and be without distinction or limitation is because it has no element to it, or to say that another way, it is nothing. Nothing, as an absolute, has no restrictions or limitations. It is free of time and of space. Absolute nothing is infinite. The nature of infinity is absolute nothing. Hard to grasp, I understand. You run into paradox again. But this isn't our first rodeo with paradox, so be open to the possibility that it is still true.

17:45 If you are stuck in and restricted to perceptions and distinctions, you won't be able to make the leap outside this limited view. I know attempts at logic won't work to make this leap, but worth a try, eh? Let's continue to push past the edge of the envelope of logic and experience, and keep attempting to make a leap in consciousness.

17:46 **Guided Meditation: Nothing**

How can everything fit into nothing? Think about it. It is really the only place it can fit since everything is infinite, even though we ignore that fact.

Bring to mind the most absolute reality you can imagine. Notice it cannot end, therefore, it must be infinite. For any of this to have a chance at being true, it must be the very nature of existence, and this nature can't be finite. Can you grasp that?

Absolute Nothing is not finite, everything else is. Nothing has no boundaries or limitations, it has no location, not even space. Where else could the entire universe—all of existence in any and every form possible—fit?

If this is still hard to get, remember the work we did with not-knowing. Here, you can't find any boundaries even though you might assume there should be some. Not-knowing may or may not be infinite, you don't know, but this lack of boundaries is similar to absolute Nothing.

Consider that although it may seem like Nothing and Infinity are polar opposites, they are actually the same, that's how it can be the source of everything. It is the absolute nature of existence. Don't get hung up on the name, concentrate on the reality. Dwell on this reality.

Contemplate the absolute Nothing that is the same as Now, Infinity, and the nature of all existence. Don't be intimidated by these grand-sounding names, grasp the nature of existence.

Ultimate Existence Is Absolute Consciousness

17:47 The paradox that the real nature of the relative is actually absolute, and that everything is nothing, makes comprehending any of this challenging. Yet, consider, if this nature is separate from anything in any way, none of this assertion could be true, could it? Even being "one" is distinct from everything and nothing. No matter what we might come up with within the perceived relative world, it would not be something else. The only possibility that can contain it all is best called nothing—no time, space, object, this or that. I could say infinite-nothing, but then you're likely to think of expansive nothingness, and that really isn't it. In this nothing there is no space or dimension of any kind.

17:48 Whatever this nature is, or whatever we call it, I'm saying that everything is a form of consciousness. Every rock and thought, animal and plant, perception and molecule, stupid thing and brilliant thing, everything that exists in any way is of this nature. Call it consciousness, or call it existence if you like, but know that every form of what was previously held as consciousness—perception, awareness, cognition, thinking, mind, experience—are limited forms of consciousness and so you can't find the true nature of this absolute consciousness using those faculties, even though they are still of this same nature. Consider the possibility that ultimate existence is absolute consciousness.

17:49 The truth is existence is consciousness, consciousness is existence. In the end, they are exactly the same. So you could call absolute consciousness absolute existence, or absolute existence absolute consciousness. But it doesn't matter, it is the same no matter what you call it.

17:50 When you eliminate you and not-you there emerges a new experience along with a new consciousness that blows the mind of this self-that-doesn't-exist. When this happens there is a deep joy that erupts from nowhere. A joy that arises from being free of being a self. Even the existing "self" that remains as a distinction—knowing it is not real—shares in this joy and is tickled by it.

Is God Absolute Consciousness?

17:51 If absolute consciousness is existence, and includes everything that exists in any way as limited forms of consciousness, it has probably occurred to some that this might be what has been historically called God. Of course, we must immediately detach such a notion from all the plethora of crap that has been imagined as God by minds that couldn't and didn't understand at all what they were talking about, and simply made up fantasies that can be known and thought and believed in. Clearly, God cannot be a personage or an entity of any kind. Entity is way down on the list of distinctions created inside of life for it to be in any way absolute, no matter how grand and inclusive is our imagination. The absolute can't be defined or boxed into our thinking or our experience.

17:52 How can infinite consciousness or absolute existence be known in our shared world of perception, experience, or mind? It CAN'T! The only way it can show up in the relative world is as a belief. The name is not it, the concept or imagination is not it, the belief is not it—not even close.

17:53 Some call what they perceive around them "God's creation." This might generate a disposition of appreciation, acceptance, and awe, but it is just a belief. And when we adopt such a belief, we are focused on the limited forms of Consciousness we perceive, and not the nature of it—or God itself. We are also pushing responsibility for this "creation" elsewhere and keeping it at arm's length. In this way, it gets us off the hook because we don't have to actually become conscious of what's True, we just need to embrace a belief that feels good.

17:54 Many centuries ago, there was a struggle about whether or not to use a word to refer to or name God. Perhaps this was because it was understood that this would degrade the reality in favor of a distinction and an idea. We can see that over the centuries this matter degraded far more than that, into cartoonish stories, images, and ideals. So, let's not talk in terms of God, it's weighed down by way too much baggage.

17:55 Leaving aside such titles, let's speak about existence or consciousness instead. The absolute nature of existence seems outside our ability to know or imagine. We are stuck within physics and biology, perception and life. In these domains, for us, everything makes sense and we know what is self and what is not self, and that is really all we need to know to be able to create the distinctions and abilities necessary to navigate through life.

17:56 When we start to consider, however, that reality is simply made up of various forms of consciousness, this creates another perspective—even if we don't directly grasp it but just hold it as a possibility. We then see everything—all objects, selves, interaction, cognition, light, movement, space, awareness, thought, and everything else—as simply limited forms of absolute consciousness. This changes our relationship to everything experienced and even to experience itself.

17:57 Yet you don't achieve such consciousness without eliminating the distinction of self and not-self. Why is that necessary if it is all the same consciousness? Because living and experiencing everything as either you or not-you keeps you stuck in a limited view of reality. Once you and not-you are gone, or transcended, reality is seen differently. Then there is no "me" or "not-me," there is only perceived distinctions that are all the same, meaning they all are just various forms of consciousness. So the rock and you are the same. Still hard to grasp that an object is the same as you, isn't it? But that's only because you remain stuck in your self. Toss that distinction, and a new experience arises. At least it's an interesting possibility to consider and contemplate.

Wrapping Up

17:58 You might think all this makes sense and just believe me about such an extraordinary possibility, but that isn't the invitation. Such belief lends itself to being too close to a religion and blind faith, which is not appropriate for this work. Certainly, adopting such a context of belief would make a huge difference in your experience, but then so does any belief system if you truly believe it and adopt it.

17:59 On the other hand, it is highly likely that you can't relate to this assertion at all and find it puzzling why I would go down such an obviously impossible road, and assume that I must have finally just gone off the rails. Perhaps all this contemplating has made me nuts, eh? Still, I stand by these assertions. Your job is to become conscious of what's true or not true about them. Indeed, it takes a very deep and unprecedented level of consciousness about the nature of existence to do so. Yet, it's not impossible, you just have to "get over your self." ☺

17:60 That's it, folks! It is a lot to take in, actually too much. The human mind can't absorb the depth of mind-bending communications that have been offered up to this point. I can only assert that they are true having become conscious of them myself, but I am at a loss to communicate them any better than I have. It is really up to you to find out what's true for yourself, beyond belief and assumption. I bet you noticed that I repeated myself over and over again. As I did, I hope your contemplations deepened each time, and you made leaps of insight, breaking through envelope after envelope (even though it's always been the same envelope). No matter how far you got, keep working on it, there's always more.

17:61 Toward that end the next section is focused on contemplation, taking up a committed practice to discover what's true no matter what it is or how it turns out. In one form or another, this is what you need to get all this. Good luck and may the wind fill your sails.

Part IV
THE STONE AND THE KNIFE

The Truth may be absolute, but our experience is not. Practices that are created with the intent to move closer to the absolute Truth, or increase our consciousness in any way, may or may not work to accomplish that end. Yet, as we scrape away at our relative experience by successfully having breakthrough after breakthrough, along with sudden and gradual understandings that increase our consciousness, we may move closer to grasping the Truth, even if we always seem to fall short of a complete and absolute enlightenment.

Perhaps the sticking point is that a relative cognition is not and never will be absolute consciousness, so there is nothing that can be done or experienced that can reach or grasp the absolute within a relative experience and mind. The leap needed to bridge this unbridgeable gap is grasping that the absolute is not separate from the relative. Instead of endlessly creeping to an infinitely distant goal, perhaps we could grasp that the real nature of the relative is absolute—and be conscious of how this is so. Beyond this leap, however, no practice will ever reach its end if the goal is to have a relative experience provide an absolute consciousness.

Chapter Eighteen

IN THE PURSUIT OF CONSCIOUSNESS

Taking Up a "Spiritual" Practice

18:1 You can become conscious of the absolute inside or outside of any practice. But the practice itself can't produce that result, only you can. A good practice may help you focus your attention on your inquiry and empower your intention to grasp what's true, but don't confuse method for results.

18:2 No method is absolute, it is an invention that may or may not be useful. Every method is only a method, and none are the Truth. No practice by itself can produce the result of direct consciousness and shouldn't be held as if it can. It may greatly assist you in doing that, but *you* have to do it, the method can't. This is what "direct" means.

18:3 Within a good practice, we tend to whittle away at our experience, eliminating beliefs and assumptions, programming and attachments, and whatever is unreal or unnecessary. This is appropriate. As we turn greater amounts of our attention and efforts to uncovering our unconscious assumptions—while working hard to become conscious of every facet and corner of our experience and reality—strangely, both our practice and the stockpile of our identity are reduced.

18:4 Sharpening a knife on a wet stone, both stone and knife are diminished. Just so, in an effective practice our self-identity, assumptions, and beliefs also become diminished, giving us the sharp edge of conscious clarity that can cut through ignorance and sever consciousness's attachment to mind, self, and perceptive-experience. Over time the practice itself also becomes simpler. This direction begins to empower the possibility of making a leap where we merge the relative and absolute into one consciousness. Yet such a leap in consciousness is extremely rare.

18:5 One thing to consider in all this, difficult as it may be, is that what is perceived—whatever we are aware of in our objective and subjective experience—is not the same as whatever is there. As Buddha said: "What you see as reality is like a 'cataract' on the eye of my true sight." His true sight, we postulate, is a direct consciousness of reality and not the indirect relative phenomena that are perception, concept, and experience. Our job is to have this same "true sight."

18:6 Any practice attempting to realize the absolute nature of existence should include both sides of the same coin. To do this, you must understand that the practice itself can't produce absolute consciousness—again, only *you* can, or should I say, only consciousness can, because it *is* consciousness, which is also the true nature of existence. So, inherent in the practice should be an awareness that it is reaching for something outside of anything that can be accomplished within it. It is as if representing the Truth without itself ever being true. It might be sort of like being in a dream and contemplating being awake—knowing that this won't succeed within the dream—but the attempt itself provides a link to the possibility of actually waking up while you're still dreaming.

18:7 So, perhaps we could say that the practice is more of a representative expression manifesting something that can't be manifest—somewhat like language represents a distinction with a form (a sound, a shape, etc.) that itself is not at all that distinction but at the same time brings the presence of the distinction to the fore. In this case, the absolute is not a distinction—even the distinction we make to think and speak of it—so it can't manifest in that way.

18:8 Therefore, this "practice" would simply act as a placeholder for the absolute within indirect perceptive-experience, pointing attention toward direct consciousness. There is a danger, however, that your practice forms the belief—which is not useful and only supports unconsciousness—that it somehow represents, and through its particular processes will produce, absolute consciousness. Or that it slips into a ritual of blindly believing in it, thus becoming something like a religion. This should be guarded against.

18:9 The intent should always be to become completely conscious of what is absolutely true. If you already are, then there is no need for a practice, but even then, you should take care that any forms of expression or appreciation or communication don't become mindless rituals, dogma, beliefs, or mere routines. And remember, there is always something more of which you are ignorant.

18:10 But if this is all a bridge too far, what do you do in the meantime? If you can't square the absolute with the relative, where should you put your attention and efforts? There is no place to put attention other than on the life you are living. The only added ingredient that transforms your life into a practice is to ask: What is it? No matter what you experience as you, life, others, relationship, existence, or anything else: What is it? What is its nature? How did it come to pass? Why does it exist?

18:11 Once you honestly and openly investigate reality and your experience of it, you are contemplating without changing a thing. You can contemplate as a separate practice, focusing on a subject and attempting to become conscious of its essence or nature. You can also investigate anything you experience, without any particular setting, posture, technique, or method. Simply want to discover what is ultimately true, even of the mundane and the normal. As I've confessed elsewhere, one of my favorite quotes is applicable here:

> *It's not that I'm so much smarter than anyone else, it's that I stay with the problem longer.*
>
> Albert Einstein

18:12 This is the only practice you really need. Seek to know everything, and eventually you may. Then all will reveal itself and the relative and absolute will become one. You'll live out the rest of your life and then fade into absolute nothing where you already are . . . or something like that. ☺

18:13 Of course, there is a lot to become conscious of that isn't absolute or even existential. Here, the goal is different, it is to improve our experience, not to grasp the truth—remember that. We could take up practices that increase awareness, improve mind and emotions, heighten sensitivity and health, discover unrecognized aspects of our experience or world, and so on. These kinds of practices are easier to understand than "spiritual" contemplative practices, and are usually less prone to mischief. We like them because they improve our experience of life. But, of course, they take work and repetition—pretty much the definition of practice—and so we may be too lazy to take them on.

Personal Problems with Any Practice

18:14 All practices are invented—even if most often by someone else—and require accomplishing something not yet attained or known. Because it isn't found in what's known, it is also not found in your experience. In other words, whatever the experience of attaining the ultimate goal of the practice is, you can't know.

18:15 Of course, you will always think you know because when being enrolled in adopting a practice, or upon creating it for yourself, you proceed only if it promises some wanted outcome. This necessitates imagining an outcome in some fashion. Yet, because of the nature of any practice that is pursuing becoming conscious of something of which you are not yet conscious, you actually won't be able to know the results of whatever such a practice promises prior to becoming conscious.

18:16 Within any practice this tends to be true, but with a practice leading to a relative development—improving or developing something physically, mentally, emotionally, or even "spiritually"—you can often observe others who've accomplished that end and see where it goes, or extrapolate the end result of the process you are engaging. For example, if you want big muscles and so practice lifting weights, it isn't hard to see others with big muscles accomplished from such practice. If you want to feel serene you might enter a practice of training equanimity and see the teachers showing signs of a peaceful composure when they are with you, and so imagine that this practice leads to your desired outcome. Just so, we imagine this same dynamic must also hold true for a practice promising direct consciousness. But it doesn't, and this is most often overlooked.

18:17 A somewhat frustrating aspect of such contemplative practices might be living with the very fact that your present experience isn't what you are trying to accomplish. It seems like you personally are as if barred from some "secret club" of obscure "knowledge" and so remain outside of the desired consciousness. I imagine this might be discouraging. But I also suspect that most often people committed to some practice don't dwell on this fact and perhaps overlook it altogether. Instead, one's attention is on making progress in the practice itself, either physically or subjectively.

18:18 A practice will almost always have physical rules to follow and mental states to achieve. The rules tell you how to physically proceed. Perhaps you must sit a certain way, adopt a particular posture, place your body on a specific cushion, gaze a certain way, breathe a certain way, focus on this or that, feel something or not feel something, and so on. It could include dressing some way or doing chores or activities or rituals. A practice will also probably involve trying to enter suggested states, think or not think in some way, focus on a subject, engage in some kind of mental or experiential routines, or create some imagined experience.

18:19 Whatever the practice consists of, this is where most of your attention is likely to go. If you start to become good at the physical and mental aspects of the practice, you begin to feel like you're making progress toward a deeper consciousness. Yet this may not be true at all.

18:20 The notion that you aren't any more conscious because you've "mastered" a practice might be difficult to hear since it sounds like you are failing at it. But be of good cheer, whatever you accomplish in the physical and mental domains are still accomplishments, and they might assist you in focusing on your ultimate goal. It is useful to notice, however, that these accomplishments themselves don't actually increase your consciousness.

18:21 Often more troublesome than the inherent mistakes and overlooked disconnects of any practice are the impinging forces of life—pain, emotion, distraction, frustration, disillusionment, boredom, and so on. It certainly isn't uncommon to become upset, frustrated, or disillusioned with some practice. Life has an abundance of distractions, and there are far more activities that bring us immediate gratification than a dreary practice.

18:22 When our practice feels like it is working and it seems we are making progress, or our fantasy of what we are doing is strong and present, we may well feel satisfied with it. Yet, a lot occurs in life—much of which feels very important and in need of attention—that can feel contradictory to or in conflict with a practice or the beliefs of the practice.

18:23 The pains that arise in the course of life can easily derail us. Emotional pain of various kinds can be overwhelming sometimes and may turn us into cynics or skeptics about even the goals of the practice. Such painful events can sideline our enthusiasm for our practice and might also motivate us to resist, suspend, or even reject it.

18:24 Such reactions may well interrupt our practice, unless we simply blindly believe in it, imagining that even in our most painful moments some mysterious "grace" will be bestowed upon us because of it. This requires that we merely follow the routines of the practice without question.

18:25 Questioning, however, should be the cornerstone of any practice to increase consciousness, and so blind faith is detrimental to real progress. Of course, we might also realize at some point that the practice we have chosen is bogus, just a fantasy built around a belief system and not an honest and grounded practice with the intent to directly grasp whatever is true about reality. These things need to be sorted out.

18:26 Even if our practice seems genuine and effective, how do we deal with the pain and distractions of life without setting aside the practice? The pull of such forces can seem overwhelming and urgent at times, and any practice can easily be set aside, as it is not urgent and is rarely in any way overwhelming.

18:27 Many people put attention on contemplation when they are mildly curious, engage in some fantasy, are bored, or feel like it might ease their dissatisfaction with life. I think managing to maintain a practice throughout ups and downs requires getting that what we're after is the truth, and that never stops being the case no matter what we experience.

18:28 We also have to grasp that no matter what we experience, our intent is to discover what's true about that very experience, as well as what's true beyond that experience. But even with such a commitment we are still likely to at least temporarily put our practice aside and succumb to pain, self-doubt, and other debilitating reactions from time to time. It's an obstacle that we shouldn't ignore but instead learn to relate to effectively. One way to do that—consistent with a practice committed to discovering the truth—is to investigate the very challenging experience we are enduring, contemplating its nature and why it exists.

18:29 On the other hand, independent of the crippling challenges of pain and self-doubt, we have the flip-side tendency of self-aggrandizement—feeling we are a spiritually superior person because we are engaging in some practice. This may or may not be obvious to us or others, since the "culture" of the practice itself might include a certain humility in its expression. Yet even within this self-deprecating idea there can easily be a sense of self-aggrandizement arising from our apparent accomplishments. Commensurate with this totally common human tendency is the possibility that an individual believes that they are actually superior because of their practice and accompanying belief system. This should be acknowledged and confronted when it is occurring and, if possible, transcended.

18:30 Of course, there is the more minor obstacle of finding time to do your practice. The demands of work, family, or just living life can all suck up a great deal of your time. Although real, I call this a minor problem for the simple reason that most practices that involve inquiry and contemplation can be done without formality or setting.

18:31 People often attach a setting or specific routine to their practice, but if you think about what it is you are really trying to accomplish, it is highly likely that this can be accomplished without any routine or setting. There are often many times throughout a day that your attention can successfully be put on such goals, and so you can contemplate at various times and in different circumstances. Certainly, a special time and quiet setting, or a group effort, or uncommon actions that accompany a practice can help one focus and put full attention on the effort. This can be very useful. It just isn't an insurmountable obstacle, especially since priorities can be made and time allotted if the commitment is real.

The Danger of Beliefs

18:32 One of the most challenging dynamics to overcome that pretty much always attaches itself to any practice is a belief system. This often shows up as beliefs that frame and explain the practice and its goals. But believing is an error. Because of its central role in the practice—giving us a rationale for its pursuit and providing an imaginary end point—it is very tricky not to adopt these beliefs as a reality and still commit to the practice.

18:33 In the beginning of any learned endeavor we are at the mercy of whatever teacher or system we choose to join. As we are newly exposed to some practice, we must believe the claims of the system since that is what is presented. Given the presented practice resonates with us enough for us to take it up, it will likely seem to agree with our already established beliefs, or at least have a convincing argument about why it is effective. Since in the beginning we don't really know how effective a practice is or how it actually works, we are at the mercy of believing in what we are told, or what we have invented ourselves if we go down that road.

18:34 So, beliefs come with the package. This dynamic is pretty much unavoidable. If you scrutinize any practice, you can observe the beliefs that are touted and how these influence the practice. But if you are clear-headed about it and look from a detached perspective, you can also discern many beliefs and assumptions not stated that are buried within it. It is very useful to dig out every belief attached to a practice, as well as every belief you have personally applied to it, and spend some time detaching from them all, viewing the practice newly once freed from them.

18:35 Beliefs are just beliefs. They are not whatever is true, they are concepts of something claimed to be true. The chances are remote that they even come close to what is really true because that's not their purpose. Their purpose most often serves a different master—to support a fantasy or a made-up cosmology, give direction or purpose to life, agree with one's self-agenda in some way, ground us in an invented "reality" of some kind, help us feel good, be an avenue for someone to make money, and so on. Those pursuits may seem useful to someone, but none are the pursuit of the truth.

18:36 In any case, it is hard to recognize beliefs as beliefs and go beyond them to search for what is true—either using the practice or discarding it. Since all practices have some beliefs attached to them, these beliefs should be clarified and scrutinized—and discarded if at all possible. Blind beliefs are a trap in any practice.

18:37 Even my own work falls prey to this dilemma. Before I wrote any books on consciousness, my committed students tended to have more breakthroughs than after the books came out. I can't say for sure, but it seems very likely this is due to the new students "believing" what I write and so filling their heads with ideas and fantasies, even as I ward them off from doing that. In so doing, they pursue concepts they developed from what they read, rather than take on a genuine open-ended pursuit of whatever is true starting from a blank slate. This occurs even after much time is spent telling them not to do that. So, take care to avoid believing. Instead, pursue whatever is true, no matter how it turns out.

The Direct Method

18:38 There are many methods that can support an increase in consciousness, and even more that can assist personal growth in various ways. To be sure, there is a great deal that can be accomplished in the relative domain—which, remember, is everything that is known or experienced in any way. Here, there's a lot to become conscious of—every facet of life and every kind of experience is ripe for deeper understanding. The nature of emotion, thought, language, communication, process, self, mind, and so on are all subjects for greater consciousness. Insights and breakthroughs can and should abound in the domain of life.

18:39 But none of this is absolute, or the true nature of existence. This nature can only be gleaned directly. Therefore, there is only one "method" for direct consciousness or enlightenment—it has to be done directly.

18:40 This "direct method" is not actually a method. A method requires process, and process in a specific form. "Direct" means there is no process and it has no form. But then, you might wonder: What are we talking about here, and what are we doing when we attempt to use the direct method?

18:41 Whatever we "do" in this regard isn't the direct part, because *doing* itself demands a process. In this form of contemplation, process and doing are kept to a minimum while also striving to be devoid of fantasies and belief systems. This sets the scene for our direct method.

18:42 The "method" itself is to keep attention on a subject of inquiry, some aspect of existence, and intend to become conscious of its true nature. There is very little else attached to it. Sometimes communication may be added in dyads to facilitate moving through mental barriers or assumptions. Or perhaps contemplating mind-bending considerations—such as most of what has been communicated in this book—is taken on to shake loose assumptions or mental routines that might have built up in the minds of contemplators, and so on. But even such additions, minus any peripherals, should always be kept to bare bones and not be confused with the direct intent when contemplating. In the end no matter what is done, we should always keep the focus on intending, without fanfare or distractions, to become directly conscious. The *direct* aspect is the *consciousness itself.*

18:43 "Direct" means there is no separation, no distance, no process, no path, no travel or activity of any kind. You are "it" so to speak. You are there. There is nothing to do to "get" there. It is not a perception of something—which is always indirect. Perception is simply a "representation" of some kind, giving partial, limited, and specialized information about the form or effect of whatever is perceived. Nor is direct consciousness an experience of any kind—it is not a concept, feeling, intuition, or any other mental activity or function of the senses. It *is* the actual thing-itself, otherwise it is not direct!

18:44 A direct consciousness is the true nature of the subject. No process makes it happen, it can't be a paint-by-the-numbers affair or accomplished via a step-by-step procedure, no matter how cleverly such a procedure might be designed.

18:45 The direct "method" is to fiercely intend to "know" a subject, focusing on it and being open to whatever is true, until a sudden consciousness occurs. There really is no more to it than that, and even this simple "action" taken to attempt direct consciousness is not the direct consciousness itself. This method is so absent of frills or steps, beliefs or activities, the mind can have a hard time dealing with it.

18:46 To be sure, the mind will be involved and do its best to solve the problem. It just won't be able to. But it should be allowed to try as hard as it can, it is how you keep your attention on the subject. It is like trying to see a "magic eye" autostereogram image. The 3D image is not seen at all, and what is seen is clearly not it. Yet you must still stare into the image for as long as it takes to make the shift and see what's there in 3D. When this leap occurs there is no doubt about what you see. It is clear and you can easily speak authoritatively about what's there because you see it in detail. If you didn't attempt to look into it, you wouldn't finally see what was previously completely unknown. This is a metaphor for contemplation. Keep focusing on the subject until you have a direct consciousness of the matter. When you do, it is completely clear and obvious.

18:47 It is best to know, however, that everything arising in one's awareness is not the direct part. Yet, consistent with the focused intent and attempt to have a direct consciousness, all that arises should not be resisted. You need to allow every contribution to the effort in whatever form it takes. Perhaps you could hold such mental actions as being rather like a well-meaning coach trying to help you in your endeavor, but no matter what is contributed by the coach, in the end you're the one who has to do it. The coach can't do it—all that activity isn't the thing-itself.

18:48 This direct method doesn't give much to occupy or distract the mind. It most often doesn't provide good feelings or a sense of accomplishment, beyond the pride or satisfaction you might feel at having committed yourself to the attempt. So, it can be a difficult road and may not be for everyone. A real and strong commitment to grasp whatever is true is requisite, and it is the only thing that could keep you engaged in this "method." Again, the direct method is to simply become conscious of what's absolutely True. This can't be done in any other way but directly.

18:49 Clearly, this asserts that direct-consciousness itself transcends all perception, experience, awareness, or any indirect method of "knowing." It is not a conclusion, no matter how conclusive it seems, or a state, or any other contrivance that will often insert itself as the "answer." We are not looking for an answer but a consciousness of whatever is true. If we can only be conscious of what we perceive or experience, then no direct consciousness is possible; our knowledge of anything would be indirect and not absolute. In life and in our experience this is always the case, but it is not with direct-consciousness.

18:50 Consciousness that is direct means we are in the very same place as the subject. We grasp its true nature because we are conscious of this nature. It is obvious because our consciousness is not separate from the absolute existence of the subject. Again, the "direct method" is to simply focus on and intend to become directly conscious of our subject until we do.

Consciousness, Awareness, Perception, and Cognition

18:51 There seems to be a lot of confusion about the differences between consciousness, awareness, perception, and cognition, since these activities all seem to be more or less the same thing, or at least to share the same domain. This domain we could call forms of "knowing." But if they are all the same we don't need four different words for them, so let me attempt to clarify the distinctions I make in this area.

18:52 Consciousness is the source of all forms of knowing as well as existence. This is a distinction not found in the English language, so I'm using the term "consciousness" in a new way. Consciousness itself has no form, yet every form of knowing is also a form of consciousness, as is every form of relative existence. Consciousness precedes and is the source of all knowing and perceptive-experience. It precedes and is independent of self and not-self, and so self-survival. This is what I'm referring to when speaking of direct-consciousness or enlightenment.

18:53 Yet, having a direct-consciousness doesn't necessarily provide a complete understanding of the nature of consciousness-itself because our attention is on the nature of the subject we're attempting to become conscious of. The nature of consciousness-itself is right there when we do have these breakthroughs, it is just most often missed. This is one reason having many such "enlightenments," increasing in depth and scope, assists in ultimately grasping the nature of consciousness.

18:54 Although we can't say that consciousness itself is a particular form of knowing, we also can't say that is it different from what is known no matter the form. It is as if the "mother" of all forms of knowing and existence. It's quite difficult to speak about consciousness since it exists prior to cognition or distinction. Consciousness as a function of a form of knowing tends to arise into awareness as insights or sudden direct understanding, but even these—free and open as they are—will be formed and limited to some degree, and so not revelatory of the nature of conscious itself.

18:55 Normally we confuse awareness or being aware with consciousness. Sometimes being conscious is held as simply being able to perceive and be cognizant, like when one is knocked out we say they are unconscious. But that isn't how I'm using the term. Consciousness is the source and context for all forms of knowing and existence. Awareness, on the other hand, is when stuff begins to become known.

18:56 Awareness is different from what I am referring to as consciousness. Consciousness is not "known," since it is the context for knowing; it is as if nowhere or exists in "nothing," or you might think of it as if it's in the background, so to speak. Awareness brings consciousness into a world of "knowing we are knowing." At its root, awareness is without specificity, although it becomes formed when it relates to whatever we are aware of.

18:57 In this way, awareness is wed to perception and mind, it is the act of gleaning that something is occurring. Usually this involves perceiving something and noticing it in the context of your internal or external environment. Awareness and perception are linked, as they seem to form the foundations for each other.

18:58 Being aware that we are perceiving, however, is different from having a perception of something. Without the act of perception we have nothing to be aware of, and without awareness a perception doesn't come to our attention, nor do we reflect upon it. When we "increase" awareness, becoming aware of something of which we were unaware, or perhaps becoming more sensitive to our surroundings, and so on, we say we are more aware.

18:59 Yet, awareness is a rather general or inclusive activity that becomes specific when something is perceived and interpreted. Being aware might apply to something in particular, that is to say, being aware of something perceived;

or it could just be being aware that we are aware, that awareness is occurring regardless of specificity—this is focusing on awareness itself.

18:60 For example, as mentioned, we could be aware of our surroundings by activating a sensitivity to and putting attention on our environment in present time. We may be mechanically perceiving what is there, but without applying attention to being aware of these perceptions they mostly go overlooked. With increased awareness, all the perceptive organs are engaged, and attention is devoted to the task of being aware of all that comprises the present moment. Bringing attention to what is perceived, known, or experienced could be called an act of awareness.

18:61 In a very different way, we could also be aware of conceptual knowledge or other forms of "knowledge" that aren't currently being perceived as a thought, such as knowing the values of a culture or the proper behavior in certain circumstances. So, we might say we are "aware" of cultural values or the context for some event, etc. If this knowledge arises specifically into our experience only then is it "perceived" or noted and brought to the fore.

18:62 The distinction between awareness and perception suggests that perception is more like a mechanical activity, and awareness is a function of putting attention on that or any activity. Awareness is the act by which we know anything is being perceived. In fact, we can perceive something without being aware of the perception. If we don't put attention on the perception and bring it into our awareness it goes unnoticed even if a perceptive activity is taking place.

18:63 For example, we can see that there are many things within our perceptive field that can be seen or heard of which we are unaware because we ignore the presence of that data, relegating it to the domain of unimportant or insignificant. This occurs a lot. But in order to consider something is so insignificant as to remain unseen, we'd have to know it exists in the first place. That puts us back in a domain of a function of awareness or a mind that works on a level that is not noticed. Even though we may be perceiving what we "unconsciously" assess as insignificant data, there is obviously some form of consciousness operating in the background, but we say we become aware of it only when it comes to our attention.

18:64 Perception, on the other hand, is a meaningless phenomenon that supplies mechanical data we must then sort out and identify. Biologically, it is an activity that uses various methods that are stimulated in different ways by the presence of something. It is as if being indirectly "touched" by or connected to the presence of some element of existence. This usually takes place when a creature forms an organ that can receive some form of data about its environment.

18:65 The possibilities for perception are infinite, yet the form it takes or method used is particular—even though possible variations are wide open. For us it primarily comes through eyes, ears, nose, mouth, and bodily sensations, but perception also applies to everything we perceive conceptually or mentally and emotionally. Yet, mere perception isn't useful without interpretation, it is just an activity that takes place and all by itself is a meaningless phenomenon.

18:66 Cognition or "recognition" is a conceptual activity that allows us to interpret and so "know" what something is. We can see that awareness and perception are necessary for cognition to take place, and it can be difficult to separate which is which. To simplify we might say cognition is the process that brings perceptive data into specific and usable forms for self-survival. Perhaps we could say consciousness is the underlying foundation for all forms of knowing or existence, awareness is the capacity to focus attention on anything, perception is the receiving of data, and cognition is making sense of it in a way that serves us specifically.

18:67 Even though cognition is the most limited form of these distinctions, it is also the most useful and the most understandable in the sense that it is easily graspable and fully formed. Through cognition the subject is placed in context, related to the self, and means something to us individually. Although through cognition we have a solid grasp of our reality or anything that is occurring, it is founded on our own self-mind and assumptions, beliefs, and programming, and so such recognition is not an accurate representation of what's real. Yet it is our most valuable tool for survival.

18:68 Freeing ourselves from the idea that what we cognize is necessarily true allows us to investigate and change unnecessary mental activity that is unhealthy or ineffective. By focusing on forms of consciousness that are more basic or prior to our cognized experience we can more readily recognize and challenge the errors and ineffective experiences that plague us. It's useful to look into these matters, they form our entire known world.

18:69 I only bring up the way I use these words so you have a better sense of the distinctions I make and can better glean what I'm talking about when I use them. Of course, sometimes I will be rigorous in their usage and sometimes I will use them more informally to keep the communication going, and you simply have to discern from the context the distinction I'm referring to. Ultimately it doesn't matter. What matters is what you grasp or become conscious of.

The Spirit of This Work

18:70 One of the hardest things to get across to people is the real spirit behind this work. I think those who study with me inevitably begin to sense it over time, yet clarifying it into a condensed communication can be challenging. Even I have difficulty telling a stranger what it is I do. There is such a big gap between the common touchstones that most of us share as an assumed reality and what I'm often trying to convey that there are no starting places for an accurate communication. To leap across the gap between the two takes a commitment and openness that is generally lacking in humanity. My inability to easily bridge this gap notwithstanding, it is the spirit behind this endeavor that is its most important component, and the principle I'd most like not to be lost when I die.

18:71 The "spirit" or driving principle behind my work is really the same in the martial and body-being investigations as it is in the consciousness work.

Simply stated, it could be said that the purpose is to discover—in every way possible and every aspect of the subject—whatever is true, including its very nature. That is the basis, but it still doesn't reveal all that is behind this endeavor. Let's unpack this a bit, beginning with the question: How does this spirit show up?

18:72 Is a strong *drive* or "obsession" to honestly and personally seek out what's really true a necessary element? Absolutely. Sometimes people ask where they can find the motivation necessary to pursue this work. The motivation is simply wanting to know what's true! This prime element provides all the motivation you need—unless, of course, you don't really want to know. From this motivation, a real interest, wonder, fascination, and curiosity should arise, without which how would your mind be stimulated to investigate the existential makeup of all that is experienced, including a deeper questioning of what might be overlooked?

18:73 You will also need a kind of *self-contained capacity* to investigate any subject. You must create the possibility that you personally can directly uncover whatever subject you tackle. This is not about having opinions, figuring out, or drawing conclusions. It is living inside the possibility that you can directly experience, for yourself, whatever is true, independent of beliefs or hearsay. Without taking on this responsibility, and so putting yourself in the driver's seat, you would be limited to guessing or to buying others' assertions, and neither of these is consistent with this work.

18:74 So, what we might call an obsession or drive to become conscious of whatever subject we take on is essential to the spirit of this work. That isn't to say it has to show up as overwhelming enthusiasm, or that you should throw up your hands because the job is "just too big." Start with a genuine wanting to know and proceed with what can be done given where you are now. You simply need to want to achieve whatever it is you are attempting and be willing to pursue it until it becomes a conscious reality for you.

18:75 Commensurate with this "obsession" is a *passion* for the work. Being enthusiastic about the pursuit is useful, but not necessary. Poetically speaking, it needs to be more like a deep fire or fervor that runs like a nuclear reactor fueling your investigations. Many challenges can arise—negative resistance is likely to occur, and you may well run into seemingly insurmountable barriers—but it's your passionate commitment that will get you through these challenges. Such passion also stimulates the brain and sharpens your mind, as well as keeps your attention and awareness always working on the problem, even in the background, to produce fruit at a later time.

18:76 *Honesty* is clearly an element as well—especially developing self-honesty to the point that it hurts and may well run counter to self-interests. No matter what the subject is, the truth can't be pursued through any kind of deception, bias, misrepresentation, lying, ignoring, distortion, or any other activity that isn't aligned with what's true. Honesty is simply aligning your experience—including your thinking, communications, expressions, and so on—as best you can with whatever you assess to be true. Again, grasp that "honest" relates to "true" and so must be a component in pursuing the truth.

18:77 Another crucial element is to look beyond convention and assumption. Taking nothing for granted, and being willing for the result to be unexpected or even unwanted or inconceivable, is essential to create the *openness* needed to pursue such consciousness. The only criterion is that the result is actually true. Because of this commitment, courage is necessary.

18:78 A degree of *courage* is also required since not only do you need to confront a self-honesty that can prove painful and difficult, you need the courage to delve into areas that may prove unfruitful or challenging. You may think you discovered something that in the end is found to be mistaken. In this case, correction needs to vigorously occur, despite any embarrassment that might arise. You might also discover something that goes against your beliefs or fantasies or desires, and therefore will have to give those up. The main commitment must be to discover what's true, beyond personal cost. Such an effort includes discovering or learning facts, figuring out how something works, or realizing the principles and dynamics behind interaction, emotion, perception, or any other life activity, as well as becoming conscious of what is absolutely True beyond human conception or experience.

18:79 I suspect when I say "beyond human conception or experience," people may be baffled by this. Am I saying that it is inaccessible? If so, then what's the point of pursuing it? To be clear, I'm asserting that human conception and understanding or even experience is not the end-all to what's possible. The goal isn't to find what can be found within the limits of our own mind or biological parameters, but to grasp what's actually true.

18:80 When it comes to what's absolutely True, this must step outside any limitation. Therefore, we have to create the possibility that we can become directly conscious independent of anything conceivable or perceivable, and independent from all hearsay or what anyone, including ourselves, asserts. Direct consciousness isn't limited to any form of experience, understanding, or conception.

18:81 Like I mentioned, a disposition commensurate with this spirit and endeavor is to put oneself in the driver's seat—meaning you must make it your own. If you look at almost any of the books I've been asked to sign over the decades, the message is inevitably "Make it your own." This sentiment is essential because if you are not at the source of personally experiencing or being conscious of anything I've communicated, or anything you are attempting to discover, it won't become real for you.

18:82 By now, everyone interested in my work knows I am strongly against anyone believing anything I say—or anything they say or anyone else says. Believing or assuming is contrary to this pursuit and is actually detrimental. This is an important point. Spinning one's internal wheels or adopting hearsay is not what true discovery is about. The practice needs to be beyond oneself because the truth isn't about oneself, it is about itself—even though oft times the "itself" is yourself. In my other writings, I've outlined quite extensively the dynamics that dominate our perceptions and experience that will always be inconsistent with any clarity in discerning the truth. Yet, here we're looking at the spirit behind our pursuit rather than anything discovered using it.

18:83 As I've pointed out, genius has a lot to do with staying with the problem until it is solved—this could be called contemplation. It is also what it takes to get to this level of consciousness and knowledge. A rather "impatient patience" is another key element that seems to contribute to this work.

18:84 If you put together what I've mentioned so far you may be able to glean the indomitable spirit behind what I do. I'm not claiming it is a complete list or fully captures this spirit, but it's a start, and points you in a direction. It seems that some of the operating principles that stand out within this spirit are:

- A committed drive and passion to discover whatever's true
- Creating a self-contained capacity and possibility that you can personally grasp what's true
- Honesty, Courage, and Responsibility (making it your own)
- Looking beyond convention, assumption, conception, perception, and oneself
- Not believing; but instead, grasping what's true for yourself
- Being impatiently patient and staying with problems longer

18:85 If you're up for it, I recommend that you work to bring each point into your experience until it is operating as a principle that governs your thinking, questioning, and searching. Maintain it for some time. When you can experience being aligned with each principle, experience them all as a function of your ongoing and daily consciousness. Then find the spirit where these principles arise naturally, and must arise for that spirit to exist.

18:86 I still can't actually tell you what this "spirit" is in some easy-to-remember sound bite. But if you consider something that inherently contains all the elements I've outlined, perhaps you get the idea. Leaping beyond the idea, grasp it as a simple and indomitable intent or principle. This intent walks a razor's edge that operates from the aforementioned distinctions as a matter of course, knowing when you or anyone is pursuing the truth, and when you or they are not. Yet you really have to do it, not just think about it.

18:87 Commensurate with our look into the spirit of this endeavor may be a disposition I adopted early on. One of the reasons I may seem to have insights, clarity, and abilities where others don't is my lack of attachment to any domain of human invention. Inevitably people fall into a particular world view, what I inaccurately call a "cosmology" or belief system about reality—traditional or modern—such as some form of spirituality, all kinds of fantasies, personal-growth perspectives, martial art dogmas, religions of all kinds, or any other invented human view about reality along with its accompanying beliefs. Adopting any such world of beliefs molds one's thinking to conform to this system, and so biases and distorts one's view of the cosmos or reality. It also limits the possibilities considered for investigation and the directions in which one will look.

18:88 Consider that most of what is presented in this book—much of which virtually no human has even considered—could only have been discovered through such an approach. Most often, however, people are unknowingly stuck in some view or belief that will prevent any real open questioning. This belief system is often simply hearsay, yet sometimes it comes from personal conclusions that are really just conjecture. Although generating a "cosmology" of beliefs—meaning an overall view of reality—is extremely common and dominant in almost all investigations claiming to seek the truth of some matter, it is a mistake.

18:89 Transcending assumptions and beliefs is necessary in order to pursue an open and true investigation or contemplation. Most people don't know that the "worlds" they believe in—whether it is a spiritual belief system, a practice of some sort, a gloomy outlook on life, an affectation of some kind, a fantasy, or any other view—are not true. They are just made up, often by others in which we join, or by oneself for various, often unconscious, reasons.

18:90 Challenging all these beliefs is an important step toward freedom and the pursuit of the truth. If after transcending the dogma and beliefs of some invented world you still find its basic framework to be useful toward some end, it can be used, but with the knowledge it is only a tool serving a purpose and is not necessary or true in and of itself. The spirit of this work includes becoming free from all such beliefs and dogmas.

Call a Practice What It Is

18:91 One of my pet peeves is people calling their practice or pursuit what it is not. This seems to happen quite a bit and is unnecessary and misleading. If people simply called it what it is then I'd have no problem. In these cases, there is always something that is being pursued and practiced. If it is accurately called what it is then we can align with that and all is well. Yet when it is represented as something it is not, we are fooled or misled, and tend to make up fantasies that aren't real at all.

18:92 For example, in the martial arts there are many arts that are not at all fighting practices—actually most aren't. Yet, many schools say they are developing fighting skills when they really aren't. Such arts might include most schools of T'ai Chi, Aikido, Karate, various Kung Fu arts, Wu Shu, and many other martial arts. I know this might sound strange to most people, but only those arts that train and compete in some form of actual fighting can be called fighting arts. Arts in this domain might be boxing, muay thai, judo, MMA, and fencing, for example.

18:93 Those arts that are primarily choreographed techniques, or are fundamentally some form of dance, or do unrealistic games, aren't really fighting arts, even though they may call themselves that. If they called themselves what they are, a form of techniques learning to do such and such, or a dance in which such and such is developed, etc., then there is no disconnect within or without.

18:94 It is the same for spirituality or any other practice. For example, sometimes people pursue more empowering or healthier states and yet call this seeking the truth. We can see that in life there is nothing wrong with, and may be lots of benefits to, pursuing empowering and healthier states. Simply call it that and we are on the same page. Call it seeking enlightenment or pursuing the Truth, and I have a problem, because it's not.

18:95 Following a belief system as if it is the same thing as trying to grasp the truth is another example. How many pursuits can you think of that when it comes down to it, there is no real or open pursuit of whatever's true no matter how it turns out? Instead, they are pursuing something believed to be true, and definitely want it to turn out a certain way. There are many such examples, more than not, I think. Religions are always based on some sort of fantasy and invented cosmology and yet they also always promote themselves as *the* path to the Truth, even though religions require blind faith instantly available, and nowhere in blind faith is there the intent to grasp whatever is true whether it agrees with your beliefs or not.

18:96 There may be something quite beneficial to some practice, but it should be called what it is. Then again, there may also be overlooked negative consequences to a practice. At least calling it what it is clarifies its real purpose and goals. To me, it isn't misleading and is far more powerful when pains are taken to call something what it is. We can pursue it or not, but at least now we know what it is we're taking up or rejecting.

Part V
NEW PERSPECTIVES

Chapter Nineteen

A FEW MORE DISTINCTIONS TO CONSIDER

19:1 So much in this book will inevitably seem out of reach or abstract, and will probably take much more contemplation and investigation to absorb. Yet, life goes on, even while such pursuits are undertaken. So, I want to provide a small look at a few possibilities that can make a significant difference in your life and can be put to work right away.

19:2 There are many powerful distinctions to make and insights to have about principles that empower your investigations and your experience of life. You can see quite a few of these in other books I've written, but let's hit a few more here that may not have been covered there. Making clear or finer distinctions in your experience always empowers your ability to more effectively engage in life, and it improves your ability to question and investigate anything.

Existential Assumptions

19:3 What I mean by existential assumptions is frequently misunderstood, or more accurately, what it takes to grasp them is. (For more of an introduction to this domain, see Chapter Twenty-Two in *The Book of Not Knowing.*) When the notion is proffered that there are some basic core beliefs or assumptions about your very existence, the character of your being—examples of such assumptions are that your being is broken or flawed, worthless or inadequate, missing something important, and so on, the kinds of things we've seen when exploring feelings of being incomplete—this domain is often seen as virtually inaccessible, taking a lifetime of contemplation to unearth. This is not a useful way to look at it. Why do you get stuck in spinning your wheels fruitlessly, and how could you more effectively hear this possibility so as to get free?

19:4 People's first approach to trying to solve this dilemma usually relates to a psychological perspective. But this is based on far too many paradigm assumptions common to psychology, as well as lots of socially accepted realities and assumptions that just aren't true. In this world, being worthless or broken is seen as a personal malady usually formed in childhood, often as a result of parenting or other social circumstances, and individuals tend to seek historical reasons to find a resolution. Frequently, this process takes a long time with little success in "curing" the psychological "disease."

19:5 Within this psychological paradigm and thinking, one tends to live inside the emotion, accepting it as real and looking for its cause. In normal life, people are pushed around by their emotions, imagining that circumstances or others are "doing it to them." Just so, in the so-called "unconscious" domain of mind, one looks for the historical events that are responsible their distress. This pseudo-psychological approach usually goes nowhere because its foundation and view remain in place and are not questioned, even though they are not true. A slightly different way to relate to these feelings is to step back and to psycho-analyze what's going on and see if you can figure out why you feel that way, such as I'm bad and wrong because... and you try to fill in the blank.

19:6 Getting outside emotional reactivity can be done in a couple of ways. One is to apply the intellect to reason out what may be going on. This provides a detachment from the emotion so you aren't stuck "inside" it, being dominated and blinded by it. Even though the rational approach may inject some impartiality in the matter, it is abstracted from the reality that is lived; and although it may help gain some perspective not entirely dominated by the reaction, it doesn't get to the root of the problem.

19:7 On the other hand, to approach it existentially means you look into the experience itself without assumptions, and certainly without social or psychological preconceptions. This is to simply approach the reality of its existence—*what is it? why is it?*—not basing this contemplation on demanding the world be the way you think it is. In this way you can unearth what's going on experientially, and in a manner that allows you to eliminate the whole thing. This is the world of unearthing existential assumptions.

19:8 An existential assumption simply refers to an assumption you have about your existence, and since it is an assumption, it isn't true. Again, this is the domain where you might feel worthless, incapable, less than, broken, flawed, that something essential in your experience is missing, and so on. You think these are aspects of your existence, as if they are simply how you are. I suggest they are assumptions, perhaps deep and life-long assumptions but mental constructs nevertheless.

19:9 Your job in this arena is to discover what they are and see that they have dominated your self-view. Then, get they are conceptual in nature and eliminate them. This doesn't have to take a long time at all, it can be done in a few minutes or hours—if not, then more time may be needed. But it shouldn't be made into a life-long struggle. When you get the existential nature of such assumptions, you experience that they are conceptually generated and so experience them as something you are doing. As pointed out many times in many places, if you are doing something, you can stop doing it.

19:10 I have mentioned this domain of experience in other books, but what I want to clarify here is the way people get stuck in psychological loops that don't go anywhere. They seem to misunderstand how to relate to the idea of existential assumptions. This domain starts by noticing patterns of emotions or behavior, usually negative, and wondering why they exist. A way to begin this investigation is to look into your core experience of being a person. After this scrutiny, you ask what is at the source of the existence of some discovered characteristic trait or emotional pattern.

19:11 To help clarify, let me take one example and work it through, so you can see some of the stuff that might arise along the way, and how you might unearth unnoticed layers to such an experience. Primarily, I want to walk you through the kind of thinking and investigating that could unfold in such a contemplation. It is only a sample to provide some specificity. It shouldn't be held as typical or used as a template, or seen as the only way to go. It is just one possibility to help show layers that might normally be overlooked.

19:12 Let's say I look into the fundamental character of my person, and perhaps I come up with or see that I am arrogant and self-centered. This might be hard to admit or embarrassing to confess, but as I look deeply and honestly into my core thinking, feeling, and behavior, I conclude this is a true statement. Yet, although this alone might seem like a big step because it's not the norm in our social culture, it is only the beginning. A solid beginning for sure, and if I go no further such a discovery or admission could strongly influence my experience and behavior, depending on how I relate to this realization.

19:13 What is at the bottom or source of the existence of this disposition? As I look into it more, and consider outside of assumptions, I further discover or see that my arrogance is based on the fact that I am afraid of others and feel less than them. At first, I don't fully understand how these are connected, but I see both are true and the latter insight seems deeper and more at the core of my person.

19:14 Yet, this is all still stuck in our human psychology and so is still limited to our social assumptions and the meaning we attribute to all these feelings. So, to make progress I consider this same experience existentially, outside of social convention. How might I proceed to do this? I could simply do it by understanding and dropping a social context, but that may not be accessible to me yet, so I might engage in some long-winded mental research.

19:15 Perhaps I back off my individual challenges and consider our shared reality more broadly. I do this to get some context and background for my personal feelings of self-importance. I see that in our western modern culture we tend to hold the individual as of supreme importance and as if it stands on its own. I begin to recognize that these are false assumptions built on evolving views that over time skewed our collective experience toward our selfish and self-serving impulses. From this trend, we started to view ourselves as important, unique, and special, as well as coming to believe that the self somehow exists independently from our shared cultural and human experience. But these assumptions are all conceptual inventions and not actually true.

19:16 Although this is just a possible contribution to my investigation, I think it may have a significant relationship to my inquiry and perhaps sets the stage for my personal experience. Besides, I find it fascinating and so I spend more time delving into it. Intellectually, I notice there are billions more others than me, and that social reality is overwhelmingly based on all of us, not me alone. Although that is only a concept, my grounded experience shows there are a lot more people than I—everywhere I look there are tons of others. So my self is always less than the many others that exist and with which I live, and collectively they have far more power than do I.

19:17 Once seen, this is obviously true, and I notice that the implications of this lopsided relationship go back to birth. Even before I could fully comprehend the vast world of other people, simply being raised by one, or a few, is still more and bigger than I am. One major thing that is overlooked is the fact that even compared to just one other (parent), my newly forming self doesn't even come close to equaling them. In the beginning of my life I am not able to do anything for myself. On the other hand, the other (usually mother) does everything for me.

19:18 As I begin to form cognitive abilities, from my viewpoint she seems to have the ability to do everything, and to know everything. I can virtually do nothing and know nothing. How can I not see myself as less-than, powerless, and not part of or equal to the other more capable and powerful human(s)? I can't avoid this comparative relationship being ingrained in my psyche. Think this goes away as I grow? Why would it?

19:19 As a baby, you must experience yourself as incapable, powerless, and ignorant. It isn't seen as a problem since you know nothing else. But as you develop, quickly you begin to compare your experience to others and find yourself on the bottom of that totem pole. (I know, it is the other way around with totem poles, but that doesn't have the same ring to it.)

19:20 You know there are currently aspects of yourself that are still a child, because even as you've developed into an adult such a reality doesn't go away just because you grow up. Living within the observation that at your core or beginning you were not in the same class as the others, and even today don't have the power to alter the accepted social reality created by a community composed of many more others than you, your self is seen as smaller and less than this larger context.

19:21 So, when considering existential assumptions, it is useful to include whatever might constitute this experience, not overlooking such fundamental stuff as the above. Once done—even if only intellectually but preferably having some experiential insight—it places us in a different position to the matter and helps pull us out of our social programming. After we get this kind of space from our own feelings and self-view, we can address these matters in a more effective way.

19:22 Although this whole "self versus other" type of contemplation is unnecessary for this work, what is necessary is to bust up the taken-for-granted assumptions our personal experience is based upon. Therefore, some such shift in looking at the experience existentially and freed of social convention is required. I just used one example that could contribute to this shift, given it didn't occur simply in my first act of contemplation without any sidetrack.

19:23 Going back to my work on observing my basic character, I can start again with a new perspective and broader range of possibilities. When I look back at my arrogance and being self-centered, for example, I can see that whatever that is is only considered wrong or bad because of social convention. Taking away the social contributions to my existence, I get to see it as what-is rather than as simply being bad. In this way, I may also see being afraid of and less than in a new light.

19:24 Of course, I have to look deep within my experience for what is real in this case and not just come to conclusions. Even after acknowledging such overlooked building blocks to my experienced self-reality, that doesn't mean it answers what is really going on with me. It may, but it may not. I have to see what's true in my own case. I can't stress enough that all the intellectual complications I laid out above are not only unnecessary, unless they are founded on experiential insights they are not useful. I'm just trying to warm you up to the task by venturing down various avenues that might well be overlooked. The most important and essential element in all this is the immediate contemplation of my felt experience.

19:25 As I deeply probe into my experience, I see my arrogance as simply a defensive act, and my fear of others as more fundamentally real than the arrogance. Grasping that my fear is founded on the deep-seated sense that I am incapable and insignificant, and so is not really based on others, I experience that the fear is also unnecessary. Still, both the arrogance and fear are reactions to the fact that I experience my very existence as having this fundamental flaw—that at the root bottom I am less than and incapable.

19:26 Previously my self-centered experience would never have thought such a thing about myself. So, in that world, I wouldn't be able to get at this kind of depth without leaping past what I used to take for granted as my self-experience to recognize these buried self-assumptions. Once I can uncover and confront being existentially incapable, I can contemplate what that really is, its nature. As I grasp this as a real experience, I also grasp that it is just an assumption, a concept that I have lived with pretty much throughout my life. Once I experience it is truly a concept, I get that it is not real or necessary, and that I am not that.

19:27 When I can see all these things as something I have created and keep alive by locking my brain onto certain concepts, I have the ability to eliminate those concepts, and the whole contribution of that existential assumption goes away. The moment I get the real nature of this self-experience, I get that it is a concept of my own making. When I truly grasp this, it becomes possible to stop it and so free my "person" from these ideas. All this can take place in a short period of time, if the will and honesty are deep enough.

Simply stated: Stop It!

19:28 An existential assumption exists right in the very experience you have of yourself now, it is not elsewhere, it is simply overlooked or buried a bit. Don't make discovering such stuff a long ordeal, just tell the truth and start from a blank slate without assumptions or preconceptions. The goal is freedom now, not one of nurturing an idea of a possible freedom later that never comes. Beyond discovering and eliminating something that already exists, we have the possibility of creating what has yet to be created.

Creating from Nothing

19:29 Obviously, creativity seems to be about bringing something into existence that doesn't currently exist. Although we might think this may involve changing what already exists in some way, this is the most minor form of creativity. Creating something that hasn't yet been created—whether a new contribution within a known domain, or something that never existed before in any form—is the essence of creativity.

19:30 When it comes to creating something that hasn't yet been created, we may still have an occurring domain to work with, such as books, paintings, dance, sports, tools, technology, philosophy, art, and so on. When we have an already invented domain, we have the basic framework and possibilities established for our creation. This makes the starting point much easier since it has already been started, but it also forms our biggest impediment.

19:31 One of the greatest challenges to creating something in a known domain is moving beyond what has been created so far, and not falling into the trap of just imitating or re-forming what has already been done. The more contributions that have been produced in some field, the harder it might be to be creative, because so many versions have already been generated and new ideas seem rather scarce. So, the opportunities and challenges are rather evenly matched. The form is supplied and easily accessed, but the form also restricts and channels us into old grooves, and this is often antithetical to creativity. Knowing this impediment, however, helps us avoid this pitfall, even though the challenge remains.

19:32 Genuine or original creativity demands that something new arises, something that has not existed heretofore. Otherwise, why call it creation? Simply moving around what's already been produced in a new way may be seen as creative, but this is generally a lower form of creativity than creating something never created before. Such a new creation may start by generating something that doesn't fit anywhere and so will necessitate creating a new domain or field in which new distinctions can be made.

19:33 Being the first to create a new domain is the most difficult because it arises from nothing and has no precedent. This pure form of creativity is also the most difficult to establish within a culture for the very same reason it is so difficult to create. Being completely unprecedented, it is unfamiliar and has no established place in our collectively perceived reality. It may be rejected outright or it may take time to be accepted. Eventually, if a large number of people co-create this new domain, it becomes a reality. Creating a new domain of consciousness or experience, or anything else that has never existed, is a very difficult task and takes profound absorption and deep genuine insight way beyond the norm. This is rare.

Leonardo Principle

19:34 Leonardo da Vinci was clearly a very creative person and a genius in multiple fields. When we take this as simply the given qualities of one person, we miss an important question. What allowed him to do all that? Perhaps it is not so much about the given qualities of a person as it is of developmental possibilities.

19:35 What if you, like da Vinci, could develop the same mental, physical, and perceptive faculties, depths of thinking and contemplation, and whatever else may be needed, to allow you to make breakthrough after breakthrough and create new inventions, works of art, philosophical thought, discoveries, and unknown possibilities yet to be found? This may seem impossible, yet why should it be?

19:36 In my book *The Genius of Being,* I noted how much you learned in your first two years of life. At that time, you made huge and, for you, groundbreaking breakthroughs pretty much daily and across a broad spectrum of human possibilities—physical, mental, interactive, communicational, emotional, and so on. How could you make such frequent and unprecedented breakthroughs now? What is the source or power that allows you to do that? Whatever this possibility is, I'm calling it the Leonardo Principle.

19:37 It might be challenging to wrap our minds around this principle because it stretches the bounds of our settled experience and remains unknown and obscure. Yet, using the springboard of da Vinci's accomplishments and imagining what source might be behind it, as well as our own development in the first two years of life, we can search for or create a principle for these creative activities—remembering to transform the principle from a concept to an experience, understanding the power it will have on our life once adopted. Aligning with this principle, even if it is ill-defined, pushes us in this beneficial direction. We can use it to stretch our experience and state of mind to new heights. Like all principles, we simply have to adopt it and let it govern our experience.

19:38 Imagine putting yourself in the place of "being" Leonardo, able to make fine distinctions in art and anatomy, physiology and other sciences, philosophy and thought, mechanical inventions of various kinds, even weapons. Don't assume this experience is simply better than most people's experience—it may be of a different nature or focus. We can see that real questioning, not overlooking the obvious, and going beyond convention would all be central aspects of this principle.

19:39 What else is needed? From such a consideration, you may be able to glean a possibility that you can seek out or try on. In order to follow the Leonardo Principle your first task is to create it and adopt it. Then, see where it leads you.

About the Correct Way to Be

19:40 I think there is some confusion in consciousness work concerning the idea of a "correct way to be." When people take up some sort of "spiritual" or consciousness practice, they are often searching for a way to be that will improve them; and when they follow a teaching, they assume that it contains in it a prescription for how they should think and behave, as well as what to believe. It should be clear to you by now that I don't provide any of these and recommend that you don't think in those terms.

19:41 Still, people seem to think that there is some particular "way to be" when becoming enlightened or conscious or whatever, that everyone should attain. I don't think so. If you are looking for the correct and universal way to be from me, you are looking in the wrong place. I don't tell people how to live.

19:42 I recommend powerful principles, and I point out a great deal to become conscious of—of which people are generally ignorant—but other than that you're on your own. There are many behaviors people can and do adopt that aren't anybody's ideal of the "ultimate best way to be," and yet this may have little to do with their level of consciousness. If you study it, you can see that even among so-called "enlightened" individuals there are many different ways each presents themselves, and usually there is quite a bit of ego clearly still present as well. The truth is the truth, a person is a person. Those aren't the same thing.

19:43 I share the principles and dynamics I've found that are occurring in humans, and people can choose for themselves what to use and how to use them. It's like teaching someone how an old-fashioned car radio works, what each knob does. Turn one knob this way or that and the sound increases or decreases. Turn the other knob and it moves from station to station. Knowing this, you can choose the volume and station to listen to. That's not up to me. My job is to show you how it works, not tell you what to do with it.

19:44 When someone becomes directly conscious of the nature of existence, this tends to alter their person to some degree and will probably change their approach to life. Yet they will still be a person, and this person will tend to continue as historically constructed. For sure, they might choose some new way to be, more than likely altering their base identity somewhat to fit the effects this new consciousness has on their mind. Regardless of any changes, in the end, they will still be a person and relate and act as such.

19:45 Whatever some "enlightened" person is still attached to will determine their self-identity and so their behavior. Given they are attached to biological life and to some degree a social life, they will maintain their body and a personality, and interact from a character, thus determining their behavior and perspective. But they don't have to believe any of it. Although I said "given" that this is so, I think it is only a rare possibility that leaves any room for it to be otherwise. Consciousness is consciousness, and it does tend to change the person to some degree—more or less depending on the depth of the consciousness—but a person is a person.

19:46 Metaphorically, we could think about it, inaccurately, as if the person is the "container"—which could be anything from a vase to a tractor, a marble to a tube of toothpaste—and the consciousness is an awareness this container has access to. In this, we see that the container will remain pretty much the same and do much of the same activities, no matter what they are aware of. Certainly, the tube of toothpaste might decide to take up swimming, or to sit in the forest like a rock, but it will probably still be moved to clean teeth.

19:47 In any case, I'm suggesting that we make a distinction between the person and anything they may or may not be conscious of. As for a correct way to be, if direct consciousness doesn't produce that in people, why would we think there should be such a thing? Certainly, in a social domain having effective parameters for behavior is appropriate and must be decided upon by the individuals who comprise that society. But in a spiritual sense where truth is the goal, I think we are best served to be suspicious of such a notion.

19:48 Conversely, independent of such concerns, we might better judge the limits of one's consciousness through the stuff they are stuck in and ruled by. If they are clearly suffering and trapped in dysfunctional mental states and behaviors, we will rightly assess this is not free or healthy. In such a case, we might be justified to imagine that their depth of consciousness is suspect. On the other hand, they may be trying to adhere to some image generated by a belief system about how they should behave, but this doesn't have anything to do with their degree of consciousness.

19:49 Although it may not indicate a correct way to be, freedom is essential to consciousness, so it will influence someone's experience and behavior. If not, you might ask why are you or they still stuck in such limitations and illusions? Sounds like there is some ignorance there, and more consciousness may be appropriate. The point is that trying to behave your way into consciousness may not be a sound method and runs the risk of turning your efforts into pretense. A way to be is a social matter not a matter of consciousness, even though one's way of being will be affected by their depth of consciousness. I know this can be confusing, so I'll let you sort it out.

Genius doesn't endow you with the right to be an asshole to others.

Getting Over Yourself

19:50 I would like once more to touch on the idea of getting over yourself. This can be a useful phrase reminding you not to take yourself, or the sound and fury, too seriously. It helps you avoid getting caught up in the self-referencing and generally self-centered world that tends to dominate experience. It assists in opening up to possibilities outside the self's views on everything and transcending bias, opinions, and beliefs. It breaks the hold of that obsessive and myopic focus on the self as the beginning and end of all reality.

19:51 One contribution to this effort is to adopt principles that are not based on the self or the whims and desires of the self. Many principles do that, if you adopt and live within a principle regardless of what it does for the self; and even when it defies or goes against the grain of self desires, comfort, or needs, it will assist in putting self in its place. Principles that do just that are: honesty, honor, integrity, commitment, mastery, contemplation or questioning, and others. When you look into it, you should see that each of these principles serves itself not you. In other words, it is bigger than you.

19:52 If you abide in one such principle you must succumb to whatever is consistent with it, and this is often not you. In this way, it kicks your ass and helps you live in a world that is not devoted solely to you, and it changes your life and consciousness in the process. This doesn't eliminate you, but it does create a much bigger, more powerful experience of life. [For more on this, visit my other books that contain more information about this subject.] But to get over yourself serves to take you even further.

19:53 To get over yourself as an ultimate goal is to eliminate the self-distinction altogether, and so the distinction of you and not-you, thereby finding and acknowledging a consciousness that is prior to and independent of all the hoopla created by the self. In this way, you get a glimpse of the consciousness that doesn't come or go, doesn't live or die, and yet embraces—while at the same time is free of—all that seems to exist.

19:54 To do this may not seem reasonable or possible. But remember, consciousness is more than what can be contained within a self-perspective. Clearly, reality isn't restricted to a self or a mind, and whatever is absolutely true can't be either. Therefore, it isn't hard for us to imagine that real consciousness stretches beyond our own cognition and perception, and way beyond our beliefs and assumptions.

19:55 When we accept the idea that consciousness creates the self, and not the other way around, we can further entertain the possibility that consciousness is everything that seems to exist. Once we step outside ourselves as the only window into consciousness, we might grasp the consciousness that is both self and not-self, arising as awareness, mind, perception, creatures, and objects.

19:56 This may not seem consistent with your current experience, but you can contemplate the matter and see where it goes. Just start by getting over yourself. It's hard to imagine a deeper or more blissful consciousness or reality. Give it a shot.

Chapter Twenty

MAKING A DIFFERENCE TO HUMANITY

What Makes a Difference?

20:1 Let's take a moment to look into and investigate what makes a difference in our shared human experience of reality and life. There is much that goes on in our individual experience that doesn't make any difference at all in our collective world, it only makes a difference in one's subjective or personal world. We have many mental and emotional activities going on, and although they dominate our personal experience, the only influence they have on our environment is how they determine our behavior and actions. Even then, this is restricted to our small sphere of influence and doesn't do anything for humanity or the general life experience we all share. So, what does?

20:2 Obviously, what makes a difference in our social reality as a whole is what everyone shares. So the collective and universally adopted creations or inventions are what create the experience humans have of life and reality. Because we create them they can change, but such a change has to be shared, otherwise our life experience and world don't change. The only time an individual makes a real difference beyond their own experience is when they create something that becomes widely adopted and used by all of us, or at least most of us.

20:3 There are many shared and widespread inventions—physical, technological, or conceptual—that have transformed the human experience and abilities. For example, try to grasp the huge contribution language has on your experience and the shared experience of all of us. It's massive. Imagine a world without communication, without the ability to coordinate, plan together, or share ideas; a world without internal dialogue, books, news, technology, science, and on and on. Think about it.

20:4 Consider how many other inventions couldn't take place without the use of language. Its very nature demands that it be shared, so it has become a universal and central aspect to our experience and world, and in ways overlooked has molded our world and ourselves. At the same time that it provides huge possibilities it also limits us to its structure and assumptions—such as self and not-self. This is but one invention, and we can see how much it changes our experience of self and life—how about all inventions?

20:5 There have been many physical inventions created over the millennia. The Romans invented a new way of building roads, they invented concrete, central heating, aqueducts, bathing houses, sewer systems, and organized a military like never before. All these things made a difference in the lives of the Romans, and as these inventions spread they made a difference to people in general. None of it could have been done without it being a collective effort. We see how such shared physical inventions like those mentioned, as well as cars, phones, plumbing, electricity, computers, and many, many more, have become aspects of our lives and our abilities.

20:6 I remember hearing that when people who'd lived to be 100 years old were asked what was the most important invention of the last century, they said: refrigerators. Most of us overlook such contributions because they seem to have always been there for us. But consider the changes in life that occurred simply by being able to keep food cold or frozen. How many other taken-for-granted inventions do you use that make a difference in your experience and abilities that go overlooked?

20:7 What about inventing ideas, can they make a difference? We see that ancient Greek philosophy and views changed people's thinking and values. The philosophies themselves may not have made a huge difference, but they allowed new ways of thinking about the human condition, thus creating democracy and new domains of thought, setting much of humanity on a different path, generating new ways of living. These made a difference.

20:8 Consider what arose from the Renaissance, the idea of personal participation in discovery and investigation, creating a platform for the emergence of modern science and the scientific method. These clearly made a huge difference in the lives of humans over the centuries. The contributions of the Buddha and others, such thinking as Zen, the possibility of meditation or contemplation, and so on have contributed to our shared experience—whether any particular person engages in them or not, just the fact they exist changes our view of things.

20:9 We can see that some of the conceptual inventions that make a difference to life are shared values, laws, standards of morality and behavior, agreements on many levels. For better or worse, shared beliefs and assumptions also craft our world. There may be a group, large or small, that shares a belief system, and we see that those beliefs alter their experience to some degree, but this applies only to those who adopt that system. What is universally shared, however, is the ability and tendency to adopt some belief system. This changes our experience of the world—again, for better or for worse.

20:10 How about what is written and spoken, and such? A phrase such as "Do unto others as you'd have them do unto you" is a pithy saying that makes a difference if adopted. Yet, even if it is not followed—and it seems it's usually not—its value is still widely agreed upon (for the most part) and so sets a standard and a perspective. "This too shall pass," although insightful and may assist individuals in getting through some encountered difficulty, doesn't seem to really move humanity. Yet if it were more deeply considered it might make a real contribution given it was universally understood. But that isn't likely, and therefore many such aphorisms or sayings don't seem to influence the experience of life very much.

20:11 One thing that could make a huge difference, however, would be to universally change how we think, what we think, and how we view reality and each other. For example, just adopting real questioning and the inclination to look into everything without basing this on assumptions or preconceived notions would change humanity. Regardless of specifics, whatever is created along those lines determines how we live life.

20:12 We can see that many inventions produce or influence our experience. The experience of humanity is founded on the principles, values, assumptions, creations, fabrications, etc., that it adopts and makes real. Just looking at our personal and shared experiences we begin to see how much of it exists because it was invented and pretty much universally accepted. As we can see by now, so many things have been overlooked that are really inventions assumed to be existential reality.

20:13 Could something I write make a difference? To individuals, yes it can. For humanity, I really doubt it, because more than likely it won't be universally shared and certainly not universally understood. Perhaps some contribution could occur if an aspect of my work, probably in a watered-down version, is universally spread and adopted. But so far none of this work has led to a broad or universal acceptance or adoption and so won't make a difference to humanity as a whole. Just attempting to understand what has been communicated in this book, we can see how difficult it would be for the majority of humans to encounter or comprehend. But think about what world might arise if it were adopted.

20:14 Notice that to contribute to or change human experience as a whole, whatever is invented has to be more or less universally adopted, be it physical or conceptual inventions. This leaves out a great deal of the personal struggles and activities you tend to experience—which you should notice do not make any difference to humanity. To contribute to the human experience broadly, whatever you generate must be widely accepted and shared. This is a sobering observation if your goal is to do that. But if that is your goal, it is empowering to notice this fact, so you can align with it and ground your efforts in a realistic direction.

Act only according to that maxim by which you can at the same time will that it should become a universal law.
Immanuel Kant

In Summary

20:15 This whole book has more in it than a human mind can absorb without a lot of unprecedented work. Contemplation is the main tool to become conscious of what's asserted, but every other useful tool should be employed as well. The field of consciousness work is immense and deep. It can be very challenging to tackle. But in my view it is also the most rewarding pursuit a human can take on.

20:16 The title of this book is *Whereof One Cannot Speak.* It seems fitting and appropriate to end with more of the quote from which the title comes, as it applies well to all the assertions and communications made.

My propositions are elucidatory in this way: he who understands me finally recognizes them as senseless, when he has climbed out through them, on them, over them. He must, so to speak, throw away the ladder, after he has climbed up on it. He must surmount these propositions; then he sees the world rightly. Whereof one cannot speak, thereof one must be silent.
Ludwig Wittgenstein

INDEX

ABOUT THE AUTHOR

Peter Ralston is one of the founders of the consciousness movement that began in the San Francisco Bay Area—the birthplace for much of the personal growth work generated in the late Sixties and early Seventies. Peter spent thousands of hours in contemplation and participated in much of the diverse work of the time.

After having several powerful enlightenment experiences in the early 70's, then maturing in his work and coming directly from the source of his own breakthroughs, in 1977 Ralston opened his *Cheng Hsin School for Internal Martial Arts and Ontological Research.* A bit later he founded a consciousness organization called the *Empowerment Institute* dedicated to contributing a powerful new direction by pressing for a deeper level of honesty and a more authentic approach than most other growth oriented or "spiritual" practices.

He also created the martial art: *The Art of Effortless Power.* In 1978 he became the first non-Asian to win the full-contact World Championships held in China. In both his consciousness work and his work in physical skill and effective body-being his approach has always been to lead students away from what is merely believed and toward a powerful personal experience of discovering for themselves what's true.

Ralston has been doing his consciousness work for many decades. In his early days he facilitated the staff of Lifesprings and Tony Robbins' NLP trainings, and did workshops for Esalen, Self-Actualizations, Empowerment, and others around the world. Although many know him for his martial mastery, he is also the author of a most powerful trilogy: *The Book of Not Knowing, Pursuing Consciousness, and The Genius of Being*. Having deepened his consciousness over the decades he is now contributing new hard earned insights and breakthroughs by adding to the trilogy-series his newest book: *Whereof One Cannot Speak*.

Ralston's other books include:

The Book of Not Knowing

Pursuing Consciousness

The Genius of Being

Ending Unnecessary Suffering

Consciousness Dialogues

The Principles of Effortless Power

Zen Body-Being

The Art of Mastery

Older books:

Reflections of Being

Ancient Wisdom, New Spirit

The Art of Effortless Power (out of print)

Currently featured workshops at his Center in the hills outside San Antonio, Texas:

Experiencing the Nature of Being (recommended as the starting point)

Transforming Your Experience of Life

Ending Suffering Workshop

Contemplation Intensive

Enlightenment and Insight Workshop

Transcending Self Workshop

And super-advanced workshops (commensurate with this book):

Transcending Life and Death

Absolute Consciousness Workshop

For more information about the work of Peter Ralston, visit the website:

PeterRalston.com